OXFORD STUDIES IN LANGUAGE CONTACT

Series Editors: Suzanne Romaine, Merton College, Oxford,
and Peter Mühlhäusler, Linacre College, Oxford

Language Selection and Switching in Strasbourg

OXFORD STUDIES IN LANGUAGE CONTACT

Most of the world's speech communities are multilingual, making contact between languages an important force in the everyday lives of most people. Studies of language contact should therefore form an integral part of work in theoretical, social, and historical linguistics. As yet, however, there are insufficient studies to permit typological generalizations.

Oxford Studies in Language Contact aims to fill this gap by making available a collection of research monographs presenting case studies of language contact around the world. The series addresses language contact and its consequences in a broad interdisciplinary context, which includes not only linguistics, but also social, historical, cultural and psychological perspectives. Topics falling within the scope of the series include: bilingualism, multilingualism, language mixing, code-switching, diglossia, pidgins and creoles, problems of cross-cultural communication, and language shift and death.

Language Selection and Switching in Strasbourg

PENELOPE GARDNER-CHLOROS

CLARENDON PRESS · OXFORD
1991

Oxford University Press, Walton Street, Oxford OX2 6DP
Oxford New York Toronto
Delhi Bombay Calcutta Madras Karachi
Petaling Jaya Singapore Hong Kong Tokyo
Nairobi Dar es Salaam Cape Town
Melbourne Auckland
and associated companies in
Berlin Ibadan

Oxford is a trade mark of Oxford University Press

Published in the United States
by Oxford University Press, New York

British Library Cataloguing in Publication Data
Data available

Library of Congress Cataloging in Publication Data
Gardner-Chloros, Penelope.
Language selection and switching in Strasbourg/Penelope Gardner-Chloros.
p.   cm. —(Oxford studies in lanuage contact)
Includes bibliographical references and index.
1. Code switching (Linguistics)—France—Strasbourg.
2. Sociolinguistics—France—Strasbourg. 1. Title. 2. Series.
P115.3.G37 1991   306.4'4'094438353—dc20   90-47444
ISBN 0-19-824993-4

Typeset by Joshua Associates Ltd, Oxford
Printed in Great Britain
by Biddles Ltd, Guildford & King's Lynn

To Piers

Foreword

Europe does not generally come to mind when linguists talk about language contact, yet it provides a rich scene for exploring a variety of issues. Penelope Gardner-Chloros's study of language contact in Alsace greatly enhances our understanding of the social dynamics underlying language choice and code-switching in a European setting. By showing how people in Strasbourg deploy varieties of French and German in diverse settings, such as when shopping or at work in their offices, we see how daily life is structured around the social meanings and relationships negotiated through use of language.

This book also gives insight into some fundamental problems of studying language contact, for example, the distinction between code-switching and borrowing. At the same time it emphasizes the importance of the social functions served by language alternation.

Suzanne Romaine

Merton College, University of Oxford

Acknowledgements

There are several distinct groups of people to whom I am most grateful for assistance and encouragement in the preparation of this book.

First of all, the person who supervised the project in its academic form, Andrée Tabouret-Keller of Strasbourg University. My thanks to her for her interest, support of all kinds, and advice at all stages of the project, are heartfelt. My immense attachment to Alsace is in no small measure due to the fact that she herself is one of its many distinguished representatives.

I am also grateful to the other members of the Group d'Étude du Langage (subsequently LADISIS, U.A. du C.N.R.S. No. 668) for welcoming me in their midst and for many fascinating discussions on language and psychology.

Georges Lüdi, Gabriel Manessy, and Marthe Philipp, my examiners, also provided me with many useful comments on the doctorate at least some of which, I hope, have left their mark on the subsequent version.

Before I left for Alsace, I discussed the project with Michel Blanc, whose courses on Bilingualism and Sociolinguistics I had attended at Birkbeck College. Quite apart from the fact that he was originally responsible for my interest in these subjects, it was he who recommended code-switching as a possible field of study in that part of France. He supplemented this recommendation with a substantial bibliography on code-switching which I put in my luggage and which, in 1981 when the subject was not as popular as it is now, proved an invaluable starting-point. We remained in touch and I owe him a great deal for sharing with me many aspects of his encyclopaedic knowledge of bilingualism.

Robert Le Page also provided me with much bibliographical help; but more important than that, he read through every page of the manuscript of this book and commented, at times in great detail, on many aspects of the argument. I only hope that the resulting book shows some of the influence which his rigorous thinking on language has had on me. Carol Myers-Scotton was also a faithful correspondent during much of the time of preparation of the book and I have benefited from discussions with her and from her own original and open-minded approach to the subject.

I am grateful also to the series editors, Suzanne Romaine and Peter Mühlhäusler, for their comments and encouragement in the preparation of this book. I benefited especially from discussions with Suzanne Romaine, herself an acknowledged expert on code-switching questions. My thanks also go to the staff at Oxford University Press for their supremely efficient handling of the editing process, and their patience with my delays.

For assistance with the field-work in and around Strasbourg I am grateful to a large number of people, many of whom must remain nameless. Among those I can list, I would like to thank the families Christoph, Schmitt, Bodé, and Rieb; Patrick Fischer, Claude Dollé, Marie-Odile Friedrich, Gilbert Salmon, Ann Reid, Huguette Fugier, Pastor Bronenkant, Reinhardt Bodenmann, Corinne Andlauer-Acker, Karine Claude, Delphine Gatti, Sanaa Johri, Marie-Angèle Nguyen, Sonya Schaal, and Véronique Wolff. I am particularly indebted to Raymond Matzen for his advice on dialectological matters and on the transcription of the dialect. My thanks also go to Alix Mullineaux and Claire Dupuis for statistical advice. I would also like to thank all the subjects of the Cité des Chasseurs interviews and Madame Gunder and Monsieur Pfeiffer of the Cité school.

Margaret Wilkerson typed the manuscript with consummate skill and I owe her many thanks indeed for her efficiency and conscientiousness.

Permission to use maps and illustrations included in the book was granted by the Cercle René Schickelé, Strasbourg; Éditions Contades, Strasbourg; and Mr Claude Lapointe, Geispolsheim-Gare. Morstadt Verlag in Kehl authorized the reproduction of the text used as an epigraph and Mouton de Gruyter, Berlin authorized the reproduction of an altered form of the Department Stores survey originally published in the *International Journal of the Sociology of Language*. All such permissions are gratefully acknowledged.

I gratefully acknowledge the support of the British Academy which awarded me a Post-Doctoral Fellowship from which I benefited during the final stages of preparation of the manuscript.

Finally, I thank my husband Piers for his constant encouragement, good humour, practical assistance of all kinds, and insightful comments at all stages of this work. If, as Virginia Woolf thought, women writing books is a sign of their emancipation, then he is largely responsible for the step I have taken in that direction.

P. H. G.-C.

London
May 1990

Contents

List of Figures

List of Tables

Gilbert hat mir von Ihren Aufzeichnungen gesprochen, Herr Grahn. Dürfte ich sie mir mal anhören? Ich studiere Soziolinguistik in Bonn und mache zur Zeit eine schriftliche Hausarbeit über das Sprachverhalten der dialektophonen Elsässer.

Ich bin baff. Kommt da so ein blondes Mädchen aus dem hohen deutschen Norden mit s-pitzen S-tiefelchen hereins-paziert, um uns von Gott und der Welt vergessenen Ixemern auf den breiten Mund zu schauen, und das Resultat davon wird dann von Doktor Doktors begutachtet, bewertet und dem sprachwissenschaft-lichen Weltfundus eingegliedert. Na, was sagt ihr dazu?

Ute lacht. Ich mag euren Dialekt, sagt sie, echt. Er wirkt irgendwie befreiend auf mich. Und doch werde ich ihn mit unserem schrecklichen wissenschaftlichen Jargon sezieren müssen. Werden Sie mir dabei assistieren, Herr Grahn?

Gern, so gern werde das der alte Schwerenöter tun, liebe Ute. Er werde sofort das Material herholen und stets zur Verfügung stehen, sobald die Soziolinguistik ihn brauche.

André Weckmann, *Wie die Würfel fallen: ein Roman aus dem Elsass* (Kehl: Morstadt, 1981).

Gilbert has told me about your recordings, Mr Grahn. Could I listen to them sometime? I'm studying sociolinguistics in Bonn and at the moment I'm writing an essay on the language use of dialect-speaking Alsatians.

Well blow me down. Some blonde from the northern tip of Germany rolls up here, hissing her Ss and asking ze kvestions of us God-forsaken Ixheimers, and her results will be laid before the eggheads, scrutinized, and then sucked into the world's stock of scientific knowledge. Well, what do you say to that?

Ute laughed. I like your dialect, she said, honest. It has a kind of liberating influence on me. And yet I'm going to have to dissect it with our frightful linguistic jargon. Would you be prepared to help me, Mr Grahn?

But of course the old rogue will help, with pleasure, Ute. He will fetch his recordings and be constantly at your disposal, for as long as sociolinguistics requires him.

1

Introduction

ALSACE is one of the countless areas of Europe with a complex plurilingual situation, which belies the persistent late eighteenth–early nineteenth-century stereotype of 'one nation, one language' which has its roots in German Romanticism (Edwards 1985; Wardhaugh 1987). At the same time, France is one of the European countries where this stereotype has been—and, to a considerable extent, continues to be—most powerful. Standard French, it has been said, has performed the same function for France as the monarchy for Britain (Charpentier, quoted Le Page 1989: 14); the French Academy continues to act as watch-dog of its purity and to issue occasional edicts on the avoidance of 'franglais', and in schools pupils continue to be taught a strictly standardized form of the language which on principle takes no account of the variety they speak outside.

The stereotype is in fact nowhere stronger than in Alsace, where a Germanic variety, the Alsatian dialect, is still to be heard on every street corner. The adulation of standard French in Alsace is still to some extent symptomatic of a sense of insecurity, a feeling of not being properly French, while wishing intensely to be so; it coexists, however, with a strong sense of regional identity and local cultural pride, associated with the 'covert prestige' of the dialect (Trudgill 1972).

From a linguistic point of view, Alsace, which is part of the Germanic dialectal continuum in Europe, offers a number of advantages. First, there are dialectological (Beyer and Matzen 1969; Philipp et al. 1984; Philipp 1965); and historical (Lévy 1929; Philipps 1975) descriptions of the dialect; the regional form of French has also been studied (Matzen 1977; Salmon 1985). Second, there are sociolinguistic studies which provide a general picture of the situation (Seligmann 1979; Schuffenecker 1981; Tabouret-Keller and Luckel 1981a; 1981b) and which can in turn be situated in the general context of regional languages in France (Marcellesi 1979; Tabouret-Keller 1981; 1985). Third, there is general agreement that the present situation is evolving very rapidly (Veltman 1982; 1983; Veltman and Denis 1988) without it being possible to predict with any certainty where present tendencies will lead.

In such a changing situation, the description of how language choices are made takes on a particular importance: 'Language choices, cumulated over many individuals and many choice instances, become transformed into the processes of language maintenance or language shift' (Fishman 1965: 73). One of the possible choices which can be made is to use both languages at the same time—code-switching. This can best be defined in a non-technical manner as the alternate use of elements from two different languages or dialects within the same conversation or even the same sentence. More technical definitions tend to prejudge some of the important questions, for example Gumperz (1982: 59) calls it 'the juxtaposition within the same speech exchange of passages of speech belonging to different grammatical systems or subsystems'; in fact, the degree of separateness of the two systems is one of the aspects of code-switching which requires investigation.

Code-switching is intimately linked with the language choices which are made and provides us with a way towards a better understanding of them. In some cases it represents a 'third choice' in its own right alongside the choice of the two varieties which are part of it (Scotton 1983; 1987*a*) and it can lead to the emergence of new forms which are different from those of both the original languages (Agnihotri 1987; Romaine 1986). It can also be the product of necessity rather than choice.

So far, code-switching has not formed the object of any major studies in Alsace (Fischer 1979; 1982) and there has been none, before the present work, at a psycho- or sociolinguistic level. Code-switching is far from being a new phenomenon in Alsace (Cron 1902, reproduced in the Appendix; Cohen-Solal 1985: 40) but in its present form appears particularly symptomatic and revealing of the evolution which is occurring.

As for Strasbourg, without being very large (250,000 inhabitants) it has considerable importance as the regional capital and the seat of two European organizations (the Council of Europe and, on a part-time basis, the European Parliament). Because of the varied social and geographical origins of its inhabitants, and in common with other urban centres which have been shown to be at the vanguard of linguistic change (Labov 1972*b*; Trudgill 1974; Milroy 1980), it is undoubtedly the place where most Alsatian–French code-switching is encountered.

The mixture which one finds in Strasbourg, at a cultural level, between traditional regional elements (e.g. architecture, dialect theatre, traditional bakeries, the Christmas market, the horticultural way of life in the suburb of the Robertsau, etc.) and French/international elements is fascinating and is echoed by the linguistic mixture which the visitor cannot help but hear when walking around or shopping. The stern nineteenth-century German public buildings are adorned with tricolours and guarded by gendarmes. The restaurants serve traditional Germanic regional dishes, interpreted with unmistakably French finesse. Signposts to villages and surnames all appear to be German until you hear them said aloud and realize that they are pronounced in accordance with French phonology—Vogel (as a surname) is pronounced /vo'ʒɛl/ and Entzheim, the airport is /ɛn'zɑɪm/; yet you will hear people speaking a type of French whose intonation patterns are those of

German with every word stressed on the first syllable. You will also hear exchanges like the following:

CONRAD   Ich bin do, morje!
         I'll be here tomorrow!

RICK   Ja.
         Yes.

CONRAD   *Y a pas de problèmes!*
         No problems!

RICK   So Got will, gell? *Bonsoir monsieur Wanner* . . . Er isch schunn haam!
         God willing, eh? *Goodnight Mr Wanner* . . . He's already at home!

CONRAD   Ja, ja, so, un ich geh jetz noch emol . . .
         Yes, yes, so, and now I'll go off . . .

RICK   *Alors à demain, monsieur Conrad!*
         So see you tomorrow, Mr Conrad!

CONRAD   Ja, *merci*, guet Nacht, *monsieur Rick!* Ja, *d'accord*, noh mache mir 's
         am Mondaa . . .
         Yes, *thanks*, good-night, *Mr Rick!* Yes, *OK*, we'll do that on Monday
         . . .

RICK   *Allez, bonsoir monsieur Conrad!*
         OK, good-night Mr Conrad!

CONRAD   Guet Nacht, *monsieur Rick!*
         Good-night *Mr Rick!*

RICK   *A demain*, gell!
         See you tomorrow, OK!

All in all, the duality which code-switching symbolizes and embodies is so omnipresent as to make it an obvious subject for any linguist to study. It is clearly most relevant to and revealing of the workings of this society; in this study I shall attempt to show how Strasbourgeois use different forms of code-switching as an integral part of their bilingual repertoire.

Finally, three methodological principles were followed:

1. A principle of authenticity of the data, that is that usage should be observed in its natural environment and influenced as little as possible by the observer's presence (hence I was not present at the recordings described in Chapters 5 and 6). No questionnaires, attitude scales, or acceptability judgements were used (Dorian 1984: 267) in order to ensure that this first description of code-switching in this context was as non-interventionist as possible.

2. A principle of methodological variety within the limits imposed by the first principle. Thus attitudes were studied principally through interviews, quantitative surveys were used to highlight the relationship between language

choice and various social and inter-individual factors, and conversational analysis was used for the linguistic description proper. The intention was that each of the techniques used should reveal different aspects of the question, thus building up a richer and more complete picture overall.

3. A principle of self-sufficiency, deriving from the fact that this work was originally carried out in preparation of a doctoral thesis.

This meant that in spite of the help and advice I received throughout the period of this study, I avoided field-work, surveys, and linguistic analyses which I could not carry out without excessive outside assistance. The size of data samples therefore had to be kept within bounds, and this study has both the advantages and the limitations of any work based principally on participant observation by a single researcher.

One of the most satisfying aspects of studying code-switching is that it elicits great interest from many categories of people, notably those who practise it. Subjects of the interviews (see Chapter 2) showed considerable perceptiveness about different types of switching and their *raisons d'être*. In everyday life, switching fulfils multiple functions implicitly recognized in society—recently noted English examples include an advertisement for car tyres which relied on the slogan: 'The best tyres in der Welt', capitalizing on the reputed durability of German products, and another for lower-cost Channel crossings in which the geographical transition is symbolized by the question: 'At this price it's rather bon, non?' The implications of 1992 are foreshadowed in a poster campaign current in England at the time of writing, which is characterized by slogans like: 'Le single market est arrivé. Where êtes you?'

All in all, I shall be happy if this work is considered as a contribution to sociolinguistic studies in Alsace, without pretending to broader applicability. On the latter, I would merely echo Romaine (1982: 284): 'If the success of a sociolinguistic theory is to be determined by its ability to say correct things about the nature of language, then it will almost certainly preside over its own demise.'

2

Language in Alsace

In this chapter I shall describe the linguistic situation in Alsace in general terms so as to provide a background for the code-switching studies which follow. It is a mistake to focus on code-switching to the exclusion of other information on the distribution and evolution of the two codes in the community; for it is only by seeing it in association with other aspects of the linguistic picture that its true significance can become apparent (cf. Trudgill 1976–7).

There are two aspects of the description: firstly, historical, geographical, political, and sociolinguistic information proper, that is to say known facts and the results of surveys; and secondly, information regarding the attitudes of speakers towards linguistic matters, explored through a series of twenty interviews carried out in the Robertsau, a suburban area of Strasbourg.

i. The Linguistic Situation

Alsatian within the Germanic Dialect Area

The term 'Alsatian' covers the various Germanic varieties spoken in present-day Alsace, which can be subdivided historically into varieties of Franconian and Alemannic (Philipp and Bothorel-Witz 1989; Russ 1989). Alsace is part of the West Germanic dialect continuum (see Fig. 2.1) and has borders with Lorraine (of which a part is also German-speaking) on the western side, Luxemburg in the north-west, Germany in the north-east and east, and Switzerland in the south.

The linguistic frontier between the German-speaking and French-speaking regions in Alsace and Lorraine follows the mountain-line of the Vosges; in the west the political frontier between France and Germany which follows the Rhine is not a linguistic frontier as such. Cutting across this frontier horizontally (and with the exception of the town of Kehl which is across the border from Strasbourg), the dialects spoken in Baden on the German side are very similar to those spoken at the equivalent latitude in Alsace.

The principal linguistic subdivisions (Fig. 2.2) are between Moselle Franconian (francique mosellan), spoken in Northern Lorraine around Thionville near the Luxemburg border, Rhine Franconian (francique rhénan), in the rest of Lorraine and the northern part of Alsace across to Wissembourg,

FIG. 2.1. Dialectal Continua in Europe
(based on Chambers and Trudgill 1980: 7)

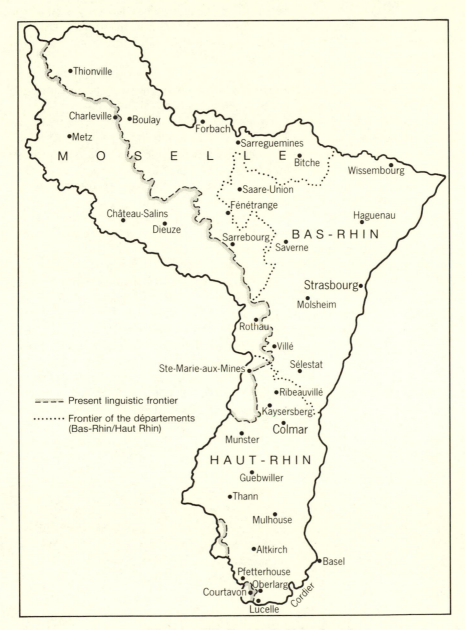

FIG. 2.2. The Linguistic Frontier in Alsace-Lorraine

Low Alemannic in most of Alsace, and High Alemannic in southern Alsace near the Swiss border. Strasbourg itself is a dialectical 'island' with various idiosyncracies; for example, the pronunciation of many words which have High German[χ] with [ʃ] as in ich ('I') = /ɪʃ/, indistinguishable from the third person singular of the verb to be, isch (High German ist).

This variation within the dialect is no greater than variation found over comparable geographical areas in countless other places. A particularity of Alsatian is, however, that it has not developed a regional koine and is separated by a national frontier from the standard variety towards which it might otherwise converge, Standard German. Consequently there is no evidence that Alsatian is becoming a more focused language due to the usual unifying influences of education, the media, greater human mobility, etc.; Alsatians from different parts of the region still find that their dialects are mutually incomprehensible and that they must resort to French as a lingua franca. German is now taught in the schools (see below) but about one third of children choose English as their second language in preference to German when they enter secondary school.

What is common to Alsatians is their pronunciation of French (still an object of derision), which is characterized principally by a Germanic stressing of the first syllable of words (ˈBonjour ˈMadame) and by an apparent confusion— actually a transfer from Alsatian lenis stops—between p/t/k and b/d/g (Philipp 1985). There are, of course, also numerous other expressions and morphosyntactic transfers (Matzen 1977; Jadin 1985) which characterize Alsatian French, although there is now mounting evidence of transfers from French to Alsatian, for example at a phonological level in the speech of adolescents (Bickel-Kauffmann 1983). It is therefore not clear and by no means certain that a regional form of French will gain acceptance alongside or instead of the dialect; the influential teaching profession, and many parents, would undoubtedly be opposed to the suggestion.

Historical Factors

Spannen Sie einen Menschen mit Armen und Beinen zwischen zwei Pferde, jagen Sie die Pferde in entgegengesetzter Richtung davon, und Sie haben genau das erhabene Schauspiel der elsässischen Treue. (René Schickelé, *Hans in Schackenloch* (1915))

(Stretch out a man by his arms and legs between two horses, chase the horses away in opposing directions, and there you have, precisely, the edifying spectacle of Alsatian allegiance.)

The historical facts relevant to the present-day linguistic situation hark back to the area's geography: the Vosges mountains are a linguistic demarcation line principally because they affected the penetration and settlement of various waves of invaders, notably the Franks and Alemanns. The various stages, going back to the Romans and beyond, are described in detail in Lévy 1929 and Philipps 1975.

Alsace's more recent political history is also highly relevant to the linguistic situation and can be divided into six major periods, of which the last four are part of living memory:

1. → 1648:   Alsace belongs to the Germanic part of the Holy Roman Empire
2. 1648–1870: Alsace belongs to France, following the Thirty Years War
3. 1870–1918: Alsace belongs to Germany, following the Franco-Prussian War
4. 1918–40:   Alsace belongs to France, following World War I
5. 1940–5:   Alsace is annexed by Germany, during World War II
6. 1945:   Alsace is returned to France.

During each of these periods the region's attachment to France or Germany was accompanied by more or less dictatorial language policy, aiming to impose either French or German on the population. For example, between 1918 and 1940, when Alsace was returned to France after being part of Germany for 48 years, the French authorities used means which now appear naïve—but may none the less have been effective—to promote the use of French, such as slogans in public places encouraging people to speak French, a tactic which was used again after World War II. In his fascinating attempt to 'psycho-analyse' his region of origin, *Psychanalyse de l'Alsace*, Hoffet claims that these campaigns were instrumental in giving rise to an Alsatian complex about not speaking sufficiently pure French (Hoffet 1951); such a feeling is still frequently encountered today.

As for the dialect, which was tolerated or even encouraged as being a form of German between 1870 and 1918 (the slogan was then: Redd wie d'r de Schnawel gewachse isch! 'Speak the way your beak grew!' (that is, the way that comes naturally, Fig. 2.3), which interestingly is now used by the present regionalist movement), it was again repressed, along with French, under the Occupation, for the Hitlerian regime wished to impose Hochdeutsch, the only variety considered to be pure and common to all 'Germanic peoples'.

Through all these political changes, the impact of which the non-frontier regions of Europe can scarcely conceive, Alsatian always remained the language of the majority (Ladin 1982: 152). The actual impact of the linguistic policies pursued by succeeding governments is difficult to evaluate, partly because it was not always feasible to translate those policies into action. According to Philipps (1975), for example, between 1648 and 1789, when Alsace was French for the first time, schoolteaching continued to be dispensed in German because French-speaking teachers were not available. Similarly, under the Nazi Occupation, the dictatorial imposition of German (even people's surnames and forenames had to be translated into German names)

FIG. 2.3. The French Cockerel,
German Eagle, and Alsatian Stork

The French cockerel and the German eagle are both attempting to make the Alsatian stork speak their language. The stork finally cries: *'I've had enough of you two, damn it all. I'll speak the way my beak grew'* [i.e. the way that comes naturally].

(Contemporary)

★ Traduction : *'J'en ai assez de vous deux... (juron). Je vais parler comme je l'entends'* (Littéralement: comme le bec m'a poussé.)

was almost certainly counter-productive as it made French into a symbol of defiance amongst the generally rebellious population.

It is noteworthy that all three of the aspects of 'ethnolinguistic vitality' identified by Giles, Bourhis, and Taylor (1977) have undergone repeated upheavals in Alsace: institutional support, status, and even demographic concentration: for political reasons there were large-scale emigrations to other parts of France both in 1871, following the Treaty signed with Prussia, and at the beginning of World War II. Today, on the other hand, on the basis of the 1982 census, 8 per cent of the population of Alsace is of immigrant origin (Tabouret-Keller 1985), the largest groups being Algerians and Moroccans (36,000) followed by Italians, Turks, and Portuguese. The presence of children of immigrant origin in the schools is an important reason—or excuse, depending on one's views—for keeping French as the only language of school instruction.

Institutional Factors

If one considers not only language policy as such but also the influence of particular institutions or 'domains' such as the media, education, and religion, then the role of institutional support can be seen to be very significant for the present linguistic situation.

The Media

After the war, as a reaction against the draconian linguistic measures imposed by the Nazi authorities (such as the fining of people overheard speaking French), the French authorities brought out an edict severely limiting the publication of newspapers and journals in German in Alsace and Lorraine (13 September 1945). The edict reads as follows: 'Only French or bilingual newspapers and periodicals may appear' (i.e. no monolingual German publications were allowed). 'Any bilingual publication must contain a proportion of text in French which is not less than 25 per cent and which will be laid down for each publication by ruling of the Minister of Information, who will be advised by the regional "Commissaire de la République" in Strasbourg or the "député" for the Moselle.'

The edict also specified that articles addressed to the young, sports articles, and all main titles as well as subheadings above a certain size should be in French, together with birth, marriage, and death announcements. A civil servant was employed to measure the number of lines in each language with a ruler each morning and address appropriate warnings to infringers, who could be punished by fining or imprisonment for six months to two years.

The effect of the edict was compounded by further regulations specifying that road signs, street names, public notices of all kinds, and advertisements had to be in French. The written language of Alsace therefore in practice became French, and this was accepted by the population who were overjoyed after the Liberation to be French again. Although they continued to speak the dialect, through these measures it was cut off from any written standard which could have contributed to its propagation and vitality.

It is interesting to note that the edict in question was only formally repealed in 1984, when a local organization threatened to bring a case before the European Commission of Human Rights relating to freedom of expression and freedom from discrimination on grounds of language, a move which would have been highly embarrassing for the French Government.

The success of these measures can partly be gauged by looking at the sales of the main local newspaper, *Les Dernières Nouvelles d'Alsace*. In 1950 they printed 30,000 copies in French and 124,000 'bilingual': in 1984 they were printing 180,000 in French, and only 55,000 'bilingual' (see Fig. 2.4). Today no newspaper in Alsace could survive by publishing a print-run of which only 25 per cent was French.

As for television, German programmes can be received satisfactorily in the south, Luxembourgeois and Belgian ones in the north; but it is thought that this facility is relatively little used except by the oldest generation. The third French channel, which is regional, recently increased the part of its programme in which Alsatian is actually spoken to twelve minutes a day, Mondays to Fridays after 7.35 p.m. (peak viewing time). To this are added three minutes

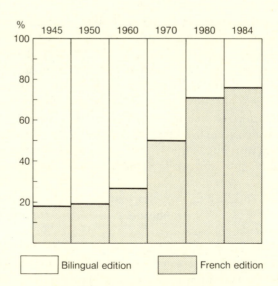

FIG. 2.4. Evolution in the Percentage of French and Bilingual Editions of *Les Dernières Nouvelles d'Alsace* printed from 1945 to 1984

of stories in Alsatian for children, three minutes of 'chronique dialectale' (dialect-related anecdotes), and, once a month, the *Grosser elsässer Owe* ('Big Alsatian Night Out'), a variety show in which Alsatian and French are both represented in songs, jokes, and sketches. Strasbourg Radio has two fifteen-minute slots a day in Alsatian. Overall, the media's contribution to maintaining the dialect is negligible or negative: to realize this one need only refer to the impact of children's programmes on the up-and-coming generation—all in French with the exception of the aforementioned three minutes.

Politics and Administration

French administration is famous for its centralization, which has enormous repercussions in the educational and linguistic spheres. The right-wing governments in power after World War II—which ironically derived a considerable part of their support from Alsace, a prosperous and traditionally conservative area—deliberately sent officials who knew no German or Alsatian to man public offices of all kinds in the region, thus ensuring that members of the public had to speak French if their requests were to be understood. 'L'homme/la femme au guichet' ('the man/woman at the desk/counter'), a powerful figure in bureaucratic France, was a French-speaker.

It is doubtful whether a Socialist government would have behaved differently: until 1971, following a tradition which harks back to the Revolution, the Socialist Party maintained the principle: 'une nation, une langue'. A change took place with Mitterrand's new Socialist Party which in 1974 put forward a bill relating to 'the place of France's minority languages and cultures in education'; I shall return to recent educational developments below. At the political level, the devolution promised to the regions by the same government proved slow and was overshadowed by the election of a right-wing Prime Minister which, in Alsace as elsewhere, drew the focus away from electoral promises to the conflict, real, potential, and imagined, between a left-wing President and a right-wing Prime Minister ('la cohabitation'). Only the Communists, the trade unions (especially the CGT), and to some extent the Centre have consistently supported minority languages and cultures.

It must be said that Alsatians as a whole have not clamoured for linguistic and cultural rights, and the Cercle René Schickelé, which represents regional interests and whose slogan is 'Our future is bilingual' is neither very powerful nor very vociferous. Political action in favour of the dialect is still tainted with a slight flavour of 'autonomism', which between the two wars was in turn ambivalently related to the German cause in Alsace and thus to Hitlerism. Politicians who wished to stamp out the dialect have played on the Alsatians' passionate desire to be French and consequent reticence to assert any claims to Alsatian individuality.

The post-war awakening of other minorities in France was also slow, and only the Corsicans were genuinely vociferous. Eventually, in 1951, the 'loi Deixonne' was passed, relating to the teaching of 'local languages and dialects'. This highly qualified measure specified that primary and nursery school-teachers could 'have recourse to' local idioms when this could be of assistance in their teaching, and in particular 'for the study of the French language'. Beyond that (note the details), any teacher *making a special request to do so* could be *authorized* to spend *one hour per week* on teaching the local language and literature. However, such teaching would be *optional* for the pupils. Perhaps the most notable aspect of this law was that it was only applicable to Breton, Basque, Catalan, and Occitan areas. Corsican, Flemish, and Alsatian had no provision made for them at all since it was supposedly considered that these languages were 'dialects' (for which read 'deviations') of other 'national' languages: Italian, Dutch, and German. And since these languages were already taught in their own right, it was argued that it was unnecessary to support the corresponding dialect. It is hard to imagine that this argument was made in good faith. The Haby Commission (1964–5), which took up and completed the work relating to regional languages, did include those which had previously been ignored; but its work never led to any substantial reforms. (For a more detailed discussion of the teaching of regional languages in France see Marcellesi and Le Greco 1975; Boulot and Boizon-Fradet 1987.) The discussion of political and administrative questions has led us inevitably to the question of education, so we turn now to the present situation in that sphere.

Education

Tabouret-Keller (1985: 21) cites the schools language policy in France as one of the principal reasons for the present evolution in the linguistic situation, that is to say the decline of the dialect, and there can be little doubt that this is correct. First of all, the centralization already mentioned with respect to administrative procedures in France also operates in the educational field; there is a half-serious joke that if you leave a school in one part of France on Saturday at lunch-time and join another class at the same level in another part of France on Monday morning, you will be able to follow the lesson where you left off. France has for decades had a centrally devised school curriculum such as has only fairly recently been introduced for certain subjects in Britain. From the point of view of language teaching, this implies a uniformity of aims and standards which has considerable repercussions in regions where a language other than French is spoken in everyday life; going to school is to some extent equated with speaking French in a particular way as well as with Standard French being the medium of instruction for all subjects. Teachers are employed by the State and can be sent all over France, so a certain proportion of them do not have any knowledge of the local language.

This was, of course, also the case between 1918 and 1940, when evidence suggests that the Alsatian dialect was still flourishing; so what has changed to make the imposition of French at school so significant in eroding the dialect now? There are two main answers to this question: first of all, an accumulation of social and economic factors, which have eroded all minority languages in Europe to a greater or lesser extent, the influence of the media, professional and social mobility, urbanization, and the struggle for jobs, all contribute to favouring a single national language (Edwards 1985; Wardhaugh 1987), whereas before the war school was the *only* place where a large number of Alsatian children heard French spoken. Second, there has been a significant psychological reason since the war why the population has willingly embraced the idea that French is the only possible school language. This psychological aspect will be explored in part ii of this chapter but, historically speaking, it can be described as follows. German was imposed throughout the school system from 1940 to 1945, a measure naturally much resented by the population. After the war, supposedly to make up for lost ground, the teaching of German was in turn totally banned by the French authorities until 1952, and then reintroduced only to a very limited extent. This equally authoritarian measure was psychologically much more acceptable to the population because of their desire to be fully French once again.

This still leaves open an important question about the relationship between the teaching of German in schools and the survival of Alsatian. In this relationship lies the artfulness of the policy adopted by the French authorities, which were basically anti-dialect: during the time when the teaching of German was banned, the dialect was tacitly assimilated to German and so no issue of preserving it separately from German could arise. When the teaching of German was reintroduced, the argument with respect to the dialect altered imperceptibly; it was then claimed that it was important to teach pupils a standardized national language with a history and a literature. How could they possibly be taught an unstandardized oral dialect which varied from village to village and, moreover, would hold up their progress in French (Gardner-Chloros 1988)?

What of the situation now? The teaching of German is, of course, no longer banned and German is offered as an optional second language in secondary schools. Furthermore, the Holderith reform, launched in 1971, led to the teaching of German in the last two years of primary school in Alsace, providing the form teacher was willing—and able—to dispense it. It is stressed in the instruction material provided ('Guten Tag, Rolf!' and Teachers' Book, 1974), however, that while certain aspects of the teaching would undoubtedly be easier for dialect-speaking children, non-dialect speakers should be able to follow the course just as readily and suffer no disadvantage, this being an important condition for the whole initiative's acceptability. Above all, the teaching is limited to half an hour a day and is not compulsory for pupils, since parents can ask for their children not to attend the German classes. As such, the scheme has in fact been highly successful but its impact is severely limited by the time devoted to it and the fact that many pupils give up German two years later when entering secondary school. Any suggestion of segregating the dialect-speaking children for classes in the dialect is still taboo and such limited classes as are now occasionally offered in 'Langue et culture régionale' over the lunch-hour have, unsurprisingly, few takers.

'Grandfather, why are there no more storks in Alsace?'

LET'S NOT SPOIL ALSACE!

TEACH THE CHILDREN ALSATIAN!

'You see son, when the storks fly over Alsace they hear everyone speaking French and so they think they haven't arrived yet and carry on flying.'

BILINGUALISM: OUR FUTURE.

FIG. 2.5. Lehre d'Kinder Elsässisch!

Finally, it is now possible, since Mitterrand's 1974 reforms, to offer an Alsatian option at baccalauréat level and at university, but naturally fewer and fewer pupils of the right age are in a position to take this up.

Religion

The Catholic Church enjoys special privileges in Alsace compared with the rest of France and is generally considered to have contributed, historically, to the maintenance of bi- (or tri-) lingualism in the region through its institutionalized use of both French and German.

Between 1870 and 1918, in order to avoid friction with the population, the Concordat concluded with Napoleon continued to be observed although Alsace was under German domination: this meant that the clergy in Alsace continued to be paid by the State and the State continued to have a voice in the appointment of bishops; the Falloux law, which guaranteed religious education, was also maintained. When France, after 1918, tried to bring Alsace into line with the rest of France, the attempt was ill-received and contributed to the rise of the autonomist movement which flourished in the 1918–40 period.

The first catechism in French for Alsace only appeared in 1945 and even today French and German—or Alsatian—are employed side by side in many services. As for the Protestant Church, which is stronger in Alsace than any other part of France and in which Luther's language carries a special significance, it continues to hold services in German, although these are becoming much rarer where there are younger congregations. Strasbourg also has a larger Jewish population than any other French city apart from Paris: in the Middle Ages it was one of Europe's 'free cities' where groups persecuted for religious reasons could establish themselves without fear. This community's traditional language, Yiddish, now scarcely spoken, has given numerous words to Alsatian.

The Sociolinguistic Picture

In broad terms the linguistic situation in Alsace can be described with reference to a diglossic distribution since the two principal languages spoken, French and Alsatian, enjoy differentiated status and are used in complementary areas of life or domains (Philipp 1978). Hug (1975) considered that the two factors which, for any individual, determined to what extent the two languages were used in everyday life were age and social environment: rural or urban. Matzen (1973) has a longer list including geographical origin, education, and training, profession, religion, and political orientation, as well as circumstances surrounding the use of the language. Such a list is theoretically infinite. We turn now to the more factual survey-based data which we have on Alsace: first the broad statistical data provided by Institut National de la statistique et des études économiques, the national census organization, and second, smaller-scale surveys on specific linguistic issues.

Institut National de la statistique et des études économiques (INSEE)

Two censuses of Alsace were carried out by INSEE, in 1946 and 1962, in which a linguistic question, 'Quelles langues savez-vous parler?' ('Which languages can you speak?') was asked. The answers provided were: 'French/Dialect/German' and 84 per cent and 82 per cent of the population respectively ticked in such a way as to show they could speak the dialect.

Then in 1979 a questionnaire entitled 'Mode de vie en Alsace' ('Lifestyle in Alsace') was sent out by INSEE (and returned by some 3,000 'heads of household') covering numerous areas of life and asking some more detailed linguistic questions. Unfortunately the principal linguistic question: 'Parlez-vous le dialecte alsacien?' ('Do you speak the Alsatian dialect?') was not phrased in the same way as in the censuses and furthermore it was not clear whether it referred to competence in the dialect or to actual use.

Table 2.1 gives the breakdown of replies to this question according to age group and includes categories for those who claim to understand the dialect but not to speak it, and those who claim not to understand it.

The overall finding, that 75 per cent of the sample replied positively to the question (92 per cent in the case of those born in Alsace) must therefore be treated with caution, for their positive replies might only imply a very passive level of competence. Furthermore in 1962 the number of dialect speakers was presumably growing simply due to the rising birth rate, whereas since then immigration has become an important factor (Schuffenecker 1981).

Table 2.2 shows the breakdown according to the birthplace of the 'heads of household' who sent in replies to the questionnaire. It is significant that the questionnaire is addressed not to speakers but to 'households' ('foyers') and overall lays much stress on the behaviour of the 'chef de famille', or 'head of household', who is likely to be male and over forty.

Table 2.3 shows in what percentage of these households it is claimed that Alsatian is spoken 'often' or 'always', in three different environments: at home, while shopping, and when going to the Town Hall or Social Security Office. There is again one set of columns for all households and another for heads of household born and bred in Alsace, plus a further breakdown for the two administrative units which make up Alsace, the Haut-Rhin in the South, and the Bas-Rhin in the North (Strasbourg being the capital both of the Bas-Rhin and of the whole of Alsace).

Table 2.1 shows a clear falling off of dialect knowledge according to age; but although the survey is now over ten years old, the overall picture which emerges is of about three-quarters of the adult population speaking Alsatian. This is probably still roughly accurate, with considerable variation between town and countryside, Strasbourg in particular being predominantly franco-phone. But although a survey of *adults'* use might not show much change overall, Veltman (1983) shows that the dialect is not necessarily being

TABLE 2.1. Distribution by Age of Replies to the Question: 'Do you speak the Alsatian dialect?'

	Age							
	16–24	25–34	35–44	45–54	55–64	65–74	75 and over	(Average)
% understanding and speaking the dialect	66	64	71	84	84	88	88	78
% understanding but not speaking the dialect	13	11	9	5	5	4	2	7
% neither understanding nor speaking the dialect	21	25	20	11	11	8	10	15
(% of respondents born in Alsace)	(83)	(90)	(93)	(96)	(97)	(98)	(96)	(93)

Source: INSEE (1979).

TABLE 2.2. Proportion of Couples Claiming to Speak the Alsatian Dialect According to their Origins

	% understanding and speaking the dialect	% understanding but not speaking the dialect	% neither understanding nor speaking the dialect
Alsatian couples	92	4	4
Couples made up of one Alsatian and one non-Alsatian	57	18	25
French couples from other parts of France	14	16	70
Foreign couples	9	17	74
TOTAL	75	8	17

Source: INSEE.

TABLE 2.3. Use of the Alsatian Dialect by Context and Origin

	% of couples claiming to speak the Alsatian dialect 'often' or 'always'					
	Bas-Rhin		Haut-Rhin		Alsace	
	All	Those born in Alsace	All	Those born in Alsace	All	Those born in Alsace
At home	63	82	55	72	60	78
While shopping	55	71	47	59	52	66
At the Town Hall or Social Security Office	41	54	32	41	37	48

Source: INSEE.

transmitted to the youngest generation even in families where both parents speak it. He compares the percentage of families where the parents claim to speak Alsatian (taking his figures from the INSEE survey) with the percentage where the same is claimed of the children. From this, it emerges that the decline in dialect use is rapid, especially in the towns. In the country, when both parents speak Alsatian, 92.7 per cent of their children speak it also; in town, in the same circumstances, only 70 per cent of the children speak it—and as Veltman points out, their command of it is probably much poorer and their active use much less frequent than that of their parents. In urban families where only one of the two parents speaks Alsatian, a mere 16.8 per cent of children speak it where that parent is the mother and 13 per cent where it is the father.

The widening gap between the urban and rural situations is one of the striking insights provided by this, and other, surveys. According to INSEE, in rural communities, 88 per cent of the respondents overall claim to speak the dialect whereas in small towns of 10,000–15,000 inhabitants, the percentage falls to 69 per cent. A separate survey in 1981 among 1,000 primary and secondary school pupils showed that in rural communities 72 per cent spoke French at home, 29 per cent in Strasbourg and surroundings, falling to 8 per cent in central Strasbourg.

As far as knowledge and use of German are concerned, INSEE's question was, again, formulated differently from that concerning the dialect or used in the earlier censuses. They asked: 'Vous-même, connaissez-vous l'allemand?' ('Do you yourself know German?') to which the possible replies were: 'Yes, I speak and write it' or 'Yes, I only speak it', neither of which necessarily implies that this ability is regularly put into practice. In Table 2.4 the percentage of householders claiming to speak German and Alsatian are set side by side; the first and third columns, which include all householders rather than only those of Alsatian origin, show that slightly more respondents in each age group claimed to speak German than Alsatian, a discrepancy presumably to be explained because some of those not originating in Alsace had learnt German as a foreign language.

TABLE 2.4. Proportion of Heads of Household Claiming to Speak German or the Alsatian Dialect by Age

	% speaking German		% speaking the dialect	
	All	Those born in Alsace	All	Those born in Alsace
16–24	64	85	56	81
25–34	69	87	63	91
35–44	72	88	70	94
45–54	84	96	80	94
55–64	87	97	81	96
65–74	90	97	87	96
75 and over	94	97	92	94
AVERAGE	80	92	76	92

Source: INSEE.

Linguistic Surveys

The characteristics of the linguistic situation outside Strasbourg are described in Tabouret-Keller and Luckel (1981*a* and 1981*b*). The latter reports on a series of surveys which involved detailed interviews in 106 homes, spread over 34 villages and 6 small towns in the Bas-Rhin. The purpose was to show the principal developments taking place in the linguistic situation; unlike the INSEE surveys, information provided by interviewees which did not fall into the categories provided was also recorded. Notably, women not infrequently claimed to speak a /ˈmeʃʊŋ/, or mixture of French and Alsatian, a category which the questionnaire had not provided for. They also claimed to speak French more often than the men did, even with their husbands: in the middle age group, they claimed to speak 30 per cent French and 20 per cent mixture, whereas none of the men in the same group reported any use of French with his wife. Children also reported using French and a mixture between themselves;

the results cast doubt on the traditional idea that the family is the place where the dialect is best preserved, since younger women admitted to a deliberate use of French when speaking to their children, as they saw it as being in the children's interest. Between the grandparents' and parents' generation on the other hand, Alsatian appeared to be the almost exclusive means of communication.

Village life appeared to be predominantly marked by the use of Alsatian whereas contacts outside the village were more often in French. Farmers in particular appear to constitute a bastion of dialect-speaking, but it should be borne in mind that at the time of this survey, they only represented 4.7 per cent of the population and were untypical in other ways too, older than the population average and more sedentary, having very often been born and bred on the farm where they still lived and worked.

The results given here only represent a selection of the extremely rich data provided by these surveys, and it is to be hoped that they will be both updated and completed by similar work in the towns, as was the authors' intention. Other smaller-scale surveys have concentrated on the younger generation and thus provide further information about the situation's likely evolution. Ladin (1982) carried out a survey among 685 bilingual pupils aged between 14 and 16 attending 15 different secondary schools in the Bas-Rhin and reportedly of very diverse social origins. The survey consisted in a multiple-choice questionnaire of more than 100 items; unfortunately, for each of the questions concerning language use or choice, three possible answers were provided: French, Alsatian, and German. Providing such a choice is misleading, especially to such a young age group for whom German is in most cases little more than a foreign language. Ladin highlights a difference between pupils at secondary schools in Strasbourg and those in the country; for the former, Alsatian was given as the first language spoken by the pupil in 53 per cent of cases, whereas for the latter it was spoken first in 86 per cent of cases; only 4 per cent of all the bilingual pupils claimed to have learnt both languages simultaneously as children.

Ladin also stresses that the tendency towards French is not only an urban phenomenon, but also a social one, linked to work places and to mechanization; among the Strasbourg pupils, most French use was reported by children whose parents were executives, in senior administrative posts, or in the professions. Cole (1975) also conducted a survey among 11–16-year-olds at the Lycée in Munster and other groups of the same age, and reported agreement (or 'convergent attitudes') with respect to the following points: that Alsatian is spoken less and less among the pupils (i.e. less among older than among younger pupils); that Alsatian will none the less not disappear; and that it is important for an Alsatian to speak the dialect (this view being held by 83 to 92 per cent of the respondents, depending on the group).

However, there was disagreement, or 'divergence', when Cole asked which age group spoke Alsatian the most at school: each age group thought the other groups spoke it more than their own.

Finally, Bickel-Kauffmann (1983) carried out a survey among 106 young inhabitants of Andolsheim born between 1963 and 1966. The majority were bilingual (74 out of 106) but the dialect was principally used by young boys between 14 and 16 and limited to the family circle and to close friends. The phonetic analysis which is the principal focus of this piece of research shows a clear influence of French phonology on the dialect in this group as compared, for example, with older speakers.

In part ii I report on the results of twenty interviews carried out in a Strasbourg suburb, in order to fill in the attitudinal background to the statistical facts outlined up to here.

ii. The Stork and the Ostrich, or Language Use and Attitudes in the Cité des Chasseurs

In this section I describe the results of twenty interviews which I conducted in late 1983 in the suburb of Strasbourg where I lived, the Cité des Chasseurs, some ninety houses which form a post-war addition to an old village which has amalgamated over time with the town, the Robertsau (Sarg 1981).

The purpose of these interviews, which were conducted in the subjects' homes, was to clarify the psychological and attitudinal background to the linguistic situation as expressed through people's reports of their own use of French and Alsatian and through their opinions on linguistic matters concerning Alsace (Gardner-Chloros 1987b). My own position as interviewer partly resembled Milroy's (1980) position in Belfast as a 'friend of a friend'. I was both trusted as a fellow-inhabitant of the Cité and considered enough of an outsider to have opinions of all kinds thrown at me, thanks to my 'neutrality' as a foreigner. I described myself as carrying out a survey on the use of French and Alsatian in the Cité, which caused no surprise as Alsatians are used to discussions and controversy about their 'linguistic question'. The interviews were conducted in French; this also was accepted without difficulty since French is the lingua franca for all relatively formal exchanges between non-intimates; at the same time, I tried to ensure that Alsatian was not excluded, or its use underestimated, by saying the odd word in Alsatian and mentioning that I understood it and had followed classes to learn it.

Socially, the Cité des Chasseurs has risen from council-housing—it is made up of wooden chalets built just after the war to house large, needy families quickly—to an owner-occupied and well-tended enclave, since the town council eventually sold the houses to their original tenants for a nominal price. The Robertsau, of which the Cité is part, has become a desirable suburb as it retains a rural air but easy access is provided by bus to town; numerous families of international origin working at the Council of Europe have settled there, though in the Cité itself hardly any of the houses have changed hands beyond being passed down to—or shared with—the next generation and their children. Among those interviewed, only one family had lived in the Cité for less than five years and almost everyone had been born and bred in Strasbourg. In only four of the families did one of the two partners come from a part of France other than Alsace; in two further cases, one partner was foreign but in both cases of German mother tongue and so dialect-speaking. My only criterion for selecting interviewees had been that both French and Alsatian should be spoken in the household, regardless of by whom and in what proportions.

Subjects interviewed were aged between 20 and 70, most being in their forties. Table 2.5 gives the occupations of both members of the couple for each of the families interviewed. It is hardly surprising, given these demographic data, to find that this population was conservative in linguistic matters and more dialect-speaking than the Strasbourg average; more than a third of the Cité inhabitants who subscribe to the local paper take the German ('bilingual') version whereas the Strasbourg average is 23 per cent (Fig. 2.3).

TABLE 2.5. Occupations of Both Members of Couples Interviewed

Occupations	Number
Members of professions (incl. teachers) and executives	6
Office employees	12
Social and paramedical workers	4
Workmen, technicians	8
Market gardeners[1]	2
Shop workers	2
Housewives	6
TOTAL	40

[1] Market gardening is the traditional source of livelihood in the Robertsau, and one of the couples interviewed ran a 'pick your own' farm.

The Cité is recognized by its inhabitants as being predominantly dialect-speaking, partly because of the high average age (the couples who originally moved in with their children after the war are now at least 60 and many much older) and also because of the Cité's ethnic homogeneity, its static population, and its village-like, cut-off character. The Cité has its own state nursery and primary school, which were once thronging with children but now, a generation later and due to the falling birthrate, are undersubscribed. It is significant that the children practically never utter a word of Alsatian at the school, either in class or at playtime, although many clearly understand it and even speak it to some extent at home (Gardner-Chloros 1983).

The interview results which follow are intended not as a static picture of the linguistic situation in a particular corner of Strasbourg, which is bound to have its idiosyncracies, but rather as an exploration, through a case-study, of some of the complex psychological factors underlying the transformation which has taken place over the last forty years in Alsace. Alsace has in that time gone from being a predominantly dialect-speaking area in which French was used in certain clear-cut domains (administration, school-teaching) to being now a French-speaking area in which some sections of the population use the dialect in some areas of their life. As I have mentioned above, official action cannot on its own explain why language shift occurs, just as political support for a language cannot on its own ensure its survival, as is clear from the case of Irish Gaelic (Mackey 1979); all such action is mediated by the group members' attitudes, feelings, and priorities. As the German popular song, much loved in Alsace, puts it succinctly, 'die Gedanken sind frei' (thoughts are free) and a language which disappears, ultimately, has no one but its own speakers to blame.

Use and Symbolic Importance of Alsatian

'C'est à dire, même une poésie, si elle est écrite en allemand, elle est beaucoup mieux carrément laissée en allemand que si vous la traduisez. C'est carrément le coin alsacien; il faut le laisser alsacien; donc il lui faut sa langue.' (Housewife interviewed in the Cité des Chasseurs)

('I mean to say, even a poem, if it's written in German, is much better just left in German than if you translate it. This is the Alsatian corner; it must be left Alsatian; so it must have its language.')

The quotation above illustrates the association repeatedly alluded to by those interviewed, between the Alsatian dialect and Alsace's separate identity from the rest of France. The dialect is so heavily invested as a symbol of regional identity that it is instantly used, I was told, even by those who are rather anti-dialect at home, when they meet another Alsatian outside Alsace or see a car with the local '67' number plates; it is an object of nostalgia and homesickness for exiled Alsatians, once again regardless of their intellectual position with respect to the language question. The dialect is described as an 'inheritance' and as part of the Alsatian's 'birthright'; even those who are against its being taught recognize that it amounts to 'a kind of identity'. This identity is, however, occasionally questioned by younger people, and older people, who emphasize how important it is to them, recognize that it is no longer so important for the young. Most feel that an Alsatian who does not speak the dialect is not really an Alsatian, even if s/he speaks a regional form of French; it is the dialect which has always distinguished Alsace from both of the two powerful nations which were engaged for so long in a tug of war over its allegiance. Thus the loss of specific Alsatian identity associated with the decline in use of the dialect is both recognized and regretted. The middle generation, those between 40 and 60, seem most acutely aware of this loss. 'We can no longer really answer your questions—we are no longer real Alsatians' was the pathetic comment of one lady who had, in fact, brought up her children in the dialect.

Sadness gives way to anger towards those who consider themselves too fine to speak the dialect and who are accused of snobbery. Young women, and in particular young saleswomen, are the main targets of this resentment, particularly when they 'pretend' not to understand someone speaking the dialect.

One cannot know, of course, whether those so accused are actually pretending or not, but their good faith is, sometimes unfairly, even more in doubt if they happen to speak French with an Alsatian accent. 'I always say to them: "Don't you understand?"' reported one nurse about her colleagues; 'You *look* as if you ought to speak Alsatian . . .'. A grandfather reported that his young granddaughter would pretend not to understand him speaking the dialect when she didn't want to do as he was asking her. 'I'll play deaf too next time you ask *me* something', he would say to her. 'You understood me perfectly.'

But while some do and some don't mind being thought of as dialect-speakers, nobody, I was told, likes to be thought of or treated as a non-French-speaker. A postal worker and a representative of the Electricity Board whom I interviewed separately both mentioned that tact required all conversations with clients, even in the country, to start in French though they might then immediately switch to Alsatian with a shared sense of relief.

The mismatches between actual linguistic competence and the competence which one wishes others to believe one possesses are of great psychological complexity. 'We're *too* near the frontier', one old gentleman repeated several times during the interview; 'That's our problem; we've *always* been too near the frontier . . .'.

At an intellectual level, many recognize the advantages of this geographical position: the Alsatians' easy access to Germanic culture, their natural role as interpreters in the broadest sense. But for many, this advantage is seen instead as a source of problems: it is the Alsatians' bilingualism which distinguishes them from the other French and which makes them 'more Germanic' than the rest, and this they still consider a disadvantage. The paradox in their attitude is not new and was described, for example, by Hoffet (1951); what is interesting is that forty years later, the paradox is still alive.

In extreme cases, there can be a pathological avoidance of the dialect which is associated with earthy values and by extension considered vulgar; I was told of three separate cases of young girls who systematically shied away from Alsatian for that reason, whereas no comparable cases were mentioned of a blanket avoidance of French.

The French Language and 'les Français de l'Intérieur'

While the dialect acts as a symbol of being Alsatian, French, for its part, is credited with the presumed characteristics of 'les Français de l'Intérieur', as the non-Alsatian French are still known in Alsace. It is considered to have a richer vocabulary than the dialect because it is the vehicle of a richer culture, to be more 'precise', more complicated, and to have greater musical qualities. Some say it is a better vehicle than Alsatian for intellectual discussions and it is recognized as having a more extensive vocabulary in certain specific (e.g. technical) areas. The majority, however, say simply that you express yourself best in the language you know best, the specialization of vocabulary in certain areas being seen as a relatively superficial difference. Some go further and defend Alsatian as more expressive, humorous, and poetic than French, giving examples of earthy designations and witticisms untranslatable into French. In one such case, after listening to my interlocutor—a market gardener—sing the praises of the dialect for some time, I asked whether he thought that French also had its own particular qualities: he put on a vary naïve 'search me' expression and said: 'Oh, I wouldn't know that . . . we don't think about such things, we don't . . . we think about the vegetables and the flowers.' What could one add, other than saying that the ostrich would seem to be a suitable rival to the stork as a regional symbol for some Alsatians.

The decline in the use of Alsatian, which is recognized by all, is not considered, at least by this group, to be due to any inherent superiority of French. As the surveys already described also tend to show, the decline of the dialect is in great part seen as due to a variety of social factors, notably urbanization and the overwhelming role of the media, especially television. The francophone policy in schools for over forty years is not held up as responsible: it is an unquestioned assumption that education takes place in French. There is still resentment and bitterness, however, that up to about ten years ago, pupils using the dialect, even at playtime, were punished in certain Strasbourg schools. Such measures do not in fact appear so much to lead to the disappearance of a language as to a functional separation of the two varieties; it was clear from the interviews that the subjects all had areas in their own lives reserved for Alsatian and others reserved for French. One employee explained to me that he always reported to his boss on his work in French, although they spoke Alsatian to each other at all other times. His answer, when I asked him the reason why, seemed to come as a revelation to him too; after a few moments' thought he said it must be because he was seeking approval for what he had done, 'like a pupil showing his work to a teacher'. Such a comment illustrates the enormous complexity of factors contributing to language choice, and simple observation of such a scene between the employee and his boss would have been unlikely to be as revealing as the interview.

Language choice also depends very heavily on the stereotypes which are held about other speakers. One elderly couple whom I interviewed said their daughter was (overwhelmingly) 'francophone'. In a later interview, the daughter in question said that unfortunately she was mainly a dialect-speaker, but that she had made sure that her own children's first language was French. By coincidence, I also interviewed a schoolteacher who had the children in question in her class; she took them as examples of young Alsatians who can't speak French properly because the dialect was always spoken in their home. Nor were such contradictory perceptions unique. The linguistic competence of others is not judged objectively, nor in isolation from other factors; judgements concerning it are part of a complex overall judgement about the person. For example, being a good French speaker appears to go with being well educated and culturally sophisticated. I was repeatedly told in connection with French, but not with Alsatian, that one had to 'speak correctly', 'pronounce correctly' or even 'turn a phrase like a Parisian would turn it'.

On the other hand, and here again one encounters an ambivalence of attitude which is likely to communicate itself to children brought up in this environment, there is clearly some residual sense of detachment from 'the French' or 'les Français de l'Intérieur', revealed partly by the denominations themselves. Similarly Alsatian is referred to by the generic 'le dialecte', or 'le patois' (slightly more derogatory), whereas French is of course 'le français'. This seems partly due to the fact that Alsatian is not considered worthy of being called a language or having a name—I was told it had 'no grammar', 'no rules', and that it wasn't really a language at all (Denison 1982)—and partly due to the fact that, as an intimate object, it does not need a specific name—like Mummy, Baby, or Darling.

Some consider themselves to be 'handicapped' compared with the Parisians, other accuse these same Parisians of being 'fine talkers who produce a lot of hot air' ('de beaux parleurs qui disent n'importe quoi'). The contradictions are still there, more attenuated and subtle than they were just after the war; memories of being ridiculed because of one's Alsatian accent while fighting in the French Army during the war, or indeed, more recently, while doing military service, were repeatedly evoked. A family in which only the mother spoke the dialect, who had returned to Alsace after spending the war years in the Dordogne, told me that at that time they had felt far more isolated than now, since the general 'mentality' was still 'very German'. On the other hand, they themselves had been not a little surprised to see the famous slogan: 'C'est chic de parler français' ('It's smart to speak French') displayed all over town. 'We didn't think it was more "chic" than anything else', they said simply.

Bilingualism and Children's Language Use

The attitude of subjects interviewed in this survey towards both Alsatian and French is, as we have seen, ambivalent and they are not willing to identify fully

LA MARSEILLAISE

Fɪɢ. 2.6. Hansi, (1873–1951) wrote and illustrated numerous works on Alsace, its legends, and traditions, while always emphasizing the region's attachment to France. Here children in Alsatian costume are pictured singing the French national anthem.

La Marseillaise, Hansi. © DACS 1991.

with either language. Theoretically, the obvious solution for children growing up in this environment would be to cultivate both languages equally so as to draw on the advantages of both; but the reality is often different. After the war, I was told, the Cité children still divided into two camps in their games: 'the Alsatians' and 'the French'—and all spoke the dialect. Now, it is almost impossible to find a child of school age in the Cité who speaks Alsatian fluently, although many understand it as it is spoken daily in their homes. The dialect has become, for them, a passive, one might even say a suppressed language.

This is not only due to the influence of school, which remains a French bastion today and which for many years, as we saw, was a place where the use of the dialect was banned entirely. It is also due to the parents' deliberate policy, which was repeatedly mentioned to me, of speaking French to their children even when they themselves spoke it poorly, which only very recently has started to give way to the opposite policy in some middle class families. As for bilingualism, it is treated as an object of suspicion and caution in practice, in spite of a theoretical recognition of its advantages—just as most parents would rather not throw their newborn baby into the water, even though they have been told that newborn babies can swim. The adults interviewed tended to consider themselves as either predominantly French-speaking or predominantly dialect-speaking, and rarely if ever described themselves or their acquaintances as balanced bilinguals.

'I am profoundly—but really profoundly—convinced', said a French teacher whom I interviewed, 'that the average—or [socially] modest—Alsatian cannot speak either French or German correctly ... The average Alsatian's lack of culture (*inculture*) is greater in both languages than that of a German with respect to German or a Frenchman with respect to French' (Martin-Jones and Romaine 1985). One need hardly add that this teacher's own large family had never been exposed to Alsatian in the home, in spite of their father's dialect-speaking background, for added to his suspicion of bilingualism was the conviction that Alsatian was not a proper language anyway. Those who took the decision to speak French to their children in spite of their own clear preference for Alsatian were often older parents, whose children were now grown up, and who were much influenced by the post-war anti-dialect policies. 'We *had* to speak French to them', I was told about that period, where 'had to' refers to an ideological commitment. 'C'était un parti pris après la Libération de parler français aux enfants', said another ('It was a decision of principle after the Liberation to speak French to the children'). Such parents are not those who regret this decision, since their children, surrounded by fluent dialect-speakers, usually also learnt the dialect, though some parents refer disparagingly to the mixture of languages to which their policy gave rise, by a jocular folk-label such as 'haggedi-baggedi' or 'charivari' ('topsy-turvy, push-me-pull-you'). Ultimately such parents feel even now that the imperfect French which they passed on has been more useful to their children than Alsatian would have been.

But there are also many younger parents, whose children are now, at most, in their teens, who took the same decision and who now regret it bitterly because they have realized that, contrary to what they thought, their children will never speak Alsatian. Like the post-war parents, they wanted to give their children a social and educational advantage by teaching them French, but this time this francophone influence snowballed with a more general social and linguistic evolution which is today eliminating the dialect entirely from young people's usage in some social classes. These parents are frustrated, as they themselves have a nostalgic loyalty to Alsatian and are bewildered by their children's total inability to speak it. 'We thought they'd pick it up later—but they don't speak a word.' Thus one can identify a whole category of parents whose present views on which language should be spoken to children are entirely at odds with their own past practice with their offspring.

As for the parents whose dominant language is French, their efforts to teach Alsatian to their children are limited to the use of a few expressions remembered from their own childhood. For example, 'Komm!' is very often used instead of 'Viens!' even by total francophones, and other short orders like 'Schlupf!' meaning put on, get into your coat, sleeve, etc. are quoted as examples. Such parents also are sometimes regretful that their children should speak no Alsatian and look to their own parents to teach their children something of the dialect—a vain hope, since those of the grandparents' genera-tion are most thoroughly conditioned to speak French to young children. Even today, in spite of the so-called resurgence of the dialect, which can be traced back to the various 'back-to-roots' movements of the late 1960s or early 1970s, very few parents actively support the introduction of Alsatian teaching or teaching in Alsatian at school. The fact that not all children would arrive equally prepared for such teaching is held up as an insurmountable obstacle; the 'overloading' of existing syllabuses is held to be another. Deep down, one suspects there lingers a much more irrational inhibition concerning the use of the Alsatians' private language in the context of a public, French place like school.

Linguistic and Psychological Repercussions of Language Attitudes in the Cité for the Next Generation

In Chapter 1 I criticized certain approaches to bilingual competence in which speakers were divided into two groups, as compound/co-ordinate, additive/ subtractive, or other (Hamers and Blanc 1989) on the basis that such approaches were reductive, and over-simplified the complexity and variety of multilingual or pluriglossic competence (Denison 1972). In this description of the interviews conducted in Strasbourg I have not attempted to explore the various individual factors, such as amount and type of exposure to the two languages, intelligence or language aptitude, etc., which contribute to the development of each individual's competence. I have restricted myself to the opinions and attitudes voiced by adults which are part of the packaging within which the two languages are presented to children, while emphasizing the complex and often self-contradictory nature of that package. It follows, if one also considers the countless individual factors which I have left out, that the bilingualism of the Cité's children cannot be described in any simple way and that clear-cut predictions as to what may happen in the future are also ruled out.

What one can say now with some confidence is that children who are actively bilingual are in a minority and the majority only speak French. On the other hand, I came across numerous signs of the children's passive knowledge of the dialect; for example, children often intervene in conversations between adults in Alsatian, usually using French themselves but showing perfect understand-ing of the dialect. Conversations between children and grandparents are not infrequently conducted with the children speaking French and the grand-parent Alsatian, each understanding the other perfectly but making no apparent attempt to accommodate to the other.

The situation in which a language which is perfectly understood remains entirely passive deserves further psycholinguistic investigation. It is clearly a different phenomenon here than that which can pertain when one learns a foreign language and one's understanding is far in advance of one's productive ability. Here one has the impression—perhaps mistaken—that if one could just say the magic word to remove the inhibition, the self-imposed rule that Alsatian is an adults' language—or a vulgar language—then countless children and teenagers who never utter a word of Alsatian would suddenly start speaking it fluently. In three cases reported to me, this inhibition was carried to an extreme point and led to a total rejection of the dialect by three young girls; the youngest, aged 6, had spoken nothing but Alsatian until she started school and according to her parents had given up speaking Alsatian almost overnight when she started learning French at school; any word extracted from her in Alsatian would be spoken with a strong French accent. On the other hand, it seems very likely, from other situations observed in Strasbourg, that the dialect, which is repressed during primary school, resurfaces in adolescent boys (Bickel-Kauffman 1983) and takes on the role of an in-language in that group, symbolizing and reinforcing male solidarity. There is clearly a lot more to be learnt about language acquisition in multilingual settings at a psychological as well as a cognitive level (Carrington 1989).

Conclusion

Through this study I have attempted to put some psychological 'flesh' on the bare bones of the statistical facts reported in part i, with reference to a small urban bilingual population, untypical, no doubt, within the capital city by its ethnic homogeneity but revealing none the less by the complex fashion in which the two languages in daily use are invested with various properties and associations.

In particular there appears not to be any clear-cut or linear correlation between a sentimental attachment to the dialect and competence or frequency of use; at times the correlation even appears to be negative, since young adults, insufficiently competent in Alsatian to pass it on to their children, appear very attached to its survival, whereas older people, for whom it has always been the dominant language, associate it with historical events which they would rather forget and are fatalistic about its possible disappearance.

As for the children, the dialect is at the same time one of the facts of their existence—the principal means of communication between some of the adults around them—and the object of a studied detachment, perhaps even of shame which those same adults have communicated to them.

The less essential the language is for actual communication, the more dominant such feelings appear to be in people's general attitude towards it, till

Linguistic Landscape and Social Reality

MONSIEUR SCHMITT, AGRICULTEUR
M. Schmitt, Farmer

MONSIEUR SCHMITT, CADRE DU TERTIAIRE
M. Schmitt, white-collar executive

'Do you like speaking Alsatian?'

'Yes, except when I'm in the presence of people from "l'Interieur" (the rest of France).'

'Do you like speaking Alsatian?'

'No, except when I'm in the presence of people from "l'Interieur" (the rest of France).'

MADAME MEYER, MÉRE DE FAMILLE
Mme Meyer, housewife and mother

GILBERT MEYER, LYCÉEN
Gilbert Meyer, schoolboy

'Do you usually speak Alsatian with those close to you?'

'Yes, except with my children.'

'Do you usually speak Alsatian with those close to you?'

'Yes, except with my parents.'

SOYO ET © COSHER FOR PASSOVER.

FIG. 2.7. Paysage linguistique et réalité sociale

it becomes an ideological or historical symbol and little more. Unfortunately for those who would wish the dialect to be preserved, for many children it appears to be a merely passive language, understood but never actually used.

It seems likely that the generation at school now in Strasbourg will be the first in Alsace to which the term 'bilingual' can no longer really be applied.

3

Principal Approaches to the Study of Selection and Switching

i. Introduction

Before describing the studies undertaken as part of this research, it is useful to consider the various ways in which language selection and code-switching have been studied up to now. Language selection (or language choice—the two terms are here used interchangeably) will be dealt with briefly: whilst it is conceptually inseparable from code-switching—since switching represents changes in the choices which are made or, in some circumstances, a 'third choice'—a full description of work done on language choice would be beyond the scope of this book. It could be taken, at the minimum, to include all the work carried out on diglossic situations, whether diglossia is defined narrowly or broadly (for a selection of important work on this question see Fishman, *et al*. 1986).

In fact, much of the work carried out on code-switching is equally relevant to language choice; but my principal aim here will be to distinguish the different levels at which code-switching has been studied and to indicate how those different levels correspond to different underlying questions and different spheres of interest.

ii. Language Choice

Diglossia, Domains, and Networks

Two fundamental articles served to draw attention to the sociolinguistic significance of language choice and still serve as a point of reference today: Ferguson (1959) and Fishman (1965). The first identified the common characteristics of situations where the question of language choice arises on a societal level, that is situations where two distinct varieties are in complementary distribution with one another. Ferguson's examples all concern regions where the distribution between a 'High' and a 'Low' variety is between two forms of a historically and/or lexically related language (e.g. classical and dialectal Arabic); but the concept of diglossia has since been extended both to the use of two entirely different languages in a single area (e.g. Spanish and

Guarani in Paraguay) and to the use of several languages or dialects in multi-lingual countries. A discussion of the concept's application in Alsace can be found in Tabouret-Keller (1984), and I shall return later to the crucial relationship, explored by Scotton (1986), between diglossia and code-switching.

Fishman's article represents an indirect development of Ferguson's; it attempts to systematize further some of the numerous possible variations between different multilingual situations. Three factors are identified as determinants of language choice: the social group to which one belongs (which has an objective aspect and an aspect dependent on one's subjective choices), the situation in which one finds oneself at the moment when the communication takes place, and the topic one is discussing. In each society there are certain characteristic *conjunctions* of such factors, which Fishman calls 'domains'. Such domains, which can be related to language use, may be situated at various different levels of abstraction. For instance, in one society there might be significant differences between the domains of home, school, and work; in another, the distinction might lie instead between intimate, informal, formal, and inter-group domains. The concept of domains has been developed by Fishman (1972) and also applied to bilingual situations, in particular those characterized by code-switching (Breitborde 1983).

The two concepts of diglossia and of domains have lately been much criticized; diglossia is seen as *precluding* rather than explaining language choice as it defines the circumstances under which a particular variety *must* be used and therefore theoretically precludes individual options. Domains, whilst still referred to in the literature, have largely been abandoned in favour of approaches centred more on the micro-level of individual interactions, for example that of Gumperz which will be discussed further in relation to code-switching. Yet the only conceptual tool which has had a comparable influence to these macro-level explanations is the concept of social networks, employed by Milroy (1980); but this alternative systematization of social relations is used by Milroy more in relation to linguistic *variation* (in Belfast) than to language choice as such. It has, however, recently started to be explored in relation to language choices in contact situations and code-switching by Labrie (1988) and Sobrero (1988). Gumperz used the network concept in a discussion of code-switched speech: 'Because of its reliance on unverbalized shared understandings, code-switching is typical of the communicative conventions of closed network situations' (1982: 71–2).

The continuing influence of these concepts is demonstrated by the fact that linguists refer to them even when they are pointing out their explanatory inadequacy in the situation which they are studying. Thus Dorian (1981: 80) remarks on the fact that topic (one of the components of domains) seems irrelevant to language choice in East Sutherland: 'Interesting in the East Sutherland context is the weakness of the *topic* factor in code-choice ... *No* topic requires English, no matter how remote from East Sutherland life or how "modern" and "technological".' Dorian found that the factors most predictive of language choice in that context were the age and identity of the interlocutor, that is factors situated on a more micro-level, or related more to characteristics of the individual than of the society.

Models of Choice

As several linguists have remarked, there are difficulties in systematizing the functioning of linguistic choice beyond a certain point. Gal (1983: 68) remarks for example that linguistic behaviour is not simply a form of obedience to societal norms, but that the speaker actively participates in the construction of the situations in which she finds herself and in the interpretation of communicative intentions. Nevertheless, several attempts at systematization have been made, one possibility being to represent the various parameters of the choice in the form of a flow-chart. This was done by Rubin (1972: 53), in relation to the choice between Guarani and Spanish in Paraguay, which she reduces to an interplay between two principal factors, power and solidarity between the speakers; by de Feral (1979: 113), in relation to the choice between pidgin, the official language, and the vernacular in Cameroon, and by Fantini (1978: 301), who explains the linguistic choice of two bilingual children in a flow-chart (see Fig. 3.1). Such representations necessarily give a very simplified picture of the interrelationships between the relevant factors; nor should they be confused with an individual psychological explanation of particular instances of choice. At best they serve to highlight statistical tendencies, but in

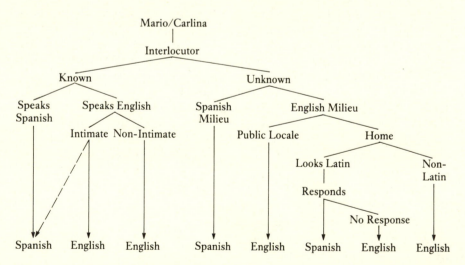

FIG. 3.1. Interrelation of Social Variables and Code-Choice in Non-Marked Exchanges
(based on Fantini 1978: 301)

a multilingual situation (as opposed to the situation represented in Fig. 3.1) they run a serious risk by presenting the varieties about which the choices are made as distinct and separate entities. In individual discourse there is likely to be a continuum between the varieties which are used (Le Page and Tabouret-Keller 1985) and code-switching represents one point or section along that continuum. Pfaff (1979: 292) writes, for example, that amongst Spanish speakers in the south-west of the United States, there is a stylistic continuum going from Standard Spanish to Standard English, various types of mixed mode being situated along the points on that continuum (such varieties, as we saw in Chapter 2 in relation to Alsace, often acquire folk labels, e.g. Tex-Mex, Spanglish, Mix-im-up, etc.).

An alternative form of systematization, but one which still forces the factors influencing choice into a one-dimensional mould, is the implicational scale, as used, for example, by Gal (1979: 102), to show with which interlocutors (ranging from God to young children) the bilingual inhabitants of Oberwärt, Austria, use German (G), Hungarian (H), or both (GH). This matrix, in which the role of the interlocutor is represented as determinant of language choice, also 'predicts' the situations where code-switching can occur, which are those where either language may be used (see Fig. 3.2).

A major difficulty with this representation, as with the flow-chart, is that it leaves out the role played by the negotiation of code-choice within a conversation. Clearly such 'negotiation'—and the use of code-switching as an intermediate or, to use Scotton's term (1988), an exploratory choice—will be resorted to more frequently in multi-ethnic situations, where interlocutors cannot 'place' one another, than in a closed village community. But there is always some room for negotiation within a conversation; for that reason I prefer to the somewhat mechanistic systematizations of language choice outlined above models of language choice which, while describing the factors which constrain choice, do not prejudge the result of that choice in a particular instance (Grice 1975).

One such model is that of Lüdi (1984: 12), developed in the context of various migrant communities in Switzerland. Lüdi outlines three 'conceptual dimensions' which help us to understand language choice: first, he distinguishes situations where the bilingual considers he has the choice to speak one or the other language from situations where that choice seems to be entirely predetermined (for example, by a monolingual interlocutor or by social pressures). This dimension is called 'determinism-freedom'; it has a social component and a component related to the speakers' repertoires.

The second dimension Lüdi identifies is called 'precoding-neocoding' and distinguishes those situations ('precoded') in which sheer force of habit practically imposes the use of a variety, from those where speakers must make an active effort of interpretation to arrive at their choice.

Thirdly, a distinction is made between 'automatic' and 'controlled' language

Number of speaker	Age of speaker	Interlocutors												
		1	2	3	4	5	6	7	8	9	10	11	12	13
1	14	H	G		G	G	G	G	G				—	
2	14	H	GH		G	G	G	G	G				—	
3	25	H	GH	GH	G	GH	G	G	G	G	G	G	—	
4	15	H	GH		GH	GH	G	G	G				—	
5	13	H	GH		GH	—	G	GH	G				—	
6	13	H	H		GH	—	G	G	G				—	
7	27	—	H		GH	—	G	G	—				—	
8	3	—	H		GH	—	GH	GH	—			G	—	
9	4	—	H		GH	—	GH	GH	—				—	
10	17	H	H	—	GH	—	—	GH	G	G	G	—	—	
11	39	H	H	GH	GH	—	GH	GH	—	GH	G	G	—	G
12	52	—	H		GH	—	—	—	G	GH	G	G	—	
13	23	H	H	H	H	GH	GH	GH	—	GH	GH	G	—	
14	22	H	H		H	—	GH	—	—	H	GH	G	—	
15	33	H			H	—	GH	GH	—	GH	GH	G	—	
16	35	H			H	—	GH	GH	—	GH	GH	G	G	
17	40	H			H	—	GH	—	—	GH	GH	G	—	
18	42	H			H	—	GH	GH	—	GH	GH	G	—	

#	Age	1	2	3	4	5	6	7	8	9	10	11	12	13
19	43	H	H	H	H	H	—	—	—	H	GH	GH	G	—
20	35	H	H	H	—	H	H	H	GH	GH	GH	—	—	—
21	40	H	H	GH	GH	GH	H	H	GH	G	G	G	—	—
22	40	H	H	H	—	H	—	—	—	H	GH	GH	—	G
23	50	H	H	H	H	G	—	—	—	GH	G	G	—	G
24	61	—	—	—	—	—	—	—	GH	GH	GH	GH	—	—
25	54	H	H	H	H	H	—	H	—	GH	GH	GH	GH	GH
26	55	H	H	H	H	H	—	—	—	H	GH	GH	—	—
27	61	H	H	H	—	—	—	—	—	GH	GH	GH	—	GH
28	59	H	H	H	H	H	—	H	—	GH	GH	GH	H	GH
29	50	H	H	H	—	—	—	H	—	H	GH	GH	—	—
30	50	H	H	H	H	H	—	—	—	GH	GH	GH	GH	—
31	60	H	H	H	—	—	—	H	—	H	—	—	GH	GH
32	60	H	H	H	H	—	—	H	—	H	GH	H	GH	GH
33	63	H	H	H	H	—	—	H	—	H	H	H	H	GH
34	64	H	H	H	H	—	—	H	—	H	H	H	H	GH
35	66	H	H	H	H	H	—	H	—	H	H	—	—	H
36	68	H	H	H	H	H	H	H	H	H	H	GH	H	H
37	71	H	H	H	H	—	—	—	—	H	H	H	H	H

FIG. 3.2. Choice of Language by Women in Oberwárt, Austria (observations)
(based on Gal, 1979: 102)

Interlocutors: (1) God; (2) grandparents and that generation; (3) black-market clients; (4) parents and that generation; (5) Calvinist minister; (6) age-mate pals, neighbors; (7) brothers and sisters; (8) salespeople; (9) spouse; (10) children and that generation; (11) non-relatives under twenty; (12) government officials; (13) grandchildren and that generation. G = German; H = Hungarian.

choices. This dimension relates to the speaker's awareness, or lack of it, regarding the choice he makes. The notion of 'automatic' or 'unconscious' choices is a recurrent one with respect to code-switching and I shall be returning to it, largely with a view to highlighting its problematic nature, later on (see Fig. 3.3).

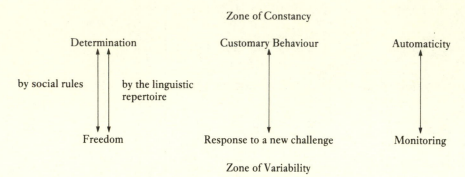

FIG. 3.3. Constancy/Variability
(based on Lüdi 1986: 222)

Whether or not one accepts the validity of the 'dimensions' chosen in this case, the advantage of such a model is that it highlights certain important factors without trying to make them part of a closed system; it is thus compatible not only with the inherent variability and unpredictability of language choice but also with the possibility of change.

The Transition Between Choice and Switching

The use of the term code-switching implies that there are two distinct entities or codes and that it is possible to move cleanly and neatly from one to the other. The same applies, of course, to terms like borrowing and interference, the use of which should instantly put us on our guard for the same reason. To talk about 'a language' is to abstract a set of patterns: syntactic, semantic, phonological, etc. from the behaviour of a group of speakers—who are themselves defined as the people who speak that language—that is in a circular fashion (Denison 1987: 66). Now it may be perfectly legitimate to talk about 'the English language', or any other language, on the basis that a sufficiently large number of people agree that a large body of written texts and a wide range of spoken productions are part of this entity, although one could of course find many borderline cases on which they would not agree (a poem in pidgin English, a schoolboy's essay riddled with syntactic and orthographical 'errors', the speech of a foreign learner of English with a very heavy accent). One is then talking about an abstraction which allows one to discuss a variety of practical issues and to exchange opinions, that is to indulge in social intercourse. But as soon as you talk of code-switching, you are inevitably placing yourself in the context of a linguistic discussion and not a general one. You are implying that there are speakers who 'switch' codes, whether in a conversation or within a single clause. Now those speakers must by definition have some, albeit minimal, competence in two different codes, and since they are *individuals*, those codes must be related to one another in their minds in a variety of fashions. There is therefore a serious question as to whether these two separate entities, the two 'languages' which we can legitimately talk about when referring to, for example, the dictionaries written for each of them or the number of children learning them as a second language at school, can still be considered to be two separate entities in the minds of speakers (Tabouret-Keller and Gardner-Chloros 1985). They may be separate at some levels, but totally indistinguishable at other levels (for instance, a speaker's semantic categories or intonation may remain the same regardless of whether he is speaking language A or B). There are also cases of code-switching where it makes little sense to talk of a base or matrix language (Clyne 1987) and a language from which some elements are taken since both languages are either equally represented or give rise to a mixed, third system (Romaine 1989). In such cases the term 'code-switching' becomes inappropriate and a term such as 'mixed discourse' must be used. In a recent study of language contact in South Africa, McCormick further found that where non-standard varieties are involved, the switch-point in a code-switched utterance could not always be assigned to one language or another (McCormick 1989: 310), and that the unassignable lexical items should be regarded as bridge elements. This leads her to a plea for a classification of code-switching based on a "speaker-oriented perspective". From an analytical point of view, Thelander (1976) has pointed to the problem of assigning mixed varieties to specific co-occurrent clusters, and by extension to implicational scale models.

What does this imply for the transition between language choice, or code choice, and code-switching? It implies first of all that we can only make deductions about the significance of speakers' changing languages in mid-conversation or mid-clause by referring to the particular social and psychological conditions which pertain there and then; for what may appear to be two separate codes to the observer may be psychologically part of a single system for the speaker. There is a clear demonstration of this fact in bilingual children's mixed productions, before they have reached the stage of being aware that there are two separate systems. Gumperz makes a similar point (1982: 66) when he discusses 'we-codes' and 'they-codes' in contact situations; the minority variety, associated with intra-group, informal activities serves as a 'we-code', whereas the majority language, or 'they-code', is associated with out-group relations and is felt to be more informal and stilted and less personal. An internal structural analysis cannot, however, reveal the functions of each code:

The process by which meaning is conveyed must be studied in terms of the stylistic interrelationship of sentences or phrases within the passage as a whole, not in terms of the internal structure of particular sentences. (Gumperz 1982: 72)

Woolard (1988) shows this to be true in relation to code-switched jokes in Catalonia. In fact, one must go even further, to understand meaning, than the 'passage as a whole'; extralinguistic information about the community and the speakers is also necessary.

An intriguing pragmatic model which covers both code-switching as the exploitation of contrasts and switched or mixed discourse as a psychologically unified mode of speech amongst bilinguals is Scotton's theory of markedness and code-choice (1986a; 1988). In certain circumstances switching does not serve to redefine the rights and obligations implicit in the conversation: it is itself an 'unmarked choice', but one which is only possible where the distribution of languages is not strictly hierarchical as it is under strict diglossia. I shall return to this important new contribution to the field in the next section, when discussing the principal ways in which code-switching has so far been studied. Types of code-switching are now being increasingly documented where it is the whole discourse mode, rather than individual switches which is considered the important factor (Poplack 1980; Scotton 1988).

iii. Code-Switching

Classifications

Many extensions and sub-classifications of the meaning of 'code-switching' have been proposed since Haugen's (1956) original coining of the term to cover situations in which 'a bilingual introduces a completely unassimilated word from another language into his speech'. Haugen himself used 'switching' to cover the alternate use of two languages, 'code-switching' when a single word is introduced, 'integration' for the regular use of material from one language in another, and 'interference' for the overlapping of two languages. Clearly our object must be to find the taxonomy which (*a*) most reliably distinguishes between the different linguistic phenomena we find in the case of language contact (I use 'reliably' simply in the statistical sense of giving rise to agreement between several judges) and (*b*) corresponds most convincingly with the attendant sociological and psychological factors.

The distinction within code-switching which has no doubt had the most enduring influence is Gumperz's distinction between 'situational' code-switching, in which distinct varieties are associated with distinct activities or situations, and 'conversational' code-switching in which the changes take place within a single conversation without there being any change of interlocutors, topic, or any other major factors in the interaction (1982: 60–1). Conversational code-switching is at times 'metaphorical' when the purpose of using variety B in a conversation which began in variety A is to introduce new connotations linked to variety B. The classic example of metaphorical code-switching is that given in Blom and Gumperz (1972) of a conversation in the Social Security office in a Norwegian village, where two villagers switch from Standard Norwegian, in which they have been discussing business, to the local dialect to discuss family and village matters. Situational code-switching is now considered almost too general to qualify as code-switching at all and increasing attention is paid to code-switching within the same conversation and especially within clauses. Situational switching is linked to the concept of diglossia and language-related domains; on a practical level, it can easily be distinguished from conversational switching. The distinction between metaphorical and other kinds of conversational switching is of a quite different order since it implies a complex judgement as to speakers' motivations, which in turn depend on an understanding of their cultural values.

Bal (1981) suggests a comparable distinction within code-switching to that between the situational and the conversational; according to him, there is 'real mixed discourse' on the one hand and changes of variety which merely reflect the implicit 'rules' of a diglossic society, which impose certain linguistic patterns which are in turn reflected in individual speech. Even 'real mixed discourse', he continues, has nothing to teach us about the internal 'rules' governing individual speech, since it is a manifestation of mixed *parole* and not of mixed *langue*. This last point is analogous to the distinction between language borrowings and speech borrowings drawn by Grosjean (1982). In practice it is extremely difficult to make a clear distinction between speech and language borrowings; at what level of abstraction is the 'system' to which these terms refer situated?

Even within a single individual, one can distinguish between the way s/he is speaking now, the way s/he speaks in general (or in other circumstances), the way s/he thinks s/he speaks, the way s/he thinks s/he ought to speak, the way s/he thinks people in general ought to speak, etc.; each of these categories may correspond to an elaborate and more or less consistent set of patterns which s/he carries around in his/her head. If you add to this the various categories of pattern which exist in the society or community where s/he lives, you exponentially increase the number of possibilities. It no longer seems realistic, in the light of our present understanding of linguistic variation and speakers' overlapping repertoires, to talk of a simple distinction between competence and performance or language and speech when discussing code-switching. If you want to decide which 'rules' the bilingual code-switcher is applying, you first have to decide what you mean by a rule (Le Page and Tabouret-Keller 1985: 193–298).

Other classifications of code-switching abound but many suffer from a lack of rigour with respect to the level of analysis which is being considered. Kachru (1978), for instance, distinguishes three categories: 'code-switching', where the change in variety is determined by 'the function, the situation, and the participants' (i.e. a category similar to Gumperz's situational switching); 'code-mixing', which is defined principally from a linguistic viewpoint in that it 'entails transferring linguistic units from one code to another', and, third, 'odd-mixing', which does not fulfil the same condition as the other two categories of being 'functionally and formally a rule-governed phenomenon' but whose characteristics are not further elaborated. The problem, clearly, with such a classification is that each of its terms is defined on a slightly different basis: 'code-switching' on a macro-sociolinguistic basis, 'code-mixing' mainly on a linguistic basis, and 'odd-mixing', apparently, as a spare category for those instances of linguistic coexistence which do not fit either of the preceding categories. Even within the linguistic description of code-switching, there is a need to distinguish the level one is talking about, and switching may be phonological, syntactic, lexical or any combination of these (Lawton 1979).

Process or Result?

'Code-switching' is an inherently ambiguous term; firstly, one needs to make clear that one is using 'code' in its most general linguistic sense, of a 'neutral label for any system of communication involving language' (Crystal 1980: 66) and not in a more abstract symbolic sense (Jakobson 1963: 63), nor as the antithesis of 'message' as Martinet (1970: 25) suggests, nor yet in any other ideologically charged sense (Bernstein 1971–2). Secondly, the word 'switching' can indicate both the 'action' of switching—and whatever mental processes that implies—and the linguistic results of multiple changes, that is, it is used as a synonym for switched or mixed discourse, and is then a purely linguistic label.

Very roughly, one can state that the first sense of switching is that adopted in a variety of psycho- and neurolinguistic studies, whereas the second definition is that which underlies the sociolinguistic approach. It is regrettable that the two traditions largely ignore one another, since each could gain essential insights from the problems which preoccupy the other. Psycholinguists seek measurable physical correlates of the 'action' of changing languages, sometimes without asking themselves what is a language for the individuals they test, and to what extent their two languages constitute separate systems. Linguists and sociolinguists, on the other hand, build up theories about significant transitions in their subjects' discourse without adequate psychological foundations: for example, code-switching has been compared repeatedly to style-shifting in monolingual discourse without any attempt to discover whether the two phenomena are genuinely comparable at a psychological level.

The whole search for a 'grammar' of code-switching, as I shall again be stressing later, implies the coexistence of two distinct entities, the two codes, and allows little room for a discussion as to how separate those codes actually are and whether they are not in fact situated along a 'more-or-less' continuum.

iv. Code-Switching and Other Marks of Language Contact

Historical Development

The study of code-switching only became possible once the results of two languages coming into contact ceased to be considered as aberrations and ceased to be compared with narrowly defined monolingual norms. Nowadays, no informed person would dispute the systematic character of interference, code-switching, pidgins, or of the process of loss in dying languages; it is now a question of describing that systematicity, at a linguistic level and from the point of view of its sociological and psychological motivation.

This change in attitude has coincided with a crystallization within the study of language, of theoretical linguistics, sociolinguistics, and psycholinguistics, to mention but three of the sub-disciplines, as separate fields of research. At least in theory, the latter two now avoid value judgements about particular speech-forms. In sociolinguistics, for example, we no longer talk in terms of 'ideals' as in Weinreich (1953: 73–4):

> The . . . ideal bilingual switches from one language to another according to appropriate changes in the speech situation (interlocutors, topics, etc.) but not in an unchanged speech situation, and certainly not within a single sentence.

For Weinreich, 'abnormal proneness to switching' was an individual personality trait found among people who spoke two languages from a tender age and mixed them without relying on any system. I have come across such individualistic, quirky switching among conference interpreters and it is clear that the phenomenon can exist at an idiosyncratic level. One should be wary, furthermore, of drawing too rigid a distinction between idiosyncratic speech habits and community norms: within a social group in which language switching is a permissible and accepted part of the repertoire, there may none the less be individuals whose switching habits owe more to their own imaginative construction than to that repertoire.

What dates Weinreich's description far more than the reference to idiosyncratic aspects of switching is the reference to the 'ideal' bilingual. The fiction that there exists any kind of 'ideal' speaker has, I repeat, *in theory* been abandoned by sociolinguists; it is associated with Chomsky's 'ideal speaker-listener in a homogeneous community' (1965: 3), that is with the theoretical school of linguistics in which language is studied without reference to the actual circumstances in which communication takes place.

Relations between Language Contact Phenomena

Once the results of language contact are no longer considered arbitrary aberrations, the need arises to classify them and describe the relations between them. A useful starting-point, which highlights the problems inherent in such a classification, is Haugen's distinction (1956: 40) between code-switching on the one hand and interference and integration on the other: whereas interference and integration are instances of the levelling down of differences between the two codes, in code-switching the distinct character of the two codes is said to be preserved. This is basically the same distinction as is drawn in the work of Poplack and Sankoff (1984) and Poplack (1988) between code-switches and loans.

Other researchers, such as Shaffer, have drawn the line differently again (1978: 267); according to him, both code-switches and loans require there to be two separate languages, and only interference is a step towards the *fusion* of the two languages. I have argued elsewhere (Gardner-Chloros 1987*b*) that code-switches and loans are in fact opposite ends of a continuum, and will return to this argument later.

We observe fundamental mistakes in such attempts at the discrete classification of linguistic phenonema. First, it is not always possible to assign a linguistic unit to one system alone; second, even if it were, and we could then speak with confidence of distinctions between 'code-switches' and 'loans' and 'interference' to be made in linguistic terms, there is a priori no reason to assume that these three categories correspond to significantly discrete categories of social and psychological behaviour.

Up to now, in the majority of works on code-switching, the essential socio-psychological correlates of the linguistic categories proposed have been lacking. Yet language contact does not take place in a vacuum; as Gumperz has pointed out (1964: 1124) the process of borrowing is not simply a linguistic process but depends on social norms which allow it to take place. In the field of pidgin and creole linguistics, to which a great deal of attention is paid today, the social and historical criteria used to try to determine whether a contact language should be regarded as a pidgin or a creole do not necessarily produce the same judgements as result from applying linguistic criteria, and it is very much questioned whether we are here dealing with discrete categories of language. Linguists tend instead to speak of the process of pidginization and of creolization—which may be taking place inadvertently in the same community, as today in Papua New Guinea. A correspondingly dynamic view is needed in the field of code-switching.

v. Which Frame of Reference?

Like bilingualism, code-switching can be studied at individual or at group or societal level. Therefore, as Tabouret-Keller writes in her critique of Breitborde (1983: 144), when seeking the 'significance' of code-switching one must distinguish its social significance from its significance in the individual's personal history and from many other possible levels of significance, including that related to an abstract linguistic analysis. Equally the reasons why a segment is in Language A or B must be distinguished from the speaker's reasons for using a mixed mode of speech.

This fundamental classification, often omitted, is a precondition for answering many of the questions which have concerned researchers in this field.

Code-switching: A Stage in Language Shift or the Product of Stable Bilingualism?

It is clear that language shift—that is, shift from the use of Language A to Language B in a community over time—does not follow a universal order, does not always include the same stages, and above all does not always proceed at the same speed (Kallen 1981; Thomason 1986). Code-switching need not, for example, always be present as one of the phases in language shift; nor can its presence be taken to imply that a particular type of shift (e.g. the 'disappearance' of one of the languages) will inevitably take place. In the case of Hindi–Punjabi code-switching in Delhi (Gumperz 1964), the constant mixing of the two languages is accompanied by a high degree of convergence between the two, particularly at lexical level; yet the two languages remain distinct thanks to a small number of differences, especially syntactic and phonological.

On the other hand, Nadkarni (1975) describes a case of syntactic convergence between two unrelated languages (Konkani and Kannada), which does not fulfil any particular linguistic 'need': Konkani has simply adopted the form of the Kannada relative clause in the community studied, on top of its own Indo-Aryan form. In spite of this convergence, due no doubt to contact extending over several generations, code-switching, according to Nadkarni, is unheard of in this community.

We thus have an instance of convergence with code-switching (Gumperz) and of convergence without code-switching (Nadkarni). An example of code-switching without apparent convergence is provided by Poplack and Sankoff in relation to the Puerto Rican community in New York, which in spite of constant switching between Spanish and English (of which a large part is intra-sentential) and in spite of the political and economic dominance of English, has resisted in a remarkable fashion the potential influence of English on Spanish syntax. In this community, the mixed mode represents 'a distinct communicative resource for fluent bilinguals' (1980: 49) and this state of affairs, in which many members of the group have three distinct varieties in their repertoire (Spanish, English, and the mixed mode) is reported to be relatively stable.

Ultimately, however, any appraisal of the stability or transitoriness of code-switching is dependent on two factors: first of all on the criteria used to identify how many codes or languages are spoken in a given community. The three varieties identified by Poplack and Sankoff may well correspond to three extreme sets of circumstances in the Puerto Rican community, but it is unlikely that the distinctions are so sharp in the speech of any given individual member of that community, even allowing for the fact that Poplack has recognized the Puerto Rican case to be an extreme one (1988). Secondly, the answer to the question will depend on the time-scale chosen: descriptions of 'stable bilingualism' should at least include comparisons between the oldest and youngest members of the group and if possible follow the changes which occur over a number of years. Gumperz and Hernandez state that we find code-switching 'each time minority language groups come into contact with majority language groups under conditions of rapid social change' (Gumperz 1969: 2). But what is 'rapid' in the life of a society is not 'rapid' in the life of an individual, and it is for that reason that explanations of code-switching must make absolutely clear which level of explanation they are addressing.

The Role of Competence in Code-Switching

Fishman (1975) wrote that in situations of stable multilingualism, speaker competence was not a variable which could help to answer the question as to who spoke what to whom, since all members of the community spoke both languages.

But although the society may itself be bilingual, each of the individuals who make up that society is bilingual to a different extent; in any given interaction, the interplay of the various speakers' competences is a very significant factor in the determination of language choice and code-switching. In Alsace, for example, where certain 'bilingual' individuals are noticeably more competent in French and others in Alsatian, a conversation might well start in French and then move on to Alsatian when one of the participants has trouble expressing something in French or comes to the conclusion that his interlocutor would rather speak Alsatian.

Researchers such as Gumperz and Bal (cf. above) have therefore drawn a distinction between two types of code-switching of which one is the direct product of diglossia in the society and the other is more closely linked to the individual and the choices he makes. Unfortunately, no empirical basis has been found which would allow us to say which kind of code-switching we are dealing with in a particular instance. Diglossia and the individual choices made within a diglossic context cannot in practice be satisfactorily separated in order to provide objective correlates for different types of switching.

The Variables Correlated with Code-Switching

Breitborde (1983) differentiates between microlinguistic factors which can help explain patterns of code-switching, that is factors issuing directly from the interaction itself, and macrolinguistic factors, that is the societal norms relevant to an explanation of code-switching (for example, which are the important 'domains' in that society). He sets himself the task of 'redressing the balance', as he sees it, within code-switching research, by concentrating on the second level of explanation.

This raises a difficult problem: on the one hand, microlinguistic theories, of which a good example is Clyne's theory of 'triggering' (1967) which will be discussed below, are often at the same time valid at a superficial level and insufficient at a deeper level. On the other hand, as Tabouret-Keller remarks in her comments on Breitborde, in a macrolinguistic theory, the factors entering into that theory (e.g. age, sex, social network) must be hierarchically arranged. But the hierarchy will depend on circumstances: the elements which make it up will vary in importance not only due to changes taking place outside the particular society but also because of the individual choices exercised by individuals with respect to the aspect of their social identity which they want to bring to the fore (Tabouret-Keller 1983: 145). Let us take an example: Rubin (1962), in a discussion of bilingualism in Paraguay, compares the use of High and Low varieties in diglossia with the use of informal 'thou' and the formal 'you' forms, since both are connected with macrosociolinguistic factors, power and solidarity. Cases of doubt as to which form to choose are cases where the two factors are at odds with one another, for example when one addresses an equal, from a social or professional point of view, with whom one does not feel solidarity.

In Scotton's terms (1986b) one can make a marked or an unmarked choice between the High and Low varieties, and one can equally make a marked or unmarked choice of terms of address. But in an individual situation—for instance, in Alsace, where one could argue that both choices, that between High and Low and that between *tu* and *vous* and *du* and *ihr*,[1] must be made in any conversation between bilinguals—it is highly unlikely that individual choice will be exercised to the same extent with respect to both decisions. One of the two decisions may be regarded as more or less obvious or automatic, or both, or neither, depending on circumstances. Neither the macrosociolinguistic nor the microsociolinguistic level of explanation is sufficient in itself, nor can the two be plausibly separated in practice; code-switching is deeply enmeshed in both.

---

[1] *Ihr* is Alsatian for HG *Sie* (polite form).

vi. Contributions and Problems of
Psycholinguistic Approaches

Code-switching, as we have seen, has been studied from various different angles and consequently several distinct approaches have been crystallized. These could be grouped together in several ways, but the most obvious division is between the psycholinguistic and sociolinguistic approaches. I shall not be going into the neurolinguistic studies of bilingualism and in particular bilingual aphasia, which are in a different way also relevant to switching (Albert and Obler 1978; Paradis 1983; Vaid 1986).

The Electric Model

Psycholinguists have often based their approach on the electrical sense of 'switch', that is to say they have concerned themselves with the nature of mechanism which allows the bilingual to change from one language to the other.

Penfield and Roberts's 'single switch model' (1959) put the hypothesis that the activation of one of the bilingual's two languages renders the other inoperative. This was followed by the two-switch model described in a series of papers by Kolers (1966), Macnamara (1967), Preston and Lambert (1969), and Macnamara and Kushnir (1971); according to this model, rather than there being a single process which allows bilinguals to change from one language to the other, there are two different kinds of switch, an 'output switch' governing the production of language and an 'input switch' governing reception. Each of these processes takes a certain time, which can be measured in hundredths of a second. In the case of the input switch, this time is measured by comparing the time taken by bilingual subjects to read a monolingual text and the time taken to read a text in which there are a number of to and fro switches from one language to the other. The latter task, not surprisingly, is found to take longer and the surplus time is divided by the number of language changes in the text. 'Switching' can then be characterized by the time necessary to accomplish it.

Such an approach is naïve about the nature of language and languages: no attempt is made to discover which *aspect* of the complex activity that subjects are asked to perform—reading a mixed language text—slows them down, although Macnamara concedes that the sheer confusion brought about by these constant shifts in 'preattentive operations', rather than the language changes as such, could partly account for the time-difference noted.

In fact, as Neufeld (1976) observes, switching is not a unitary phenomenon but has several different components: phonological, lexical, semantic, etc., which need not all function simultaneously. The time taken to switch must therefore depend on the experimental task which the subject is given. For example, Neufeld considers that the mental stocking of the two languages is more unified at lexical level than at other levels; this could have consequences for the type of switching which creates the greatest confusion in the subject.

The Experimental Approach

A more subtle model is put forward by Albert and Obler (1978). Instead of a switch with two positions, they suggest that bilinguals move from one language to the other by means of a continuous flexible control system which is sensitive both to changes in the linguistic and the non-linguistic environment, and which never totally excludes either language.

More recent work by Dechert (1982) on the HIPS, or Human Information Processing System, goes further in the same direction. Though he does not deal with switching as such, Dechert compares linguistic capacities with an information processing system, in which various inter- and intra-linguistic plans and programmes compete to organize the material. Errors, hesitations, and accidental structural mixtures are due in the second language as in the mother tongue to the more or less conflictual interplay of these strategies.

What kinds of experimental studies are carried out to confirm such hypotheses? One example is Albert and Obler's bilingual version of the 'Stroop Colour-Word Task' (1978), which, in its original monolingual version, is used in the area of perceptual psychology to explore the conflict between visual and linguistic information: subjects are asked to state the colour of the ink in which a number of words are written, these words in fact being colour-names different from those of their ink-colour; thus the word 'red' is written in green ink, etc. In the bilingual version used by Albert and Obler, a further difficulty is introduced, as some of the words are in one language and some in the other and the subject furthermore has to name the colours sometimes in one language and sometimes in another. The principal result which emerges is that subjects make fewer mistakes when the word is written in their second language than when it is written in their mother tongue; one may conclude that bilinguals can more easily exclude linguistic information in their second language than their mother tongue (a capacity called 'gating'), although they are affected, to a lesser extent, by conflicting signals in their second language also.

A comparable experiment was carried out by Taylor with word associations (1971). Bilingual subjects were asked to provide as many associations as came to mind in whichever of their two languages they wished, to words which were sometimes in one language and sometimes in the other. On average, associations given in the same language as the stimulus were more numerous than those given in the other language, from which it was concluded that intra-linguistic links are stronger than inter-linguistic ones.

Such psycholinguistic experiments present a number of problems: first and foremost, deductions are made concerning normal linguistic functioning on the basis of an experimental activity which is only very remotely similar to it. Second, in spite of considerable human and technical resources and statistical processing, the actual results of the experiment are frequently meagre and ambiguous; the statistical level of significance reached is often minimal and the results of the various sub-tasks do not all lead to the same conclusion. On the other hand, of course, like any properly conducted experiment, such tests have the advantage of being replicable in principle, which introduces an element of objectivity into this complex and intangible area. But results, however objective and well-documented they may be, are only of interest if they contribute to answering a question which is important in itself.

A more recent psycholinguistic model which is relevant to code-switching as it occurs in natural speech is that of Green (1986). An inhibitory control mechanism is proposed which suppresses L.2 when L.1 is being used mono-lingually. In spontaneous use, this suppression of L.2 is held to be *external*, that is, not within the L.2 system itself, leading to dysfluencies in L.1 when L.2 expression of a concept is more available than one in L.1. Furthermore, 'in the case of code-switching, there need be no external suppression of L.2 at all; at least in the simplest case, such as continuous word association, the output can be free to vary according to which words reach threshold first.'

The work of Grosjean (1985*a*; 1988) and Grosjean and Soares (1986) also represents an attempt, at a psycholinguistic level, to uncover the complexity of language processing and production process in bilinguals, who, it is argued,

should be studied as such and not always in comparison with monolinguals. Instead of being the sum of two monolinguals, bilinguals are competent 'native speaker-hearers' of a different type; their knowledge of two languages makes up an integrated whole that cannot easily be decomposed into two separate parts. (1986: App. A)

Compound/Co-Ordinate and Independent/Interdependent Bilingualism

Researchers have also made use of code-switching to explore the distinction between compound and co-ordinate bilingualism. This distinction refers to the individual's linguistic history and is based on the hypothesis that compound bilinguals have two signifiers, one in each language, for each concept signified; such people are generally early childhood bilinguals who learnt both languages simultaneously. Co-ordinate bilinguals, on the other hand, are those who, having learnt the two languages in different contexts, have different sets of associations for words in language A and their 'equivalent' in language B.

Psycholinguists now tend to prefer to the compound/co-ordinate distinction another, similar distinction which need not be related to the individual's linguistic history, that is the distinction between 'independent' and 'inter-dependent' bilinguals. (One should point out that some *socio*linguists continue to use the compound/co-ordinate distinction, somewhat loosely.) At any age, the bilingual's two languages may be more or less independent of one another, and their degree of independence may fluctuate within the individual's life, according to the circumstances in which the two languages are used. An example of extreme interdependence might be provided by a professional translator, for whom every word or expression in L.1 elicits an equivalent in L.2; an example of extreme independence could be that of someone who spends their annual holidays in a place where they speak a language other than their mother tongue and for whom the two languages are therefore never juxtaposed in time.

The advantage of this distinction, compared with that between compound and co-ordinate bilingualism, is that it allows a person's bilingualism to be described with reference not only to their linguistic history but also to other factors, intellectual or related to personality and situation: on the other hand, both sets of distinctions assume that there are two separate units, the two languages, which are related in a variety of possible ways to a third and quite separate unit, 'meaning'. Clearly this is an over-simplification of the ways in which linguistic and semantic systems are related to one another in the bilingual's brain.

The distinction derives behavioural, but not theoretical, support from the various experimental tasks designed to confirm its existence. These consist, for example, in tests designed to show a difference between the way in which independent and interdependent bilinguals switch from one language to the other; the hypothesis is that independent bilinguals will find the transition from one language to the other more laborious, whereas interdependent bilinguals can move from one language to the other in a more automatic or unconscious way. If true, this should presumably have repercussions for the way in which they code-switch. Jakobovits (1968) makes use of a battery of tests including the timed decoding of mixed-language texts, timed translation of lists of words of which some are in L.1 and some in L.2, grammatical tests, Cloze tests, subjective evaluation by the subjects of their own competence in the two languages, etc. Subjects whose general level in the two languages is considered equal are classed as compound—or interdependent—bilinguals if they perform well in the tests requiring rapid transitions to be made between the two languages. Lambert and Rawlings (1969) found that bilinguals whom they had classed as 'compound' could provide more word-associations to a bilingual word-list than the 'co-ordinate' bilinguals faced with the same task.

Here again, the results must be treated with a degree of caution. First, the results of these tests, which are intended to distinguish the compound from the co-ordinate bilinguals thanks to their performance, are in fact the only information which we have about them: we are neither concerned with their personal histories nor with the contexts in which they use their two languages. Their type of bilingualism is therefore purely defined by the test, and the definition of the different types of bilingualism is therefore circular: group A is made up of compound bilinguals because they obtained such and such results in the test, and obtaining such results indicates that one is a compound bilingual.

Secondly, performance on some of the tests, for instance those where the task involves translating, is very much affected by practice or experience at carrying out that particular task, and we have no information about how practised subjects are.

Thirdly, the reason given for the difference between the result of the two groups is not entirely convincing: Jakobovits suggests that compound bilinguals react more quickly because they are only replacing one linguistic 'label' by another, whereas co-ordinate bilinguals must seek out an equivalent in their semantic systems. But we do not know for certain—and again it begs the question—that in translating from one language to another one can bypass semantic processes, whatever one's linguistic history.

Finally, from the point of view of the tests' contents and the ways in which linguistic capacity is measured, 'language' or 'language A' is often simply identified with a list of words. At best, therefore, one is measuring or describing the subjects' lexical knowledge, which cannot be simply equated with their knowledge of the language, let alone with their ability to use it.

General Critique

In formulating a more general criticism of the kind of psycholinguistic research on code-switching described above, it is important to meet scientists in this area on their own ground rather than judging them in relation to criteria external to their purpose.

As we have seen above, code-switching may concern related or unrelated languages, dialects, sociolects, etc. Within any such combination, what is likely to make the switch more or less difficult from a strictly psycholinguistic point of view is partly the social values attributed to the two varieties but above all the linguistic 'distance' between them: the structural, lexical, phonological differences between the two varieties. But so far psycholinguists (with the exception, at a theoretical level, of Neufeld) have tended to ignore the different kinds of transition which are subsumed under the term code-switching; the psycholinguistic process of switching languages is studied as if it were a single unitary one. One could argue that experiments such as those described above cannot be carried out unless such a simplification of the underlying question takes place; if that is so, one must question the usefulness of setting them up, with the elaborate means which they necessitate, in the first place.

vii. Contributions and Problems of
Sociolinguistic Approaches

Sociolinguistic approaches to code-switching can be divided into those which put more stress on the 'socio-' and those which emphasize the '-linguistic' aspects of the subject. But within both tendencies code-switching is generally viewed as part of a broader set of phenomena emanating from language contact. This is because sociolinguists who observe and analyse language as used in real life are inevitably confronted with the fuzzy edges of the phenomenon, for example, the borderline between code-switching and borrowing or the different implications of switching from a dialect to a standard language and switching registers. Indeed, for practical purposes one may divide work in this area into that where code-switching is considered as an aspect of other phenomena such as accommodation or language shift and that where it is studied in its own right.

Code-Switching as an Aspect of Various Sociolinguistic Phenomena

Code-Switching and Bilingual Behaviour

Code-switched speech can be considered as a compromise between the two component varieties where these carry different connotations or social meanings for speakers and interlocutors (Scotton 1982). As such it can form part of linguistic accommodation as defined, in particular, in the work of Giles since it is one of the processes which allows one to 'converge' or 'diverge' from one's interlocutor (Giles and Smith 1979): one can 'converge' by using the language in which one's interlocutor is most at ease to the extent that one is able, having recourse to switching when one's level of competence is insufficient; one can 'diverge' by introducing elements from the code in which one's interlocutor feels less at ease into one's own discourse, so as to distance oneself from their manner of speaking while still being understood. One can also indulge in mixed discourse, where speaker and interlocutor are equally bilingual, in order to reinforce the sense of a shared, mixed identity and to maintain the status quo of the bilingual situation (Tabouret-Keller 1983: 147). However, as far as I am aware, code-switching has not as yet been considered in any detail in relation to accommodation theory. A theory which places code-switching in a broader sociolinguistic context is Scotton's theory of marked-ness and code-choice, explored in a series of articles (1983; 1986*a*; 1986*b*; 1987*a*; 1988). Unlike accommodation theory, the markedness model does not make assumptions, which are difficult to verify empirically, about individual speakers' motivations. Instead, and this is particularly clear from the paper in which Scotton sets out the relationships between code-switching and diglossia

(1986*b*), the choice of code, and consequently code-switching also, is seen as reflecting the rights and obligations which attach to each code in that particular community and which the speaker wishes to bring to the fore in that particular interaction. Mixed discourse, and arguably switching itself, is ruled out in strict (Fergusonian) diglossic contexts as each of the varieties available is exclusively allocated to certain kinds of situation. In other kinds of bilingual context, where the division of roles between the two varieties is not so strict, one can switch in order to mark shifts in the aspects of social relationships which one wishes to emphasize as the conversation develops. Mixed discourse can itself, in such contexts, constitute an unmarked or neutral choice in that it allows the rights and obligations associated with both varieties to be present simultaneously in the conversation, whereas the choice of one of the two varieties on its own would carry a specific set of connotations which may not be desired.

Multi-Dimensional Character of Code-Switching

Sociolinguists concerned with various aspects of bilingualism have considered code-switching to be a possible stage in a complex process of linguistic development and change, from a variety of different angles: Kuo (1974), in a study of Chinese migrants in the United States, considers code-switching a stage in their linguistic assimilation: the first generation only speaks Chinese at home, the second frequently indulges in code-switching; it seems likely that the third or fourth will only speak English. T'Sou (1975) studied the same group but emphasized the function of code-switching as an indicator of individual acculturation processes; to the extent that an individual still code-switched between English and Chinese it could be considered that his assimilation was still incomplete. Auer and di Luzio (1982) considered, on the basis of their work among Italian migrant children in Germany, that code-switching represented a stage in their linguistic development which was not only dependent on their age but also on their network structure and on their attitudes towards the two nationalities and cultures.

Various studies of bilingual child language acquisition have shown that children brought up speaking two languages go through a stage when they use lexical items from Language B in the context of Language A if they have not yet acquired the equivalent in Language A (Ronjat 1913; Leopold 1939–49; Swain 1971; Lindholm and Padilla 1978). Such 'mixtures' apparently affect between 2 and 4 per cent of such children's utterances and disappear as the child acquires the equivalents in both languages. These results concern situations where the child is presented with two separate languages rather than with actual code-switching, however, and further work needs to be carried out in order to determine how a child presented with code-switched speech reflects the mixed character of the input in his or her own speech (Tabouret-Keller

1969). A third possible situation is that described by Agnihotri in his study of Sikhs in England (1987): there children and adolescents to a certain extent create their own mixed forms from the two idioms spoken around them; they are themselves at least in part responsible for the development of a code-switched form of speech.

Finally, according to Weinreich, a correlation between age and linguistic behaviour represents 'the synchronic manifestation of language shift' (1953: 94). As it is rare to find communities where there is no correlation between the speakers' ages and the use of code-switching, it seems likely that code-switching is always an indicator that change is occurring—though apparent stable monolingualism in a community does not of course conversely imply that no change is occurring. There are also cases where internally motivated language change (e.g. structural simplification), the type traditionally studied by historical linguists, can on closer examination be seen to be attributable to language contact whether or not there is any overt code-switching in the community (Thomason 1986).

Trudgill provides an interesting example of the relationship between code-switching and language shift in his research on Arvanitika, an Albanian dialect spoken in Greece and in the process of being replaced by Greek (1976–7). Trudgill explains the difficulty which he encountered in distinguishing between reduction (loss of some aspect of the language) and simplification (in which the forms change but all the functions are preserved), this distinction being obscured by the compensating role of code-switching, in this case the importation of Greek forms into Arvanitika. Lavandera (1978) reports a similar phenomenon in Buenos Aires where migrants of Italian origin switch between their own dialect of Argentinian Spanish, Cocoliche, and standard Argentinian Spanish to compensate for reduced stylistic options available to them in either code. This remark is highly significant as it suggests that code-switching may be a key element in understanding certain cases of shift. At any rate, it would seem essential to consider its role in any study of the decline of a variety, bearing in mind that it may manifest itself at a variety of levels, including the phonological (Caramazza, *et al*. 1974).

The Rehabilitation of Code-Switching

The second group of sociolinguists, who make code-switching the principal focus of their research, have contributed to its no longer being considered an aberration, as Weinreich implied, by demonstrating its communicative uses on the one hand and by attempting to extract its linguistic patterning on the other.

Gumperz and the Functions of Code-Switching

Gumperz's basic distinction between 'conversational' and 'situational' switching, which has been described, had considerable influence on subsequent research. Clearly, however, it is more of a theoretical distinction than one which can be used in practice when analysing bilingual conversations; for in practice how is one to distinguish between switches brought about by diglossic parameters and others? Only rare and extreme cases will be clearly attributable to the existence of a particular social 'rule' outside the speaker. Quite apart from the knowledge of the speaker's motivations which such a decision implies, it requires a further judgement to be made regarding the delimitation of the varieties between which switching takes place. Even Blom and Gumperz's classic example of conversational code-switching in a Norwegian village (1972) was later criticized by Norwegian linguists who claimed that the Hemnesberget dialect and the official language were not clearly distinct entities but points on a continuum.[2]

Gumperz's contribution to code-switching studies is, however, considerable, ranging geographically from India to Norway to the United States. As early as 1964, Gumperz remarked that alternation between Hindi and Punjabi in Delhi must clearly be functional as the two varieties had already converged to such an extent that the few remaining differences would also have been wiped out if they did not serve a specific purpose. In 1967, on the basis of three case-studies from different language groups (Hindi–Punjabi, Kannada–Marathi and Spanish–English in New York), Gumperz stressed the necessity for 'ethnographically oriented linguistic measurement', that is for an analysis of bilingual speech which takes account of the norms of the bilingual society in question. In 1969, with Hernandez, he developed the idea that the choice of a particular variety has a significance which depends on the social presuppositions shared within the group. In 1970, he gave a series of examples of the different possible functions of code-switching in a conversation, such as the reinforcement of an important message, quotation, indication of the principal addressee of the message or the introduction of specific connotations linked to the other language. In 1982, he synthesized the results of his other studies and stressed again that code-switching shows that members of a group have their own socially defined notions of code and grammatical system. 'Code-switching', he writes, 'provides evidence for the existence of underlying, unverbalized assumptions about social categories, which differ systematically from overtly expressed values or attitudes.'

Gumperz's contribution to the 'rehabilitation' of code-switching is linked to his repeated demonstrations that it is not an arbitrary or random phenomenon, but an additional 'communicative strategy' to those available to monolinguals.

[2] Personal communication by Gjert Kristoffersen.

Bilinguals, for Gumperz, are not fundamentally different from monolinguals simply because the varieties they use are connected with what are generally called 'different languages':

Rather than characterizing members as speaking particular languages it seems reasonable to speak of speech behaviour in human groups as describable in terms of a linguistic repertoire consisting of a series of functionally related codes. (1972: 145)

Numerous researchers explored and analysed the functions of code-switching in different parts of the world along the lines proposed by Gumperz: Parkin among different ethnic groups in Nairobi (1974); Di Pietro among Italians living in the United States (1978); Scotton among workers in three African cities: Kampala, Nairobi, and Lagos (1976); Scotton and Ury in further African contexts (1977); Hasselmo among Swedish immigrants in the United States (1970); Garcia (1980) and Fantini (1978) by carrying out case-studies among bilingual children. The results of some of the taxonomies developed will be taken up later in the book.

Linguistic Analysis: From the Identification of Regularities to Code-Switching Grammars

The second aspect of the rehabilitation of code-switching has consisted in a series of attempts to show its systematic character, at lexico-semantic, grammatical, and functional levels. In particular the school of research associated with the work of Poplack and Sankoff attempted to show that there are universal constraints governing code-switching, that is to say a certain number of predictive rules concerning the position in the sentence where code-switches can occur, which cut across language combinations and socio-linguistic contexts.

Linguistic Regularities

Among the earliest pieces of work on the linguistic regularities of code-switching one must mention the work of Clyne among German immigrants in Australia (1967; 1969; 1981). Clyne identified a phenomenon which he called 'triggering': he noticed that the use of linguistic elements shared by the bilingual's two codes (for example, recurrent, culture-specific importations from English when they were speaking German) often provoked a switch into the language of that imported element, which then carried on being used for the rest of the sentence or utterance. More recently, Clyne has developed the notion of triggering in relation to other aspects of the patterning of code-switching including its syntactic characteristics and convergence between the bilingual's two codes (Clyne 1987).

Timm studied the speech of Mexican immigrants in the United States (1975) and Russian–French switching in *War and Peace* (1978), and noted a number of grammatical regularities in the switch points, for example that the switch almost never took place between a pronominal subject and its verb or between two verbs, for example, where one is a complement of the other. Lipski (1978), who also based his work on Spanish–English switching, summarized the grammatical observations made by Timm, himself, and others and reduced them to a few general principles, concerning for example the relation between the number of switches per sentence and the length of the sentence. He postulated the existence of an 'anticipatory mechanism' which controls the match between the first part of the sentence, in Language A, and the second part in Language B: 'Only after production of the sentence has passed the point where transfer to the other language would not entail a radical shift of syntactic structure does the actual code-switch occur.' Although his approach was mainly linguistic, Lipski by implication raised the psycholinguistic question as to whether the two language systems are activated simultaneously or consecutively; as we have seen, the problem with such a question is that it implies that there are two clearly distinct systems in the speaker's mind whereas this cannot be clearly demonstrated.

Code-Switching Grammars

Poplack (1980) and Sankoff and Poplack (1981) took up some elements of previous work on the syntactic regularities of code-switching, but also carried the underlying hypothesis much further. Initially on the basis of work carried out among Puerto Ricans in New York, they proposed that there were only two grammatical constraints on where code-switching could occur in the sentence: the 'equivalence constraint', similar to Lipski's generalization described above, according to which switches can only take place where the grammars of the two sentences map on to each other, and the 'free morpheme constraint', which states that switching cannot occur between two bound morphemes, for example between the stem of a verb and its ending.

Subsequently, and although this approach has continued to flourish (e.g. Woolford 1983), numerous researchers in many different sociolinguistic contexts have found counter-examples to the proposed restrictions (Maters 1979; Martin-Jones 1980; Bentahila and Davies 1983; del Coso-Calame, *et al.* 1983; Romaine 1985; Berk-Seligson 1986; Scotton 1987*b*; Eliasson 1989; etc.); there are also a number of counter-examples arising in the data recorded in Strasbourg which are described in Chapter 6.

Poplack and Sankoff's method of dealing with such counter-examples was twofold: on the one hand they postulated that a number of cases which do not conform with their constraints are not in fact code-switches at all but 'nonce loans', a concept which will be examined below. On the other hand, they dismissed such counter-examples as unrepresentative of the community-wide norms which allow intra-sentential code-switching to flourish in certain bilingual communities; according to them it is these norms, and not the exceptional cases, in which we should be interested. Let us consider each of these claims separately.

Nonce Loans

Poplack and Sankoff's most detailed statement as to what they understand by loans (1984) gives four distinguishing criteria for them: frequency of use, native-language synonym displacement, morphophonemic and/or syntactic integration, and acceptability; however, they admit that not all these criteria will be satisfied in all cases which they want to consider as loan words, and each of them may be satisfied by words which are not. Code-switching they consider to be an entirely separate phenomenon, 'simply the alternate use of the two languages in discourse . . . without any necessary influence of one language on . . . the other.' They suggest that there is a continuum between nonce (or one-off) loans and established loans (Poplack, *et al*. 1987; arguably this is a contradiction in terms, since how can something which happens only once become established?) but no continuum between code-switches and loans.

Scotton (1987) questions the status of 'nonce loans', showing that these forms, which by definition occur only once, behave in a manner more similar to code-switches than to established loans on a number of criteria, notably because they occur (*a*) as vehicles of microlevel social negotiations, and (*b*) with greater frequency in communities which use switching as an unmarked choice.

These are already significant reasons for doubting the viability of nonce loans as a separate category from code-switches. To this one must add the doubts which numerous authors have expressed regarding the validity of the free morpheme constraint on which the category of nonce loans depends. Eliasson (1989) gives examples of word-internal switches gleaned from seven different authors, and adds his own examples taken from switching between English and Maori, which are typologically far apart at many levels. If one assumes that all these examples are loans, then at the phonological level alone one is led to make what are, at the very least, large assumptions:

from this it follows that the phonological structure of Maori would be enriched by several new vowel qualities, fourteen more consonant phonemes, consonants in syllable-final position, and a mass of totally unprecedented consonant clusters. If we shrink back at this unattractive consequence, we will be forced to view them as part of a separate system, for they are after all regular and systematic. But this system has the quite peculiar quality of being ephemeral, yet recurrent: a nonce system that keeps flipping in and out at will. It is clear that the theory forces us to untenable conclusions . . .

In the Alsatian data (Chapter 5) intra-word switching is rarer and occurs principally in verb formations modelled on a traditional pattern of borrowing from French into German. On the other hand there would appear to be many

switched words, in specific semantic categories from which loans are also
taken, which are on their way to becoming loans in the community but are not
yet considered to be fully established as such (Tabouret-Keller 1989)—should
one perhaps refer to 'recurrent switches' as an intermediate category preferable
to nonce loans? For these and other reasons I have argued (Gardner-Chloros
1987*a*) that all loans must start off as code-switches and that there is a relationship of degree or a continuum between the two (Garafanga 1987). Haugen
(1972*a*) also argues for a historical definition of borrowing since synchronic
criteria as to what constitutes a loan are not watertight.

What is in fact the advantage of introducing this new category? Arguably it
has been brought in so as to get round some rather serious difficulties with the
idea of 'constraints'. This has recently been illustrated in the case of the
Punjabi compound verb (Romaine 1989). Romaine shows how Punjabi–
English bilinguals violate both equivalence constraints and constraints based
on Government and Binding Theory (Di Sciullo, *et al*. 1986) when combining
Punjabi 'operators' (e.g. 'kǝrna'—'to do', 'hona'—'to be/become') with a major
category (noun, verb, or adjective) taken from English instead of Punjabi (e.g.
lobbying kǝrna, involve hona). When Sankoff, Poplack, and Vanniarajan (1986)
found analogous examples in Tamil–English switching, where the Tamil
operator 'pannu' is combined with English forms, they got round the problem
that these forms violate their constraints by treating all instances of such
English forms as borrowing; the same applies to phonologically unintegrated
English words which they found with Finnish morphological elements
(Poplack, *et al*. 1987). According to Romaine, the error here is to assume that
the grammatical norms of the two languages in isolation provide the basis for
determining what is grammatical in the mixed code, whereas in fact the mixed
code has its own norms. 'Poplack's defence of the structural integrity of
linguistic systems is motivated less by the evidence than by the desire to justify
the validity of a particular theoretical model of code-switching' (Romaine 1989:
286). As Eliasson (1989) also points out: 'the notion of momentary borrowing
comes to serve as an auxiliary theoretical concept whose function it is to
protect the original theory from criticism'.

Community Norms and Counter-Examples
Secondly, and perhaps even more importantly, the emphasis on community
norms rests on the idea that code-switching is a relatively focused phenomenon, so much so that one can talk in terms of its rules and their exceptions.
This may be the case in some communities, but it seems more likely that in
most there are a range of functionally related varieties, incorporating more or
less code-switching, of a more or less grammatically intricate nature, depending on context and a range of other sociolinguistic factors. Language shift and
language change (e.g. convergence) are both related to the fluctuating power-
play of these varieties. Furthermore, the linguistic phenomena which make up

code-switching are not susceptible to black-and-white categorization (Chapter 6); they are used in different combinations, at different times by the same people in such a way that it is impossible to assign some to 'rules' and others to 'exceptions' on any empirical basis.

For example, as we have seen, a number of instances which Poplack would term 'exceptions' are cases where switching takes place within the word (contradicting the free morpheme constraint)—but there are certainly rules, by which I mean regularities, in the way that code-switched words behave, waiting to be investigated. To call them exceptions is to imply that they are arbitrary or unsystematic, when in reality the problem is that they do not fit into the rigid categorization proposed. In order to cope with them Poplack places her arguments within a variable rule framework, that is one in which there is only a certain probability that the rules proposed will apply in a given situation. An exception is therefore not considered a falsification of the rule, nor even an incitement to reformulate it, but merely a case where that rule does not apply. In Popper's terms (1959), having seen a black swan, we do not concede that our original statement 'All swans are white' has been falsified, but say instead that the bird in question is not a swan.

There are two points to be made in relation to this argument: first of all, it seems to me too easy to dismiss cases which do not fit the scheme as exemplifying a different phenomenon to code-switching, because then as I mentioned above the theory about code-switching is circular and cannot fail to be verified. It seems more realistic to say that there are many kinds of code-switching, some linguistically integrated with the surrounding language and some not, and that it remains to be discovered with what psychologically or sociolinguistically significant distinctions these various types of code-switching correspond.

Second, the variable rule argument is part of a much larger debate (Cedergren 1973; Cedergren and Sankoff 1974) about the nature of language and the best form of scientific method. Suffice it to say here that there is an inherent problem in saying that some instances of code-switching, borrowing, or what-have-you do not conform with a particular 'rule' which one has enunciated. The problem has to do with what is meant by the word 'rule'—a prediction as to what 'must' happen given a particular set of circumstances or a simple generalization on the basis of observed behaviour? For a full discussion of the various possible meanings of this word and the confusion to which it can give rise in linguistic discussions, compare Le Page and Tabouret-Keller (1985).

In her more recent work Poplack (1988) admits that 'ad hoc constraints on where code-switching can occur are not generalizable from one language to another or even across different studies of the same pair in different contexts'; but she maintains the category of nonce loans, which are not taken into account when discussing the characteristics of code-switching. She also maintains that code-switching should not be confused with any kind of borrowing, incomplete language acquisition, or interference—that is, phenomena which she considers unrepresentative of community-wide bilingual norms.

I have explained above why I do not think that such a classification is appropriate for an ever-fluctuating, creative, and unregulated aspect of speech such as code-switching. If code-switching is tied up with language change at all, how could that change ever occur if people—in particular young people—did not violate or, better, rewrite the rules by using forms never heard before?

Thanks to the copious work undertaken by Poplack and her associates and their focus on the notion of rules which govern code-switching, it is now apparent that a much more sophisticated and psychologically plausible approach to the shifting regularities of bilingual speech is required. We must be grateful to them for having provided that focus; but we must move on.

viii. Methodological Problems

I have stressed that no single exclusive approach to code-switching is likely to yield positive results in all cases and that different approaches may be more or less productive in different contexts. The type of observation which is valid and informative among Puerto Ricans in New York is not necessarily so in Strasbourg or Athens.

The Quantitative Problem

The major methodological problem inherent in all sociolinguistic research—the collection of sufficient authentic data and their analysis in the most appropriate manner—is acute in the case of code-switching. For unlike, say, phonological variables which may be present and observable dozens of times in the same stretch of discourse, it is rare for code-switching to be as frequent as that. In a discussion recorded over half an hour, there may only be a single instance of code-switching; yet there is no reason a priori to think that instance any less interesting or significant than switches which follow one another in quick succession in another passage or context.

In fact, to select out the switches in one's data and to analyse them *en masse*, as is done for example in many grammatical studies, while it may seem to be an economical way of proceeding is a technique by its nature designed to neglect the significance of the sociolinguistic context.

Acceptability Judgements

In order to describe the patterning which characterizes code-switching in variety X, one therefore has either to gather a very large sample of switches in each of the categories in which one is interested or else to have recourse to speakers' judgements as to what is an acceptable 'mixed sentence' and what is not, as, for example, did Timm (1975).

But, as has been pointed out by others, such judgements are of particularly doubtful value in the case of code-switching as it is not a 'recognized' form of speech in any sense of the word and so it is not clear what norm speakers can refer to in making their judgement. Bentahila and Davies (1983: 307) add that the use of this technique does not allow us to tell *why* certain examples of code-switching are not considered acceptable:

Thus, while a certain category of switch may be theoretically possible, as evidenced by examples found in actual speech, it is certainly not likely that all invented examples illustrating such a switch will be judged equally acceptable; whether or not the respondents find them natural will also be influenced by whether they can see any motivation for the switch.

Such a remark confirms the necessity for semantic and contextual information in analysing this speech mode.

For these and similar reasons I believe strongly in basing code-switching research only on examples of naturally occurring speech, not even trying to influence it to the extent of getting the interviewer herself to switch strategically at certain points in the interview in order to test the speakers' reaction (del Coso-Calame, *et al*. 1983). In manipulating speech, you never know quite what aspect of the subject's reaction will in turn be diverted from its normal course, nor what the correlation is between that altered reaction and normal, unconstrained, linguistic behaviour.

The Direction of the Switch

The two methodological problems described above are connected with the linguistic description of code-switching. But, as we saw, it is at least equally important to try and understand the functions of code-switching, and in doing this one has to sort out which level of explanation to choose: individual, group, society. Having decided that, there remains the problem of generalizing about a particular variety, for the same one can have a quite different meaning according to the situation (Scotton and Ury 1977). Singh (1983: 71–3) shows for example how in India the vernacular language (English) can on occasions take on the role of a 'we' code and local vernaculars the role of 'they' code among certain groups with social aspirations.

In analysing code-switched discourse observed in Strasbourg, I have at times focused on individual instances of switching and at times on the functions of code-switched speech as such. While the functions of individual switches are frequently found to be the same in different communities, the functions of mixed discourse need to be explored separately in each of the communities where this mode of speech is found, preferably by long-term participant observation. For in some countries it is impossible or meaningless to talk in terms of a 'base' or 'matrix' language and a language from which the switched segments are taken (Clyne 1987).

One observation that seems to be reinforced time and time again is that the two codes may often be mixed in such an intricate manner as to make any explanation in terms of 'interference' and 'system' look very inadequate and artificial. (Agnihotri 1987)

Switching as a functionally unmarked mode (Scotton 1986*a*) has numerous and complex linguistic concomitants.

ix. Conclusions

Code-switching can be studied at so many different levels that researchers from a variety of disciplines have turned their attention to it, often without taking account of the work carried out in related areas.

This does not imply that a satisfactory theory could be found to cover all known instances of code-switching and all ways of approaching the problem; indeed, I am mistrustful of theories which claim to provide too universal an explanation for such a complex phenomenon with its endless psychological and sociological ramifications. It is both a great advantage and a snare of code-switching that within the mass of language it represents a tangible, apprehensible 'moment' which can be isolated and analysed.

For if we are too bound by existing concepts, then we will never progress beyond trying to measure and describe the workings of this transition from one 'language' to another, without ever asking ourselves what these two different entities are, and what makes them different.

Code-switching is, ultimately, a means which individuals use to articulate their personal structures of meaning on to the constraints on the use of languages which are imposed by the society in which they live. It is unlikely that anything other than a pluralistic approach will allow us to come any closer to understanding such a complex phenomenon.

4

The Surveys

One of the main premisses of this book, as we have seen in Chapter 3, is that code-switching is one of a range of possible manifestations of language contact which are interconnected in a complex fashion at a linguistic and at a psychological level. This argument rests partly on evidence presented in this chapter and in Chapters 5 and 6 (Conversational Analysis); partly on a view of the bilingual as a psychologically complex entity and not simply as the sum of two monolinguals (Hamers and Blanc 1989; Grosjean 1985 *b*; Romaine 1989); and partly on the assumption that a 'language' in the abstract (i.e. as described in a grammar, dictionary, etc.) is not the same thing as 'a language' as known and used by an individual (Le Page and Tabouret-Keller 1985: 188 ff.) and that therefore an individual using two 'languages' is not simply alternating between two distinct systems which exist outside him but is instead exploiting—and creating—a complex system of his own.

Before going into the linguistic evidence, however, one needs to gain a rough idea of how and where the two languages, French and Alsatian, are represented in the community in which they coexist. To this end I carried out what are traditionally known as quantitative surveys, though these are mainly not on a scale which guarantees representativity of the population of Strasbourg as a whole. Large-scale studies along quantitative lines sometimes have the disadvantage of allowing the finer contextual issues to fade into the background.

One method which is used (Poplack 1988) when mathematical representativity is the aim is the recording of very large samples of speech from which only the switch-points are extracted and analysed. But code-switching, as we have seen in Chapter 3, raises multiple questions which, I would argue, can best be tackled by using various methodological techniques in parallel with each other. Until we understand the phenomenon better, I consider it a mistake to decontextualize its study, since our best insights about it may well come from trying to answer the deceptively elementary questions of where, when, and between whom it occurs.

i. Language Selection and Switching among Strasbourg Shoppers

Future studies of language in its social context should rely more heavily on rapid and anonymous studies, as part of a general programme of utilising unobtrusive measures to

control the effect of the observer . . . They represent a form of nonreactive experimenta-
tion in which we avoid the bias of the experimental context and the irregular
interference of prestige norms but still control the behaviour of subjects. (Labov 1978*a*:
69)

The aim of the first survey, which is broadly based on Labov's well-known
survey in three New York department stores, was to collect quantitative data on
the use of French and Alsatian in Strasbourg, and on switching between the
two. In Chapter 2 we noted the importance of age, context, and topic in
determining language selection; in addition to expectations deriving from the
presence of these factors, an understanding of the appropriate *situational norms*
is relevant. These norms are, on the one hand, common to many different
social groups, such as the rule that 'the customer is always right', which makes
the customer's variety dominate in customer–salesperson interactions
(Genesee and Bourhis 1982) and on the other hand they are enmeshed with the
particular diglossic configuration in question: thus in Strasbourg an Alsatian-
speaking customer might well refrain from imposing her language because
there is a conflicting norm tending to prefer French as the language of public
conversations with interlocutors one does not know personally.

Hypotheses and Variables

The hypotheses tested in the study were therefore derived both from existing
information on language use in Alsace and from the norms which were
expected to govern the situation which was observed. The first parameter was
social class: it was expected that in stores of higher social standing, more
French and less Alsatian would be spoken than in those of lower prestige, the
independent variable being *the store*.

Both *topic* and *setting* affect language choice. Topic in the strict sense could
not be used as a variable here, owing to the limited nature of the exchanges
observed. Setting was represented by the different *departments*: departments
selling *necessities* such as food or other practical items were expected to call
forth more Alsatian than those selling *luxuries* such as perfume or hi-fi, which
are tied up with social aspirations and the aesthetic side of life. Older
customers were expected to use more Alsatian and less French than younger
customers, the independent variable being *age*; the age of the salesperson with
whom they were communicating was also expected to affect language choice,
though less so than the age of the customer.

Since conversations in department stores are public rather than intimate, it
was expected that both customers and salespersons would gravitate towards
the prestige norm; that is, speak more French and less Alsatian than in private.
It was therefore predicted that whatever the figures obtained, less Alsatian and
more French would be spoken between customers and salespersons than

within groups of customers or within groups of salespersons: the independent variable was therefore the *ingroup/outgroup* distinction.

It is known from studies in different parts of the world that switching between languages or varieties need not always have the same motivation or significance (Singh 1983); the intermittent use of a variety in which one is not fully competent may for instance be used to indicate ethnic allegiance to that variety; alternatively, switching may be used by speakers who wish to converge towards a prestige norm but are unable to sustain discourse all the time in that variety. This second possibility provides a likely explanation for much of the switching from French to Alsatian in Strasbourg, since French enjoys more social prestige than Alsatian but not all speakers are perfectly at ease in it. It was hoped that the amount of switching observed when different combinations of factors were at play would, first, indicate whether this hypothesis was worth pursuing and, second, suggest further lines of enquiry regarding language switching in Strasbourg.

Method

While providing less commercial scope than New York, Strasbourg conveniently possesses three departmental stores of distinct social character: *Printemps*, a branch of the well-known Paris store, just off Place Kleber, the main square in Strasbourg's commercial centre; *Magmod*, equally central and having if anything a larger surface area, but more old-fashioned both inside and out, noticeably dowdier, and less luxuriously appointed; and *Jung*, in the suburb of Schiltigheim which, though attached to Strasbourg geographically, has its own identity, its own politics, and its own shopping centre.

Preliminary discussions with a number of Strasbourgeois revealed a clear consensus as to the stores' social stratification, *Printemps* being considered the most modern, chic, and pricey and therefore likely to be the most French-speaking. *Magmod* was felt to have an 'older', dustier image, while keeping up with *Printemps* in some respects—for example, both *Printemps* and *Magmod* devote their whole ground floor to luxuries such as cosmetics, leather goods, gifts, and jewellery. *Jung* was considered to offer goods of a lower quality, to be cheaper, more provincial. Its ground floor is the main hub of sales activity: women's clothes, men's clothes, food, stationery, records, jewellery, cameras, and so forth jostle cheek-by-jowl on small counters. Only furniture, hardware, and a few other departments are on other floors. The top floor of *Jung* is devoted to furniture, but I was never able to observe language use in that department, as it was usually empty. Only once, an elderly female customer and a saleswoman of similar age were observed, having a thoroughly enjoyable gossip, in very loud voices as they had the floor to themselves. The language used was, predictably, Alsatian. *Jung* and *Magmod*, on the other hand, are more similar to each other as regards food sales, each incorporating large supermarket-style food departments with checkout counters at the end; *Printemps* has instead a small exclusive food hall on the top sales floor, where some of the choicest Strasbourg suppliers have individual counters.

Customers' and salespersons' language use was observed and recorded on small predivided cards in each of the three stores; only women were considered since men were in a tiny minority in both groups. The main focus of the survey was the language used by customers in speaking to salespersons, of which 254 instances were observed, sometimes by making repeated use of the same salesperson, as in the case of queues at the checkout counters. *Ingroup* conversations between customers and between salespersons were also observed, amounting to a further 292 instances. The collection of these data took some thirty-five hours. This contrasts with the six and a half hours taken by Labov to gather 264 instances of possible use of postvocalic (r); the longer time required here is explained by the fact that whereas Labov was able to elicit the data by asking for an item which he knew to be on the 'fourth floor', the data in this case were simply observed without any intervention by the researcher.

Greetings and thanks in French were ignored, since 'bonjour', 'merci', etc. are used in Alsace regardless of the language in which the rest of the conversation is held. Where the salesperson spoke first, the language she used was not recorded either: as one would predict for such a relatively public and formal situation in Alsace, this language was always French—with one interesting exception. The exception was observed in the china department of *Magmod*, where a young customer was asking a young saleswoman—in French, as one would expect—where to go to make arrangements to deposit her wedding list. The young saleswoman hesitated, whereupon another middle-aged saleswoman who had been involved in a conversation in Alsatian with a colleague, but who had overheard the question, interrupted herself, came over to the customer, and directed her to the appropriate department in Alsatian. The incident was so exceptional that one can safely attribute it to an oversight, a failure to switch when circumstances required it, resulting from the saleswoman being immersed at the time in an Alsatian conversation. A mental note was therefore kept of the *first language which the customer was heard to use*. Where this was French, further eavesdropping revealed whether the customer subsequently *switched to Alsatian*. If she did, this was recorded as a *switch*. Where the customer *started* in Alsatian, this was simply recorded as a conversation in Alsatian; it was not expected that a customer starting in Alsatian (and so, in a sense, *conceding* her inability to carry out the discussion in French) would switch into French. No separate category was therefore provided for this.

However, I remained alert to the possibility of this happening and the consequent necessity to provide such a category. In the event, the original expectation was fully confirmed and it was not necessary to provide a category for switches from Alsatian into French on behalf of customers. There were, however, some instances of customers who started in French, switched to Alsatian, then back to French, back to Alsatian, etc. These cases were simply counted as *switches*—meaning from French to Alsatian, since in this study it was not the code-switched mode but the first, highly revealing switch which was the focus of attention. The third possible category provided on the cards was for conversations entirely in French.

Both customers' and salespersons' approximate ages were noted down, thus permitting an analysis not only by *age of customer* but also of the interaction between different age groups. Three age categories were used: under 30, 30 to 45, and over 45, in order to speed up data collection.

The independent variable corresponding roughly to *topic* was represented, as explained above, by a somewhat arbitrary division of departments into *necessity* and *luxury*: necessities were considered to be food, clothes, furniture, and basic household equipment; luxuries were everything else: gifts, cosmetics, records, stationery, books, etc. The distinction was tenuous in *Printemps* and to some extent also in *Magmod*, where luxurious food, clothes, and so forth were still categorized as necessities. As the outcome shows, the shaky validity of the distinction was reflected by a lack of significant results on this question; the price of items would perhaps have provided a better guide.

The language used in conversations between customers and between salespersons—classed as *ingroup* conversations—was more summarily recorded without note being taken of the speakers' ages or the departments in which they were. The same three categories of language use were employed, thus permitting a comparison between these *ingroup* conversations and the customer—salesperson *outgroup* exchanges. The switching category, while still representing a middle category between pure French and pure Alsatian, was somewhat more broadly defined than in outgroup conversations: discussions between customers and between salespersons have a less specific purpose and are less brief than those between customers and salespersons. Consequently the switching category here included any kind of switching to and fro, regardless of whether the beginning of the conversation had been overheard.

One problem was that many department store transactions are frustratingly silent: the customer browses, chooses, hands the item to the salesperson operating the cash register together with the required sum and walks away with her purchase and her change, not having exchanged a word. In other cases, it was not possible to overhear the very beginning of the conversation and some conversations recorded as 'Alsatian' may in fact have been conversations which started in French and switched to Alsatian ('switches'); thus the amount of switching is if anything underestimated.

Finally, there appeared to be no case in which a salesperson, however young, failed to reply in Alsatian to a customer who addressed her in Alsatian (though there must presumably have been some non-Alsatian salespersons). There may also have been non-Alsatian customers in the sample who spoke only French and who remain unidentified, since it was possible to avoid only the two or three customers who were evidently not Alsatian from their colouring.

All in all, the method used and the situations observed would tend to underestimate the amount of Alsatian and of switching among Strasbourgeois in general. This is illustrated in the disparity between the number of customers starting conversations in Alsatian or switching to Alsatian in this survey, which averaged out at a mere 28 per cent overall, and the percentage of families in the Bas-Rhin claiming to speak Alsatian 'often' or 'always' when doing the shopping in the INSEE survey, which was 55 per cent (this of course included local shopping rather than being limited to the big stores in Strasbourg).

The results

Stores

As can be seen from Table 4.1, almost 30 per cent of customers in *Jung* started speaking to salespersons in Alsatian, compared with just under 20 per cent in *Magmod* and 8 per cent in *Printemps*. This follows the expected pattern, and a chi-square performed on the data was significant at the 1 per cent level ($x^2 = 17.491$, dfs = 4, p $< 0.01 > 0.001$). Switching, however, does not follow the same pattern: just under 15 per cent of customers switched in *Jung*, but the next highest was *Printemps* where over 10 per cent switched. Under 5 per cent of customers switched in *Magmod*.

TABLE 4.1. Use of Alsatian, French, and Switching
by Store

	Jung	*Magmod*	*Printemps*
Alsatian %	28.1	19.1	8.0
French %	57.3	76.1	81.8
Switching %	14.6	4.8	10.2
N	82	84	88

Departments: Necessity and Luxury

General

Overall, more Alsatian was spoken in *necessity* than in *luxury* departments, and *luxury* departments gave rise to a little more switching as well as more French (Table 4.2). These differences were, however, not large enough to produce a significant chi-square ($x^2 = 2.284$, dfs = 2, p > 0.05).

TABLE 4.2. Use of Alsatian,
French, and Switching by Store
Department

	Necessity	Luxury
Alsatian %	21.7	14.4
French %	69.0	75.2
Switching %	9.3	10.4
N	129	125

Breakdown by Department and Store
A breakdown by department and store showed that Alsatian was spoken less in luxury departments than in necessity departments in all three stores, though the difference was small in *Printemps* (Table 4.3). In *Printemps* and in *Magmod*, the converse was also true: French was spoken *more* in *luxury* departments than in necessity departments. *Luxury* departments in *Jung*, however, presented an interesting exception: instead of giving rise to more French, they gave rise to more switching, suggesting that speakers felt they ought to speak French but were unable to keep it up.

Customer Age

General
The customer's age was the single most significant factor determining language use, and the biggest difference is to be found between the over 45 age group and the two younger groups (Table 4.4). Chi-square was significant at the 0.1 per cent level ($x^2 = 57.193$, dfs = 4, p < 0.001)—it should of course be recalled that it was only possible to guess customers' ages. Note also that switching does not only occur in the group where *most* pure Alsatian is spoken, but also in the group where *least* pure Alsatian is spoken, that is the youngest group.

Breakdown by Customer Age and Store
The breakdown by customer age and store shows that the oldest age group speaks most Alsatian in *Jung*, less in *Magmod*, and less still in *Printemps*, where, however, they go in for a lot of switching (Table 4.5). The group which switches most *overall*, interestingly, is the youngest group of shoppers in *Jung*. For that reason *Jung* shows a marked difference between age groups 1 and 2, unlike *Magmod* or *Printemps*.

TABLE 4.3. Use of Alsatian, French, and Switching by Department and Store

	Jung		Magmod		Printemps	
	Necessity	Luxury	Necessity	Luxury	Necessity	Luxury
Alsatian %	30.6	24.2	25.7	14.3	8.9	7.0
French %	59.2	54.6	68.6	81.6	80.0	83.7
Switching %	10.2	21.2	5.7	4.1	11.1	9.3
N	49	33	35	49	45	43

TABLE 4.4. Use of Alsatian, French, and Switching by Age of Customers

	→30	30–45	45+
Alsatian %	2.9	5.6	40.2
French %	86.8	87.7	47.4
Switching %	10.3	6.7	12.4
N	68	89	97

TABLE 4.5. Use of Alsatian, French, and Switching by Customer, Age, and Store

	Jung			*Magmod*			*Printemps*		
	→30	30–45	45+	→30	30–45	45+	→30	30–45	45+
Alsatian %	4.2	16.7	60.7	0.0	0.0	39.0	4.0	0.0	21.4
French %	70.8	73.3	28.6	100.0	95.8	53.7	92.0	94.3	57.2
Switching %	25.0	10.0	10.7	0.0	4.2	7.3	4.0	5.7	21.4
N	24	30	28	19	24	41	25	35	28

Breakdown by Customer Age and Salesperson Age

Since the age of salespersons was also noted in all the conversations observed, a second breakdown was made to show the interaction between the customer's age and the salesperson's age (Table 4.6). As expected, the highest number of conversations in Alsatian (68.6 per cent) occurs between salespersons and customers who are both in age group 3. Equally, the lowest number occurs between customers in groups 1 and 2 and salespersons in group 1 (0 per cent). The older the salesperson, the less customers are inclined to speak French (with one exception, which is discussed below, customers in the middle age group appear less inclined to speak French if the salesperson is of their own age than if she is older). Young, middle, and old customer groups *all* switch most with the middle group of salespersons. The relevance of the *situational norm* which states that the customer calls the tune rather than the salesperson is demonstrated by the fact that whereas 20 per cent of customers in the oldest age group start in Alsatian even with a young salesperson, only 15.4 per cent of young customers are prepared to start in Alsatian to accommodate an older salesperson. This finding is echoed below where the switching results are reported.

TABLE 4.6. Use of Alsatian, French, and Switching by Age of Customers and Age of Salespersons

Customer Age	→30			30–45			45+		
Salesperson age	→30	30–45	45+	→30	30–45	45+	→30	30–45	45+
Alsatian %	0.0	3.1	15.4	0.0	7.1	13.3	20.0	28.1	68.6
French %	95.5	84.4	76.9	93.9	78.6	86.7	70.0	56.3	22.8
Switching %	4.5	12.5	7.7	6.1	14.3	0.0	10.0	15.6	8.6
N	22	32	13	33	42	15	30	32	35

Ingroup v. Outgroup

General

As mentioned above, data were also collected in each store regarding the language in which salespersons conversed among themselves and the language used by customers with other customers (Table 4.7). These two sets of data, though kept separate from each other throughout, are both regarded as instances of *ingroup* interaction while conversations between customers and salespersons are labelled *outgroup*.

TABLE 4.7. Use of Alsatian, French, and Switching by Groups of Interlocutors: Ingroup or Outgroup

	Ingroup customer–customer	Ingroup salesperson–salesperson	Outgroup customer–salesperson
Alsatian %	28.5	34.6	18.1
French %	64.8	51.2	72.1
Switching %	6.7	14.2	9.8
N	165	127	254

The *switching* category has a slightly different significance here from elsewhere: whereas in customer–salesperson conversations the Alsatian situational norm requires that the salesperson begin in French, and the prestige norm also requires that the customer speak French or at least start in French, within groups of people who know each other different norms apply. Switching in such groups may either imply difficulty in using French in a sustained manner or the more deliberate use of a code-switched mode as referred to above, the motivation of which would require a separate investigation. The conversations also tended to be longer, allowing time for several switches to and from each language. For these reasons switches *in either direction* were noted down as *switches*. In common with the switching category elsewhere, this category still represents an intermediate one between speaking French exclusively and speaking Alsatian exclusively.

The average figures for all three stores showed that more Alsatian was spoken *within* groups of customers or salespersons than *between* customers and salespersons. Conversely, customers made an effort to speak French to salespersons more than they would with their fellow-customers. A chi-square performed on these data was significant at the 0.1 per cent level ($x^2 = 20.11$, dfs $= 4$, p < 0.001).

Breakdown by Groups of Interlocutors and Store

The same trend was reflected in each of the three stores taken separately
(Table 4.8). In *Jung*, salespersons also spoke more Alsatian among themselves
than did customers, but adapted as in the other stores to speaking more French
when in outgroup conversation with the latter. In *Magmod*, customers and
salespersons were fairly well matched when engaged in their respective
ingroup conversations—and, notably, spoke as much Alsatian as did customers
in *Jung*—but the amount of Alsatian spoken in customer–salesperson interaction was dramatically lower. In *Printemps*, there is less Alsatian overall;
unlike the situation in *Jung*, salespersons speak less Alsatian among themselves than do customers but are among the highest switching groups (18.2 per
cent). As in the other cases, when interacting with customers the amount of
Alsatian drops.

Switching is highest within salesperson groups in *Printemps* and *Magmod*,
but within customer groups and between customers and salespersons in *Jung*.

TABLE 4.8. Use of Alsatian, French, and Switching by Groups of Interlocutors and
Store

	Alsatian %	French %	Switching %	N
Jung ingroup customer–customer	34.0	51.1	14.9	47
Jung ingroup salesperson–salesperson	60.0	30.0	10.0	30
Jung outgroup customer–salesperson*	28.1	57.3	14.6	82
Magmod ingroup customer–customer	37.2	58.1	4.7	43
Magmod ingroup salesperson–salesperson	37.7	49.1	13.2	53
Magmod outgroup customer–salesperson*	19.1	76.1	4.8	84
Printemps ingroup customer–customer	20.0	77.3	2.7	75
Printemps ingroup salesperson–salesperson	13.6	68.2	18.2	44
Printemps outgroup customer–salesperson*	8.0	81.8	10.2	88

* Figures are from Table 4.1.

Switching

Introduction

In Figure 4.1, all the data presented in Tables 4.1 to 4.8 are given in the form of
three sets of bar charts, showing the use of French, Alsatian, and switching
respectively. The information we have about each bar is set out beneath it, and
the bars are ranked according to the percentage of French, Alsatian, and
switching in each kind of transaction. Thus the first bar shows that in *Magmod*
(with no specification as to department), customers under 30 speaking to salespersons (whose age is not specified) spoke French in 100 per cent of the cases

observed. The last bar on the same line shows the situation where the least pure French was spoken (only 22.9 per cent of the cases observed), which was in conversations between customers and salespersons both in the over 45 age group. Three points are worth recalling: (i) ingroup conversations (CC and SS) were only broken down by store, not by age or department; (ii) switching covers situations where neither pure French nor pure Alsatian was spoken, but as explained above was more broadly defined for ingroup (CC and SS) than for outgroup conversations (CS); (iii) each bar does not represent a situation discrete from each of the others, but a different way of dividing up the exchanges which were observed. The only distinction which is made invariably is that between ingroup (CC and SS) and outgroup (CS) conversations.

Patterns of Switching and their Social Motivation
It is clear from an overall view of the data that whereas the selection of French and Alsatian provides support for the original hypotheses, the pattern of switching is not a function of the same rules. For example, whereas French is spoken most in the order *Printemps*, *Magmod*, *Jung*, and Alsatian in the opposite order, switching takes place most in *Jung*, then in *Printemps*, and least of all in *Magmod*, that is, it is most prevalent in the two extreme linguistic environments. The same comment applies to customer age: whereas customers speak French in the order young, middle, old, and Alsatian in the reverse order, switching takes place in the order old, young, middle. The same amount of switching can occur where there is a very high use of Alsatian (e.g. customers over 45 in *Jung*) and where there is a very low use of Alsatian (e.g. customers between 30 and 45 in *Jung* or customers under 30 in general).

Careful study of Figure 4.1 is, however, repaid by the emergence of several patterns which cast light on the social motivations of switching. Inevitably, the interpretation given here is more subjective than the data on simple language selection presented so far; it relies partly on those data and partly on the attribution of motives to speakers (Rampton 1987).

The first likely motivation to emerge for switching can be termed *accommodation to the linguistic environment*. Such a motivation fits in well with approaches which consider switching to be a 'compromise' way of speaking, a means of reconciling opposites (Scotton 1976), since the relevant situations are marked by contrasts or opposition in the data. The highest rate of switching (25 per cent) is found among the youngest group of shoppers, who are also the most French-speaking, when they are in *Jung*, that is the most Alsatian-speaking store. The second highest rate is found among the oldest shoppers, who are the most Alsatian-speaking, in *Printemps*, the most French-speaking store. The third highest rate is to be found in the luxury—and so French-speaking— departments of *Jung*, the store where people are most likely to be Alsatian speakers (the opposite, buying necessities in *Printemps*, the most French-speaking store, also gives rise to a fair amount of switching).

French

%	N	Store	Dept	C/Age	S/Age	In/Out
100	19	Ma	-	Y	O	CS
95.8	24	Ma	-	M	-	CS
95.5	22	-	-	Y	Y	CS
94.3	35	Pr	-	M	-	CS
93.9	33	-	M	Y	-	CS
92	25	Pr	-	Y	-	CS
87.6	89	-	M	-	-	CS
86.8	68	-	Y	-	-	CS
86.7	15	-	M	O	-	CS
84.4	32	-	Y	M	-	CS
83.7	43	Pr	Lux	-	-	CS
81.8	58	Pr	-	-	-	CS
81.6	49	Ma	-	-	-	CS
80	45	Pr	Nec	-	-	CS
78.6	42	-	M	M	-	CS
77.3	75	Pr	-	-	-	CC
76.9	13	-	Y	O	-	CS
76.2	84	Ma	-	-	-	CS
75.2	125	-	Lux	-	-	CS
73.3	30	Ju	-	M	-	CS

Alsatian

%	N	Store	Dept	C/Age	S/Age	In/Out
68.6	35	Ju	O	O	-	CS
60.7	28	Ju	O	O	-	CS
60	30	Ju	Lux	-	-	SS
40.2	97	-	O	O	-	CS
39	41	Ma	O	O	-	CS
37.7	53	Ma	-	-	-	SS
37.2	43	Ma	-	-	-	CC
34.6	127	-	-	-	-	SS
34	47	Ju	-	-	-	CC
30.6	49	Ju	Nec	-	-	CS
28.5	165	-	-	-	-	CC
28.1	32	-	O	M	-	CS
28.1	82	Ju	-	-	-	CS
25.7	35	Ma	Nec	-	-	CS
24.2	33	Ju	Lux	-	-	CS
21.7	129	Nec	-	-	-	CS
21.4	28	Pr	-	O	-	CS
19.1	84	Ma	-	-	-	CS

Switching

%	N	Store	Dept	C/Age	S/Age	In/Out
25	24	Ju	-	Y	-	CS
21.4	28	Pr	-	O	-	CS
21.2	33	Ju	Lux	-	-	CS
18.2	44	-	-	-	-	SS
15.6	32	-	O	M	-	CS
14.9	47	Ju	-	-	-	CC
14.6	82	Ju	-	-	-	CS
14.3	42	-	M	M	-	CS
14.2	127	-	-	-	-	SS
13.2	53	Ma	-	-	-	SS
12.5	32	-	Y	M	-	CS
12.4	97	-	O	-	-	CS
11.1	45	Pr	Nec	-	-	CS
10.7	28	Ju	O	-	-	CS
10.4	125	-	Lux	-	-	CS
10.3	68	-	Y	-	-	CS
10.2	88	Pr	-	-	-	CS
10.2	49	Ju	Nec	-	-	CS
10	30	Ju	M	-	-	CS
10	30	Ju	-	-	-	SS

French (ctd)

	72	70.8	70	69	68.6	68.2	64.8	59.2	58.1	57.3	57.1	56.3	54.5	53.7	51.9	51.1	49.1	47.4	30	28.6	22.9
N =	254	24	85	129	35	44	165	49	43	82	28	32	33	41	127	47	53	97	30	28	35
Store	-	Ju	-	-	Ma	Pr	-	Ju	Ma	Ju	Pr	-	Ju	Ma	-	Ju	Ma	-	Ju	Ju	-
Dept	-	-	-	Nec	Nec	-	-	Nec	-	-	-	-	Lux	-	-	-	-	-	-	-	-
C/Age	-	Y	O	-	-	-	-	-	-	-	O	O	-	O	-	-	O	O	-	O	O
S/Age	-	-	Y	-	-	-	-	-	-	-	-	M	-	-	M	-	-	-	-	-	-
In/Out	CS	-	CS	CS	CS	SS	CC	CS	CC	CS	CS	CS	CS	CS	SS	CC	SS	CS	SS	CS	CS

Alsatian (ctd)

	18.1	16.7	15.4	14.4	14.3	13.6	13.3	8.9	8	7.1	7	5.6	4.2	4	3.1	2.9	0	0	0	0	0
N =	254	30	13	125	49	44	15	45	88	42	43	89	24	25	32	68	33	35	22	24	19
Store	-	Ju	-	-	Ma	Pr	Ma	Pr	Pr	-	Pr	-	Ju	Pr	-	-	Pr	-	-	Ma	Ma
Dept	-	-	-	Lux	Lux	-	-	Nec	Pr	-	Lux	-	-	-	-	-	-	-	-	-	-
C/Age	-	M	-	-	-	-	M	-	-	M	-	M	-	Y	Y	-	M	M	Y	M	Y
S/Age	-	-	O	-	-	-	O	-	-	M	-	-	Y	Y	M	Y	Y	Y	Y	M	-
In/Out	CS	CS	CS	CS	CS	SS	-	CS	CS	CS	CS	CS	CS	CS	CS	CS	CS	CS	CS	CS	CS

Switching (ctd)

	10	9.8	9.3	9.3	8.6	7.7	7.3	6.7	6.7	6.1	5.7	5.7	5.7	4.8	4.7	4.5	4.2	4.1	4	2.7	0	0
N =	85	254	129	43	35	13	41	89	165	33	35	35	35	84	43	22	24	49	25	75	15	19
Store	-	-	-	Pr	Ma	-	Ma	-	-	-	Ma	Pr	Ma	Ma	Ma	-	Ma	Ma	Pr	Pr	-	Ma
Dept	O	-	Nec	Lux	-	-	-	-	-	Nec	Nec	-	-	-	-	-	-	Lux	-	-	-	-
C/Age	Y	-	-	-	O	Y	O	M	-	M	M	M	-	-	-	Y	Y	M	Y	-	M	Y
S/Age	-	-	-	-	O	O	-	Y	-	-	-	-	-	-	-	Y	Y	Y	-	-	O	-
In/Out	CS	CS	CS	CS	CS	CS	-	CS	CC	CS	CS	CS	CS	CS	CC	CS	CS	CS	CS	CC	CS	CS

Key: No. of cases = N

Store: Printemps = Pr   Age: Under 30 = Y   Department: Dept.   Ingroup communication = In   Customers = C   Salespersons = S
Magmod = Ma   30–45 = M   Luxury = Lux   Outgroup communication = Out   Customer to customer = CC
Jung = Ju   Over 45 = O   Necessity = Nec   Salesperson to salesperson = SS
Customer to salesperson = CS

FIG. 4.1. Percentage of French, Alsatian, and Switching

This interpretation of the facts is reinforced by the *lack of switching in the most neutral linguistic environment*, that of *Magmod*, which occupies the middle rank as regards the use of Alsatian overall but the lowest rank as regards switching. In outgroup conversations, the youngest and the middle age group in *Magmod* use very little Alsatian and switch very little also. The older group of customers uses quite a lot of pure Alsatian (39 per cent) but also switches relatively little (7.3 per cent). Both customer and salesperson ingroups use quite a lot of Alsatian (37.2 and 37.7 per cent respectively); customers in fact use slightly *more* Alsatian among themselves in *Magmod* than in *Jung*, but the rate of switching between customers is much lower than amongst salespersons, indicating less linguistic insecurity.

All the data on *Magmod* suggest that it imposes relatively little pressure on speakers to use one or the other language, so their language selection is more a function of characteristics independent of the immediate environment (such as age) than of aspects of that environment, and they have little tendency to switch.

The second type of motivation or reason for switching appears to tie in with *external pressures* to use one language rather than the other, which can be due to the *situational norm or to other social expectations*. With regard to the first kind of pressure, we note that older customers switch to Alsatian slightly more often with young salespersons than do young customers when speaking to older salespersons (10 and 7.7 per cent respectively). This would appear to confirm that although there is accommodation in both kinds of circumstances, the customer's variety is more often imposed on the salesperson than vice versa.

As far as other expectations are concerned, we turn here to the figures for switching in ingroup conversations between salespersons. This occurs in the order *Printemps* (18.2 per cent), *Magmod* (13.2 per cent), and *Jung* (10 per cent), which is the exact reverse of the order in which these same groups use Alsatian. It seems more than likely that there is an expectation that sales staff will use French, be it a specific expectation formulated by employers or a general expectation on the part of customers or society at large. In *Printemps*, salespersons are awarded a bonus for linguistic competence in languages other than French, but Alsatian does not count as a language in the bonus system. But many salespersons prefer to use Alsatian among themselves, so they switch to and fro by way of compromise, most of all in the store in which they are under the heaviest pressure to speak French, and in decreasing order of that pressure.

The last possible factor affecting the rate of switching which will be discussed here is the *influence of the interlocutor*. It is fairly clear that mutual accommodation takes place from the data on language selection: whereas customers over 45 address sales staff in the same age group in Alsatian in 68.6 per cent of cases, they only address sales staff under 30 in Alsatian in 20 per cent of cases; equally, young customers appear never to address young salespersons in Alsatian, but do speak Alsatian to salespersons over 45 in 15.4 per cent of cases. Switching, however, is most prevalent among all three customer age groups when the salesperson is in the *middle* age group. This may betray uncertainty about the linguistic preferences of the salesperson; the customers' own preferences are also reflected in the fact that older shoppers switch most with this ambiguous group, shoppers in the middle group slightly less, and the youngest shoppers least (15.6, 14.3, and 12.5 per cent respectively). The influence of the interlocutor is perhaps the most intangible of the three types of motivation which have been discussed, due to the complexity of speakers' reactions to one another and the difficulty of apprehending which aspect of their identity they are bringing to the fore.

An interesting case in point is the language selection and switching pattern for customers between 30 and 45 in conversation with salespersons over 45. Whereas this group switches quite a lot with salespersons in the same group (14.3 per cent), no switching was encountered when this group spoke to older salespersons. Instead, more pure French was spoken than with the middle group (86.7 per cent instead of 78.6 per cent), which is the reverse of what interpersonal accommodation would indicate.

The 30–45 age group is probably made up of more balanced bilinguals than either of the other groups, that is of people who have a real choice as to which language to use, yet their lack of switching and low use of Alsatian with older salespersons stands out from the normal pattern of differences between the age groups. Their usage is therefore likely to be the result of a deliberate policy, which in turn probably rests on a heightened awareness of linguistic issues and differences. Its motivation requires further investigation: they might be paying their older interlocutors a deliberate compliment in treating them as French speakers, or they might be indicating their own allegiance to a younger, more French-speaking generation; or even both at once. The interlocutor has, here, still exercised an influence on language selection but not one which at first sight goes in the direction of interpersonal accommodation.

Concluding Remarks

The study provided useful quantitative data which supported the original hypotheses of language selection in a relatively formal and constrained situation in Strasbourg. Further attempts to quantify selection and switching patterns will be based on different constraints: for example, language use as regulated by the different conventions of conversations in small, local shops or other work places (see further surveys).

Furthermore, although it is true that such studies 'avoid the bias of the experimental context' and also 'control the effect of the observer', correlations between language use and apparently objective variables such as the store, the department, etc., reflect social reality better than psychological reality: the shoppers in *Printemps* who used a lot of French were not doing so merely because they were in *Printemps*, but also because they were different people from those in *Jung*. Psychological reality is less amenable to objective verification, but quantitative data relating to it can at least clear the ground for a more qualitative analysis.

Thus this study has not revealed the motivations underlying language switching in Strasbourg but has at least made it easier to ask relevant questions about those motivations. It is now clear, for example, that the original assumption that switching reveals a desire to converge to the prestige norm is inadequate: the group which switches more than any other appears to do so in order to fit in with its surroundings, since it is made up of people who are more at ease in the prestige norm, French, than in Alsatian; accommodation would therefore appear to be as relevant a motive as prestige. This in turn underlines that code-switching can have several different motives/ *raisons d'être* within a single sociolinguistic context.

It should at least by now be clear that, much as some instances of code switching are so distinctive and sophisticated as to constitute a separate mode of speaking, this mode cannot be studied quite independently from the factors governing selection of the two varieties which make it up. The results of this study show that, at least in this context, an understanding of language selection is a necessary, though not a sufficient condition for understanding switching.

ii. A Working Day in a Strasbourg Insurance Office

We find ourselves fortunate in that the patterning within this variation is by no means obscure: it does not require the statistical analysis of hundreds of speakers' records as linguists traditionally feared . . . On the contrary, we find that the basic patterns of class stratification, for example, emerge from samples as small as 25 speakers. (Labov 1978*b*: 204)

Introduction

The second survey was conducted in a different context from the first and is also very different in terms of methodology. The Department Stores survey allowed a large number of instances of the use of French, Alsatian, and switching to be collected but no qualitative analysis, however superficial, could be performed as it was essential that the observer remain as much as possible in the background, which placed a severe limit on what could be observed.

In this second survey, I recorded seven and a half hours of conversation, that is, the equivalent of one working day (though the recordings were in fact spread over three days), in a central Strasbourg insurance office.

I was granted permission for the recording on condition that clients' anonymity was maintained and the employees were, of course, aware of the recording although clients were not. I was present for much, but not all, of the time when the recordings were made so as to observe the relevant context and comings and goings. The tape recorder was placed successively on the desks of the three employees who received clients, while I sat in the small waiting area, apparently reading magazines and awaiting my turn. Twenty-one clients were received during the recordings (anything between ten and thirty represents a normal working day). A large part of the work is carried out on the telephone and I therefore recorded another 58 telephone conversations between clients and the employees, although I was only able to hear both sides of the conversation in a few cases (when no clients were in the office the telephone volume could be turned up so that both sides could be heard). Twenty-two conversations between the employees in the office were recorded, and forty telephone conversations with the company's central office where clients' files are held; the three office employees speak daily to those at the central office and know them well as the register and content of their conversations show. The three employees, two men and a woman, aged between 28 and 35, are all bilinguals who regularly use French and Alsatian outside work.

Compared with the Department Stores survey, there are clearly fewer sources of variation here: there is only one social setting instead of three; there is no equivalent to the luxury/necessity subdivision and no systematic breakdown by age, owing to the smaller numbers involved. On the other hand, I was able to explore in greater depth the ingroup (employee–employee)/ outgroup (employee–client) contrast and to add some remarks about the apparent influence of different modalities (face to face v. telephone conversations). It was also possible to register variations somewhat more subtle than the three primary categories of French, Alsatian, and switching adopted in the Department Stores survey. Methodologically, this survey lies between the first, quantitative one and the conversational analysis which follows; there was no call to use any statistical calculations beyond percentages.

Information Necessary for an Interpretation of the Results

Discourse Units

In the first survey exchanges observed between salespersons and customers were generally speaking limited to a few sentences on each side, and I remarked then that 'switching' was not the same phenomenon in the various dyads observed.

In this context I prefer to speak not in terms of 'exchanges', which implies functionally and linguistically limited discourse, but in terms of conversations. Stretches of discourse observed were longer and more discursive and the 'utilitarian' parts of the conversations (requests for information and relevant replies concerning insurance matters) were usually mingled with more social and general talk; the contents and register of the discourse observed here are extremely varied (Coupland 1984).

Nevertheless, it was possible to count conversations since the tape recorder was on one employee's desk at a time and changes were clearly marked by the coming and going of clients, and by phone calls: a change of conversation in fact signifies a change of interlocutor, and a first count could therefore be made, along the same lines as the previous survey, of the number of conversations in French, Alsatian, and in a mixture of the two (Tables 4.9 and 4.10). In the case of face-to-face conversations, it was also possible to note to what extent language selection and switching followed a similar pattern in both speakers.

TABLE 4.9. Face-to-face and Telephone Conversations

	Face-to-face	Telephone	Total
Employee–client	21	58	79
Employee–employee	22	40	62
TOTAL	43	98	141

Physical and Linguistic Context

The situation observed is formal rather than intimate and this formality is reinforced by the following considerations: Clients who come in must first take a seat in the 'waiting-room' area where there are armchairs and magazines; when an employee is free, the client goes to sit down before his or her desk. The employees' desks are close to one another and the telephone frequently rings on one or another of them. Thus all conversations, whether face to face or on the phone, can be overheard to a large extent by everyone else in the office if they are not speaking themselves. This situation must clearly affect language choice.

The three employees recorded are all young and although all three are fluent bilinguals,[1] it is likely that many clients assume they prefer to speak French. This assumption is of course reinforced by the fact that as in the Department Stores, clients are first addressed in French (unless they are known to the employees as Alsatian speakers). Moreover some Alsatian-speaking clients were diverted away from this recording by the presence during part of it of a fourth employee, a gentleman over 60 who came in to help out on a part-time basis and who had some long-standing Alsatian-speaking clients who always came to him if he was there.

[1] Some job advertisements in Strasbourg specify that a bilingual is required (as opposed to a monolingual French speaker). Observation of clients in an office like this one shows that this can be highly necessary.

TABLE 4.10. Face-to-face and Telephone Conversations: Language Breakdown

| | Face-to-face | | Telephone | |
	Employee–client	Employee–employee	Employee–client	Employee–employee
Alsatian %	9.5 (2)	0.0	3.4 (2)	7.5 (3)
French %	76.2 (16)	59.1 (13)	89.7 (52)	60.0 (24)
Switching %	14.3 (3)	40.9 (9)	6.9 (4)	32.5 (13)
TOTAL	(21)	(22)	(58)	(40)

Finally, the whole setting of an insurance office in a smart and central part of town exercises some francophone influence on clients. Insurance contracts and all attendant documentation are in French, as is all the terminology: *police d'assurance* 'insurance policy', *tous risques* 'all risks', *assurance* 'insurance', *dossier* 'file', *prise en charge* 'cover', *sinistre* 'accident', *client* 'client', *expert* 'assessor', *franchise* 'excess'. There seemed little point in classifying some of these as loans and some as switches since all are invariably used in French in this context regardless of the language spoken; it is not particularly informative to know whether they are also used in French in other contexts since they are by definition specific to this context. They have not, however, been counted as code-switches in the analysis which follows.

All in all, clients are likely to speak more French in this environment than they would if they were deciding which language to use purely on the basis of their own competence. The following examples tend to confirm this: first, that of two clients speaking French with strong Alsatian accents and repeated hesitations and periphrases such as 'What do you call it, the front window . . .' meaning the windscreen; second, similar hesitations and periphrases used by the employees, who as we will see, frequently speak Alsatian or switch when clients are not present. The short exchanges which take place between them in front of clients are consistently in French, though this might also be due to their awareness of the recording. The observer's—or the tape-recorder's—effect is, however, unpredictable and does not always result in more use of the prestige or High language. In the conversations analysed in the next chapter, those subjects who knew they were being recorded would, if anything, speak more Alsatian than otherwise, by their own admission.

Survey Results

Choice of Language

I explained above the way in which discourse is presented on the recording and in this context, that is to say as a series of separate conversations between an employee and a client or two employees, either face to face or on the telephone. Naturally, employee–client conversations differ in many respects from those between employees but it is not the object here to catalogue those differences; the most obvious of those is that employee–client conversations are much longer, a fact which should be borne in mind when assessing Table 4.10.

There were almost the same number of employee–client and employee–employee face-to-face conversations, varying in length from a couple of sentences to more than five minutes. Very few of them took place exclusively in Alsatian; on the other hand, conversations involving switching were frequent between employees (40.9 per cent). Such mixed conversations never represent cases where A speaks French and B speaks Alsatian: at least one of the two switched in each case.

On the right-hand side of the table, I was only able to hear both sides of the conversation between employees and clients in half the cases (29) and in a third of cases (13) when there was a telephone conversation between employees. In most cases language choice as between the three categories was mutual, and there were only two short conversations, between employees and on the telephone, in which one person spoke Alsatian and the other French.

As in the case of face-to-face conversations, switching is much more frequent between employees (32.5 per cent) than between employees and clients (6.9 per cent). Alsatian, once again, is rarely spoken on its own. It is also interesting to note that employees speaking to clients on the telephone (and calls are usually made by clients rather than employees) seem to speak French even more often than when the client is in the office (89.6 and 76.2 per cent), whereas between employees the proportion of French spoken on the phone and face to face remains constant, although there is more switching face to face (40.9 per cent instead of 32.5 per cent) as there is with clients also (14.3 per cent instead of 6.9 per cent). The face-to-face situation may encourage informality, and therefore be more conducive to switching, or there may be inhibitions about switching on the telephone, when one can give no extra-linguistic clues that one is about to do so (e.g. pointing at a document in French while switching into French, or pushing back one's chair and smiling to indicate friendly informality while switching to Alsatian). It would seem worth while confirming the statistical significance of this finding through a larger-scale study in the future.

Translinguistic Markers

As mentioned in Chapter 1, code-switching cannot be separated in a theoretically satisfactory fashion from other translinguistic markers, but for the purposes of a practical analysis some, admittedly arbitrary, lines must be drawn.

Before describing the type of code-switching encountered here, therefore, here briefly are the principal other kinds of translinguistic markers encountered in this context.

(i) insurance-related terminology (*constat à l'amiable* 'accident statement', *référence* 'reference', *appel* 'appeal', *franchise* 'excess') which in certain utterances is so dense that all the grammatical 'cement' is in Alsatian but all the lexical elements are in French.

Bris de glace, Sie verliere ke *franchise*. D'Lampe vorne, diss koscht hitzedaas e Packele Geld. Sie wechsle *carrément* de ganz *optique*, gel. Diss isch versichert. Diss isch *remboursé intégral*, gel, ohne *bonus* ze verliere. D'franchise ghejt nitt uf *bris de glace*.

Broken glass, there's no *excess* to pay. The lamp in front costs a packet these days. They *just* change the whole *headlamp element*, you see. That's insured. That's *fully reimbursed*, you see, without losing your *no-claims bonus*. The exclusion doesn't apply to *broken glass*.

Sometimes the terminology is not strictly insurance-related but simply legal or office-related:

Mache Se e *photocopie* von de *document* un' schickes es ihm.
Make a *photocopy* of the *document* and send it to him.

(ii) Alongside this terminology made up largely of nouns are a large number of conversational expressions (*rien à faire!* '*nothing to be done!*'), exclamations (*d'accord!* '*OK!*'), and greetings/phatic expressions (*bon, enfin, très bien, de rien, au revoir, merci bien* '*good, well, fine, don't mention it, goodbye, thanks very much*') which are particularly frequent on the telephone.

(iii) There are also a number of typically Alsatian verb coinages of which some are generalized and some not (depanniert, remplaciere, clignotiert 'rescued, to replace, indicated') and 'hybrid creations' (Haugen 1972*a*) such as *satisfaction* krieje ('to get *satisfaction*') in which the part of French provenance is, at least in part, phonologically integrated with Alsatian ('*satisfaction*' for example carried the typical Alsatian first-syllable stress but preserved the French nasal o at the end).

(iv) Other French expressions which are less integrated, apparently, with the Alsatian cement than those above, and which have perfectly current Alsatian equivalents:

effectivement	*par rapport à* geschtern
in actuality	*compared with* yesterday
logiquement	*remboursé intégral*
logically	*fully reimbursed*

(v) Place names and proper names in French: *rue des Païens*, *Place de la Gare*, *Centre Traumatologique*. Some of these names have Alsatian equivalents (d'Papierfawrikstross for *rue de la Papèterie*) but it is rare to hear these in Strasbourg. If anything, street-names tend to be Gallicized even if their component elements might be said in Alsatian in another context.

Owing to the abundance of these various translinguistic markers, at first sight one might think, in such a context as Strasbourg, that intense language mixing is in progress; in fact the *type* of mixture in such circumstances *can* be very limited, that is restricted to lexical or invariable, ready-made expressions. In future studies it would be useful to correlate the types of switching which occur with the overall frequency of switches.

Style-Shifting

The apparent disadvantage of only having observed three employees (in conversation with seventy-nine clients and a maximum of forty other employees over the telephone—some were doubtless repetitive combinations) is counterbalanced by the opportunity to observe variations in these three people's speech. The principal variations have to do with the different levels of formality employed to speak (*a*) to unknown clients, (*b*) to known clients, (*c*) to colleagues on work questions, and (*d*) to colleagues on other matters, practically a social register which could be used between friends. Each of these levels is clearly correlated with language choice, level (*a*) being almost guaranteed to be French and level (*d*) almost guaranteed to be switching. One particular set of examples is telling:

(i) Employee Mrs F is explaining to a young female client in the office how much it costs to insure different car models; the client gives no hint of being Alsatian and Mrs F's speech contains no word of Alsatian, no trace of accent or other translinguistic marker that I could identify. On the other hand, both young women make their speech less formal by 'swallowing' certain syllables in a manner very characteristic of spoken, informal French but which has no regional connotations: *quat* for *quatre*; *qu'ce soit* for *que ce soit*; *cinq cent francs d'franchise* for *cinq cent francs de franchise*; *j'crois* for *je crois*.

(ii) On the telephone to another employee whom she knows well (and with whom she uses the *tu* form) Mrs F and her interlocutor repeatedly interrupt their discussion of a client's insurance policy to exchange private comments, for example, about the weather. Markers of slangy speech like those above are multiplied in these asides:

Comment t'as fait ça?	*ça chauffe*
How d'ye do that?	it's boiling (weather)
Ouais	*C'est dingue, y'a tout qui colle, eh!*
Yeah	It's incredible, everything's sticky, eh!
l'gars	*tu parles*
the bloke	you don't say
hein?	*mille trois cent balles*
eh?	a hundred and thirty quid (slang for francs)

But in this case various regional markers are used to reinforce the familiar tone of the conversation, for example, stressing the first syllable of certain words (*Comment il s'appelle?*, *d'accord*, *C'est horrible*) and use of *jo* to draw attention to what one is about to say; *jo tu crois que* . . . and *hoppla* to end one topic of conversation and move on to another.

(iii) A good friend/husband/boyfriend of Mrs F rings up to speak to her and Mr B takes the call; she rushes to the phone and knocks herself against the edge of the desk. Mr B teases her for being in a flutter (*affolée*) over the call; still nursing her bruise and laughing at the same time, Mrs F, taking the receiver, says with an Alsatian accent taken to the point of caricature, which amusingly emphasizes her discomfiture, '*Écoute j'ai <u>cogné</u> le <u>bord</u> là où il y a le <u>téléphone</u> dessus . . .*' '*Listen I knocked the edge where the telephone is . . .*'.

In other circumstances, as we will see, Mrs F is quite capable of speaking Alsatian fluently and also of rapid, dense switching. The examples above show how, even within what is ostensibly 'French', a bilingual such as she is able to play with a stylisticrepertoire enriched by elements of the other language in ways which a monolingual cannot. This example, in which the speaker uses different portions of her bilingual repertoire for different sociolinguistic effects, lends support to Coupland's (1985) comparison of code-switching and style-shifting: 'the difference between monolingual and bilingual behaviour lies only in the choice of linguistic symbols for socially equivalent processes'.

Switching

We saw above that certain conversations in which a larger number of French elements are inserted in an Alsatian grammatical base are not in fact cases of dense switching, since the French elements are all lexical or set expressions. This is often the case of employee–client conversations:

(i) CLIENT   Ich hab e *sinistre* g'hett.
             I've had an *accident*.

(ii) MRS F   *Constat à l'amiable* isch praktisch.
             An *accident statement* would be practical.

(iii) CLIENT   (after a conversation in Alsatian) *Bon, merci bien, mademoiselle*.
             Good, thank you very much, miss.

      MRS F   So, für diss nitt, *au revoir monsieur*.
             Don't mention it, *goodbye sir*.

The lexical switching (*sinistre, constat à l'amiable*) merely reflects sociolinguistic reality—French dominates in certain areas of public and professional life and so French vocabulary must be used unless one wishes to distinguish oneself as a dialectal purist; but the use of French expressions (albeit that the greetings which appear in French above are very general in Alsace) may reflect a desire to maintain a symbolic presence of both languages in the conversation— perhaps even, at some level, to 'pretend' one has spoken French when one has in fact spoken the dialect. I shall return to these distinctions in Chapter 4; they are problematic because they rely on assigning motives to speakers without having any basis, outside the conversation itself, for doing so.

There are examples of longer switches 'triggered' by the very limited switching just described (Clyne 1967). For instance, after several minutes of speaking Alsatian to a client on the telephone, Mr L is led to use longer stretches of French by the use of various short French expressions (*attendez voir*, *je vois*, *écoutez donc*, *bien sûr*, *non*) in the following passage:

(iv) MR L   Ja . . . was . . . ah ja, *attendez voir*, jetz, *voilà maintenant je situe mieux*, doch, *euh, je vois. Ecoutez* ihr—*je crois qu'on a fait le necessaire, hein* . . . Ufböje tun ihr nix? Also dann isch ken Problem, *hein. Donc, euh* . . . Ja, *bien sûr, non* . . . *Du moment, euh, que vous faites que de la démolition, il n'y a pas de problème, hein* . . . *Voilà, d'accord.* Ja, isch ken Problem . . . *D'accord, au revoir, hein.*

       Yes . . . what . . . ah yes, *just a minute*, now, *yes now I've got there*, yes, um, *I see. Listen* you—*I think we've done what's necessary, eh* . . . You're not doing any building? Then there's no problem, *eh. So, uh* . . . Yes, *of course, no* . . . *If you, uh, if you're only doing demolition, there's no problem*, eh . . . *There we are, fine.* Yes, it's no problem . . . *OK, goodbye then.*

Switching in conversation between employees often serves to structure the discourse by highlighting some elements, sometimes by repeating them in the other language just as one might through other devices such as pausing or emphasis, or showing that one is moving from one topic or register to another. This is one of the best attested functions for which switching is used.

(v) MR L   (speaking about mail addressed to a colleague) *Ça peut être des tas de choses, hein?*

       It could be all sorts of things, eh?

   MRS F   *Oui, je sais, oui. Mais l'autre fois il m'a aussi dit d'ouvrir tous les courriers. Je m'suis fait piquer dans ce patelin, oh*, ich bin verstoche, e Katastroph!

       Yes, I know, yes. But last time he also told me to open all mail. I've been stung in that village, oh, I've been stung something dreadful!

Highlighting one part of a sentence by switching can in itself serve a variety of purposes of which emphasis as such is only one. It can also, for example, be a way of engaging sympathy for an omission, especially if the switch is from the 'formal' variety to the more friendly intimate vernacular:

(vi) MRS F   (on telephone) *Parce que quand il m'avait téléphoné à l'époque, je me souvenais très bien. Et puis, je lui avais répondu qu'il n'en avait pas besoin. Il me semble. Et après* isch's mir üss'm Kopf g'falle. *Et après, quand j'ai appris pour les caravanes, je me suis dit mince, il faut quand même assurer.*

       Because when he phoned me at the time, I remembered very well. And I told him then that he didn't need it. I think. And then I quite forgot about it [*lit.*: it fell out of my head]. *And then when I heard about the caravans, I thought, heck, he does need some insurance.*

A clear example of topic-/register-related switching is provided by Mr B, when he rings up a colleague to check a point concerning a client. As is particularly clear from the tone of voice adopted by both of them, the conversation, which is in Alsatian, at first provides an excuse for some flirting and it is only when some more serious, factual business has to be transacted that they finally move over to French.

(vii)   MS W   Wanner.
                          Wanner.

        MR B   *Bonjour, Madame Wanner.* Wie geht's bi eich?
                          Hello, Ms Wanner. How are things with you?

        MS W   Mhmh.
                          Mhmh.

        MR B   Kannsch mi?
                          Do you know me?

        MS W   Ja, kann i di.
                          Yes, I know you.

        MR B   Jo, jo. Hoer, kennsch du ebbs lueje?
                          OK, OK. Listen, can you look something up?

        MS W   Ja.
                          Yes.

        MR B   Benali Mohammed. Kannsch denne?
                          Benali Mohammed. Do you know him?

        MS W   Jo, diss isch jetz egal ob er jetz Benamou odder Benali heisst. Diss isch für mich selwe.
                          Yes, it's all the same if he's called Benamou or Benali. It's all the same to me.

        MR B   Ja.
                          Yes.

        MS W   *Attends*, ich luej.
                          Wait, I'll look.

        MR B   *Merci.*
                          Thanks.
                          . . .

        MS W   Ja, *j'ai sa carte*.
                          Yes, *I've got his card.*

        MR B   Kennsch du mir d'Referenz genn?
                          Can you give me the reference?

        MS W   Vun wellem?
                          Of what?

        MR B   Vum *sinistre*.
                          Of *the accident*.

        MS W   Vun wellem?
                          Of which one?

MR B   O verdeckel. Hett er so vil?
           O heavens. Has he had so many?

MS W   *Il en a un en juin. Il en a un en juillet.*
           He has one in June. He has one in July.

MR B   Jetz achtung.
           Good gracious.

MS W   Einmol geje Dorner un einmol geje Kientz.
           Once against Dorner and once against Kientz.

MR B   Oje! Jetz der vun *juillet* allewäj, hop.
           O dear. Let's deal with the *July* one.

MS W   *Mais t'as une facture ou quoi?*
           But do you have an invoice or what?

MR B   *Non, euh, euh.*
           No, uh, uh.

MS W   *Qu'est ce que t'as?*
           What do you have?

MR B   *Il aimerait bien savoir où c'est qu'il en est, niveau règlement sinistre*, was weiss doch ich.
           He'd like to know where he stands, when he'll be paid back for the accident, what do I know.

MS W   *Ah bon, parce que celui du mois de juillet, on l'a réglé 2050 F, et celui au mois de juin n'est pas réglé.*
           Ah, because the July one's been paid, 2,050 F, and the June one hasn't yet.

MR B   *Ah voilà, c'est celui-là alors.*
           Ah, that's it, it's that one then.

MS W   *Mhm, je vais voir ça.*
           Mhm, I'll look into that.

MR B   *Merci.*
           Thanks.

These examples illustrate the variety of motivations for switching between people who know one another well and have no inhibitions about changing languages. The significance of the 'inhibition' factor is considerable—witness the following two examples in which employees switch on the telephone: in the first, the employee, Mr L, politely starts the conversation in French, goes in for some switching when the client asks him in a friendly manner when he is going on holiday, and steers back to French for the business part of the call:

(viii) MR L   *Allo, Monsieur A? Bonjour, comment ça va?* (Client asks him when he leaves on holiday) D'nächst Wuch . . . *14 juillet* . . . *Enfin cette semaine* . . . *Trois jours* . . . Naan, s'isch nimmeh wit! . . . (Insurance related question) *Voilà, exactement* . . . *Oui* . . . *Oui* . . . *Mmh* . . . *Oui* . . .

> *Maintenant vous avez une chose: au niveau de la planche à voile au point de vue responsabilité civile elle-même vous êtes couvert* . . .
>
> *Hello, Mr A? Hello, how are you? Next week . . . 14th July . . . This week in fact . . . Three days . . . No, it's not far off now! . . . Yes, exactly . . . Yes . . . Yes . . . Mmh . . . Yes . . . Now there's one thing about this: for the surf-board, you are covered for third-party risks* . . .

By contrast, in the next example the use of Alsatian, or rather, as it turns out, of switching, is initiated, most unusually, by the employee, Mr B. This is an irreverent choice—connected with Mr B's personality (Titone 1987)—which is dependent on the fact that his interlocutor is a young man whom he feels he can patronize. The client is surprised to be addressed in Alsatian and goes back to French which feels more natural for a conversation with an unknown inter-locutor.

(ix) MR B   *Compagnie X, bonjour.*
               X Company, hello.

     CLIENT   *Bonjour, Monsieur M, s'il vous plaît.*
               Hello, Mr M, please.

     MR B   *Monsieur M* isch nitt do.
               Mr M isn't here.

     CLIENT   Isch nitt do? *Vous pouvez lui laisser un message?*
               Isn't there? *Can you leave him a message?*

     MR B   Ja.
               Yes.

     CLIENT   *Vous lui dites de téléphoner à Monsieur P. P. 66.33.40.*
               Could you tell him to telephone Mr P. P. 66.33.40.

Finally, there are a few examples of mixed discourse, that is of a form of speech in which switching is so frequent that, from a psychological point of view, the choice of that form is clearly much more significant than the reasons why individual switches take the form they do.

(x) MRS F   Do isch d'Madame F. *De bureau de Saint-Paul. Bonjour.* Wissen'r
               warum ich schunn widder anruef? Unseri mache schunn widder uf
               siewene zwanzig Grad . . . Jo, *c'est impossible*, hein. *Madame Jund, quand*
               elle est arrivée ce matin, il y en avait 29 . . . Do het se Tüer e bissel
               ufgemacht. Mir kann awwer ken . . . Ich weiss nitt. *Ce gars était là l'autre*
               jour un dann het er ebbs gemacht, het g'saat . . . *Et puis tout d'un coup ça a*
               fait clic et effectivement ça a remarché; vendredi il faisait bon, angenehm *et tout.*
               Et aujourd'hui ça va être pas tenable parce que's gibt ken Luft, hein . . . Sie-
               wene zwanzig Grad, isch e bissel viel . . . Ja, *j'compte sur vous, hein. Merci*
               Monsieur Raab, au revoir.

               It's Mrs F. here. The *Saint Paul office. Hello.* Do you know why I'm
               ringing up yet again? Ours have gone up again to twenty-seven degrees

... Yes, *it's impossible*, eh. *Madam Jund, when she arrived this morning, it was 29*... So she opened the door a bit. But we can't ... I don't know. *This guy was here the other day* and then he did something, he said ... *And then all of a sudden it went click and it did work again; Friday it was fine*, pleasant *and everything. And today it's going to be unbearable because* there's no air, eh ... Twenty-seven degrees, it's a bit much ... Yes, *I'm counting on you, eh. Thanks. Mr Raab, bye bye*.

Such examples occur in conversations between employees and the example above was delivered at high speed on the telephone. Mrs F was amused when the passage was later played back to her—but the only reason she herself was able to suggest for her switching in this passage was that her interlocutor had been switching also; while 'reason' seems an inadequate word here, the mutuality of switching is undoubtedly one of its characteristic features.

Summary and Concluding Remarks

This second survey in a public place in Strasbourg again shows a predominant use of French in this context in spite of the presence of numerous bilinguals. The use of unmixed Alsatian is particularly rare: it occurs in less than 10 per cent of employee–client conversations in the office; switching is also infrequent in this type of conversation. In telephone conversations with clients, conversations are also in French in almost 90 per cent of cases.

On the other hand, switching is very common when the employees are talking to each other (40 per cent of conversations) and between employees and clients who are well known to them. A much more limited type of mixing takes place in Alsatian conversations, even between people who don't know one another well, which merely involves the use of French vocabulary items connected with insurance matters; another limited type of switching is that which involves the insertion of ready-made conversational expressions from language A in language B (this occurs in both directions in the data). Longer switches involving whole sentences or parts of sentences often mark major discourse movements or 'footing' (Goffman 1981); finally, the use of mixed discourse appears to be characteristic of situations where bilinguals in conversation with each other are unhampered by notions of formality.

Overall this survey throws light on the relationship between various linguistic choices (including the choice of different kinds of switching) and corresponding interpersonal factors in this context. Many of the remarks made here will be confirmed and expanded in Chapter 5; the method used, semi-quantitative, observational rather than participant, and relying at the same time on recordings, was found to be a useful compromise between various more traditional sociolinguistic techniques.

iii. Language Use and Switching in and around Strasbourg

Further surveys were carried out in a variety of contexts in and around
Strasbourg in order to throw further light on the circumstances—physical and
otherwise—in which French and Alsatian are used and on the relationship
between their use and code-switching.

A Bakery was chosen in order to contrast the atmosphere of a small shop
with that of the big department stores in the first survey; a plumbers' merchant
was chosen in order to explore a male-dominated environment as opposed to
the female-dominated one of the other shops; a survey was carried out in
Eckwersheim, a village a short distance from Strasbourg, in order to highlight
any gross differences between town and country; and observation in a primary
and a nursery school and a questionnaire sent to nursery-school teachers were
used to counterbalance the emphasis on adults in the other surveys. Finally,
the subjects of the Cité des Chasseurs interviews (Chapter 2) were asked
various specific questions about switching: their replies indicate which are the
categories of switching identified by speakers themselves and give an idea of
the range of their opinions.

The Bakery

I was given permission to sit behind the counter in a bakery in a well-to-do area
of Strasbourg (Place Brant), for approximately three hours, in order to observe
the customers' language use. One hundred and two customers, thirty-six of
whom were men and sixty-six women, came in while I was there. Most of them
were regulars and so well known to the middle-aged wife of the baker who
served them. She herself was a bilingual: she told me that she spoke Alsatian
with her husband but that when speaking to customers she would follow those
customers' preference unless she did not know them, in which case she would
address them in French. With her help I was able to set aside eleven customers
who were definitely not of Alsatian origin and whose choice of French was
therefore unremarkable. Of the remaining ninety-one per cent, 72 per cent of
men and 85 per cent of women spoke only French; 28 per cent of men and 10
per cent of women spoke only Alsatian, and 5 per cent of women (no men)
switched. There was evidence that language choice was related to age as well as
to sex (older and male customers being more likely to choose Alsatian).

The very low rate of switching (a mere three aged ladies make up the 5 per
cent) was no doubt related to the very limited nature of the verbal transactions
and the strict definition of switching which was again applied: greetings and
politeness formulas (*s'il vous plaît*, etc.) were not counted, which often only left
the customer's request, reduced to its simplest form: 'e *baguette*', '*une* stolle'.
Some kinds of bread, as these examples show, have French names and some

have Alsatian names in Alsace (irrespective of the language one is speaking), but these were considered to be loans rather than switches; the language of the utterance was considered to be determined by the language of the article where this was all there was to go on. Clearly, on occasions this led to apparent absurdity where what the customer said was, for instance, 'E *baguette, si'il vous plaît* ... *Merci* ... *Au revoir*' and the whole utterance had to be counted as Alsatian although eight words out of nine were in French. Similar problems of assignment to one or the other language recur in the Conversational Analysis and are by no means an insignificant aspect of the analysis of code-switching in general. They show the danger of decontextualizing such an analysis, as I repeatedly point out, and above all of systematically assigning utterances to one or the other 'base' language when this may have no meaning for the speakers involved.

The Plumbers' Merchant

Subsequently I spent a morning sitting behind the counter at a plumbers' merchant in an industrial zone of Strasbourg, with a view to observing language use in a more male-dominated environment than in the other surveys. Of the thirty-three customers who came in, all were men and a large number were plumbers (and wore overalls); some were private individuals, in two cases couples. Next door to this counter and inside the same large hangar-like building was a bathroom showroom where people could come and select bathroom fittings, which could then be supplied and fitted by the company, and the private customers who came to the counter had usually been sent over by the showroom staff. There were eight male employees working at the counter and with the equipment stored behind the counter which was on ceiling-high rows of shelves extending to the back of the building. Of these, seven were of Alsatian origin and one was Spanish.

Of the thirty-three customers, twenty spoke Alsatian, eleven spoke French, and two switched, the same strict definition of switching being applied as in the previous survey. The plumbers, who were regulars, tended to speak Alsatian and the private customers, who were not known to the staff, tended to speak French, but the terminology used being overwhelmingly French, this would also 'trigger' longer bouts of French within basically Alsatian conversations. Among themselves, the employees spoke mainly Alsatian with the exception of the Spaniard and one other young employee who felt more at ease in French.

Overall it was noticeable that in what might have been expected to be an Alsatian stronghold, the prestige language, French, had infiltrated itself beyond what would have been strictly necessary for communication, through (i) the unavoidable presence of French terminology—the rows and rows of small plumbing equipment behind the counter all carried French labels (*douchette* 'small shower head', *raccord* 'connection', *joint* 'washer', etc.); (ii) the presence of even a very small minority of French speakers, that is, the showroom customers and two of the employees. To find an Alsatian stronghold in Strasbourg, one would clearly have to seek out exceptionally homogeneous circumstances such as were not met here.

Switching appeared to be limited to certain clearly defined situations and linguistic configurations: on the one hand, 'spillover' from the use of French terminology in Alsatian sentences, for example: Hein, *les crochets-supports?* 'Eh, *the support-hooks?*'—said by an employee to a customer with whom he was otherwise speaking Alsatian, and on the other hand whole conversations in French when the customer was (*a*) not known and (*b*) a private person rather than a plumber. In spite of what was said above about this situation lacking the characteristics of an Alsatian stronghold, the lack of switching would appear to indicate that speakers here fall into clear categories with respect to having a preference for Alsatian or a preference for French. There is apparently little motivation for switching in any dense fashion among most of the employees and their customer-colleagues.

Eckwersheim

The next survey was carried out in a village some 14 km. from Strasbourg, Eckwersheim. One of the purposes of the survey, which took the form of interviews, observation, and a questionnaire, was to identify any clear and striking differences between linguistic behaviour in town and in the country which would throw more light on language choices in Strasbourg; it is that part of the information obtained which is reported here. A 1982 census showed the population of Eckwersheim to be 906, of whom approximately one third worked in Strasbourg, a further percentage in other smaller towns roundabout, and only eight were employed on the land (*Encyclopédie de l'Alsace*, 1985). Eckwersheim's 'commuter-village' character is reinforced by the presence of a housing estate inhabited mainly by people having moved out from Strasbourg with a second such group of houses under construction. On the other hand, there is still a village life centring around the primary school, the shops, café, restaurant, town hall, and to some extent the Protestant church.

A questionnaire was distributed with the local paper from which fifty-one replies were received, representing a 20 per cent response, or some 5 per cent of the village population. Ninety-eight per cent of those who replied claimed that they were able to speak Alsatian, whether less well than, as well as, or better than French. This high figure should be contrasted with the village teachers' detailed reports of 46 per cent of nursery and primary schoolchildren able to speak the dialect. A question concerning language use as opposed to knowledge produced the following result: respondents claimed to use *both* French *and* Alsatian in the village in the following circumstances.

at the baker's	31% of respondents
at the grocer's	31% of respondents
outside church	33% of respondents
at the restaurant	24% of respondents
at the Town Hall	33% of respondents
outside the school	33% of respondents
at the school fête	27% of respondents

It should be mentioned that two influential figures, the mayor and the headmistress of the school, who might have exercised a strong francophone influence, claimed when interviewed to be very much in favour of maintaining the dialect. The above figures are of interest because they show us the circumstances in which switching could theoretically arise in public circumstances among about a third of the population, assuming that those who answered the questionnaire were typical (the questionnaire was presented in French and in German so as not to exclude any—presumably older—respondents whose principal written language was German). The questionnaire was complemented by surveys at the grocery/tobacconist and at the café/bar. At the grocer's almost all the customers spoke Alsatian although more than half used French terms, conversational expressions, and/or used French for prices and other figures. Only one (out of twenty-six observed) switched more elaborately. At the café/bar, which was observed at its busiest time, on Sunday after church, everyone spoke Alsatian with the exception of some French vocabulary ('*billet*', '*tombola*', '*jus de fruit*') and of one customer who apparently wanted to speak French with the innkeeper's wife but ended up, partly due to the latter's resistance, switching.

The most notable overall result of the survey is that in spite of being partly a commuter-village, very close to Strasbourg and influenced by the presence of a mainly French-speaking housing estate, in Eckwersheim the language of adult communication remains Alsatian and even switching is restricted to its most superficial forms, although it is acceptable to use either language in many circumstances. This provides a marked contrast to the urban surveys which showed a much more mixed usage. The enormous falling off of dialect use among children seems, however, to suggest that there will be a considerable change at the next generation.

The Next Generation

Apart from the teachers interviewed in Eckwersheim, ten interviews and class observations were conducted in nursery and primary schools in and around Strasbourg; this completed the information obtained through a questionnaire returned by 137 nursery schoolteachers in the Bas Rhin, the purpose of which was to establish roughly what proportion of children can and do use each of the two languages and what their teachers' aims and attitudes are with respect to linguistic matters. It should be mentioned that in France nursery schooling is part of the normal State school system provided for every child; although it is not compulsory it is considered an important preparation for entering primary school (Cours préparatoire) at six, and a large proportion of children of all social classes attend. Nursery-school teachers are therefore significant informants about the likely future of the linguistic situation and their views and practices are likely to be highly influential; in the case of monolingual dialect-speaking children, they represent the child's first sustained contact with the French-speaking world outside the home.

Among teachers themselves, almost half (47 per cent) said they spoke the dialect and French equally well: a further 25 per cent claimed to speak the dialect, though less well than French, and only ten per cent said they did not understand the dialect at all.

As to the reported language competence of the children, according to the teachers the situation is as shown in Table 4.11. The last category (children who do not understand the dialect) was significantly correlated with living in larger towns; however, even those children who can speak the dialect were said to use it at home and only very few of them at school (22 per cent).

TABLE 4.11. Reported Linguistic Competence of Children

	% (3110 children)
Speaking only dialect	3
Speaking both dialect and French	23
Understanding but unable to speak dialect	17
Unable to understand dialect	57

As regards the teachers' views on the children's bilingualism, these should be read bearing in mind what has been said above about nursery school being considered a preparation for primary school. At primary school, intellectual activities including the three Rs are presented through the medium of French, and teachers consider that ability to master these is directly correlated with competence in French. Forty-eight per cent thought the fact of speaking the dialect was a slight disadvantage with regard to the children's ability to speak French and a further 22 per cent considered it a serious disadvantage. A third of teachers considered dialect knowledge to be at least a slight disadvantage even with respect to the children's *understanding* of French. This negative opinion, which is not backed up by the results of scientific studies on the effects of child bilingualism (e.g. Paradis and Lebrun 1984) can be explained in several ways. Firstly, by factors connected with the socioeconomic background of the dialect-speaking children rather than with their bilingualism as such. Secondly, by the importance given by the teachers to the ideal of a uniform (i.e. non-regionally marked) form of French: 72 per cent considered it important or very important that the pupils' French be uniform with that spoken elsewhere in France from the point of view of vocabulary, 78 per cent from the point of view of grammar, and 52 per cent from the point of view of accent or pronunciation. Clearly such uniformity is less likely to be found among children in contact with the dialect than among those who are not. Thirdly, connected with the second point, the mixing of the two languages is stigmatized and is the object of correction by the teachers: dialect speakers were said to use Alsatian structures when speaking French and French vocabulary when speaking Alsatian. Their knowledge of the dialect is therefore seen as disadvantageous because it leads to mixing.

Paradoxically, however, over a third of teachers replying to the questionnaire thought the dialect should be encouraged at nursery school and 49 per cent would at least occasionally have Alsatian songs, stories, and rhymes in class (this is permitted under the latest Nursery School directives).

Once again, the interviews and class observation, as well as some of the inherent paradoxes in the replies to the questionnaire show a clear sentimental attachment to the dialect on behalf of adults which is at odds with their more intellectual convictions about the necessity for fluent competence in a-regional French.

Speakers' Views on Switching

Part of the interviews carried out in the Cité des Chasseurs, reported in Chapter 2, consisted of a discussion relating to code-switching. Subjects were all aware of its existence and had a variety of names to designate it, though these tended to be personal rather than widespread: Co-opefranzeeisch 'Co-op French', Charivari 'hustle and bustle', *notre charabia à nous* '*our Double-Dutch*', *le vrai strasbourgeois* '*real Strasbourgeois*', etc. They tended either to admit that they, like everyone around them, code-switched ('*Nous le faisons tous, plus ou moins*'), or to say that although it was a generalized habit, they themselves deliberately avoided it. Attitudes towards it ranged from considering it quite natural in a bilingual context (*normal*) and thus acceptable or even endearing (*sympathique*) or amusing, to considering it a bad habit (*une manie*), irritating and impolite. It was often said, in a variety of ways, that switching took place automatically, unconsciously, without the speaker doing it deliberately or without his being aware of it. (Lüdi (1984), finds the same with respect to some cases of language choice in a bilingual context; he refers to it as a type of 'conditioned reflex').

Subjects were further asked what they considered to be the reasons for switching; their varied and perceptive replies can be classified in the following manner:

(i) Reasons connected with the roles occupied by the two languages in Alsatian society, in particular the fact that certain professional and technical areas are the preserve of French, which leads to the use of French vocabulary in Alsatian sentences and sometimes to longer switches triggered by such terms.

(ii) Reasons related to speakers' competence: on an individual level, this might mean that certain words or notions came up in one or the other language, whether or not these are related to a specific specialized area as above. Some carried this further and said that there were people who had 'no mother tongue', who switched from one language to the other because they did not speak either well enough to avoid doing so. On an interpersonal level, there could be differences in competence between speakers taking part in the same conversation such that *either* there were language changes between speakers (this phenomenon tended to be considered as a variety of switching) or, in group situations, compromise forms of speech had to be found so that everyone could understand and participate equally.

(iii) Finally, various psychological reasons for switching were also mentioned (i.e. reasons connected with speakers' motivations or intentions, whether conscious or unconscious). Switching to and fro in a conversation where everyone was behaving likewise was seen as a way of showing one's belonging to a particular group, that of bilingual Alsatians with a dual set of references or a dual culture (Scotton 1987). Switching could be seen as a self-indulgence, a way of speaking while exercising the minimal possible effort and thereby of enjoying the experience of talking. Using Alsatian words, expressions, or asides in a French conversation could be a way of giving a verbal nudge or wink, a sign of complicity which could deflate the formality of, for example, a business conversation. Using French in an Alsatian conversation could on the other hand be a way of indicating one's fundamental Frenchness, one's immersedness in French culture and values. Several speakers referred to the fact that any of these possible reasons for switching could give rise to a linguistic habit: the reasons given need then not necessarily be present for the switching to continue in whatever form one had got used to.

The lucidity of the subjects of these interviews concerning the reasons for switching contrasts strongly with the fact that they characterize it as a non-deliberate, unconscious mode of speech—the unconsciousness is clearly not carried over into their reasoned perceptions.

Conclusion

It emerges from these studies that code-switching occurs in various forms in circumstances where the use of either French or Alsatian is possible, but that it does not necessarily occur *most* in cases where the distribution beween French and Alsatian is closest to fifty–fifty.

Thus in the Department Stores study, switching occurred most in the more extreme linguistic environments, when speakers' competence was at odds with that environment and they were therefore making an effort to fit in with their surroundings or their interlocutor; in the middle-range store where either language was equally acceptable the lowest rate of switching was recorded. The type of transaction observed is, however, decisive in determining both the amount and type of switching which occurs. In shops—be they department stores or small shops such as the baker's shop in Strasbourg or the grocer's shop in Eckwersheim, what people say to each other is limited both in form and in substance and switching is therefore limited, on the whole, to terminological needs. The same applies where speakers are constrained by social and situational expectations as to how they should behave: in the Insurance Office, it would clearly be considered bad manners for the employees to switch abundantly when talking to clients and there is a marked contrast between such conversations, where such switching as occurs is mainly terminological (and therefore one-way, French terms being used in Alsatian utterances), and conversations between employees (or employees and customers when they know each other well and are not obeying formal rules), where switching can be very dense (Wunderlich 1988).

It appears to be difficult, in Strasbourg, to find a public, 'observable' context in which either French or Alsatian is completely ruled out; naturally the more speakers are present at once the more likely it is that both languages will be represented at least to some extent. At the plumbers' merchant, the majority of subjects were predominantly dialect-speakers and the context was also conducive to the use of Alsatian (or of the Low variety), but French had slipped into the linguistic picture by various means and there appeared to be no actual resistance to its use.

Speakers' age, as the surveys described in Chapter 2 all indicate, is a highly significant factor in language choice in Alsace, and one of the best places to find unmixed French would appear to be in a school context. This was supported by the situation in Eckwersheim where almost all the adults apparently used the dialect at least to some extent but teachers reported that almost half the children could not. In Strasbourg schools the situation is far more extreme and in some classes no children have any active competence in the dialect, though passive competence can often be detected if one shows persistence. Teachers' attitudes are highly ambivalent, being marked both by attachment to the dialect and a conviction that the children should be helped to speak 'pure' French as this is directly related to their future academic success. Such mixing of languages as does occur among the children is considered a bad thing, though this judgement is certainly related to the fact that those children who do speak the dialect and therefore *are in a position* to mix the two languages often come from less privileged or less intellectual home backgrounds.

For here as elsewhere there is a lack of discrimination as to the effects of bilingualism as such and the language 'problems' identified in individual children: as in any other part of the world, some speakers, children or adults, do not master the most prestigious form of the prestige variety, French, to a level which satisfies the 'guardians of the language', amongst whom many teachers must be classed. If these speakers happen to be bilinguals, that is to say master some other variety as well to a greater or lesser extent, then the sheer fact of that bilingualism is taken as the reason for their lack of mastery of the prestige language (Martin-Jones and Romaine 1985). This is an over-simplification of a problem which requires detailed investigation on a number of levels; it is not proven that knowledge of another idiom necessarily compounds these children's difficulties in French even though they naturally will not speak the same kind of French as a non-dialect speaker (Milroy 1985).

In the next chapter, different kinds of switching will be exemplified systematically on the basis of transcribed conversations. But one can say already that the information gathered in this survey reinforces the data in Chapter 2 on the decline of Alsatian among children. The kind of switching found among children deserves further investigation in this context as it is likely to reflect this decline whereas switching among competent bilingual adults might reflect nothing more nor less than that competent bilingualism (Poplack 1980).

Finally, it emerged from the interviews conducted in the Cité des Chasseurs that speakers were aware of the prevalence of code-switching around them, in spite of the fact that they described it as an 'unconscious' form of behaviour on behalf of speakers. It was considered acceptable behaviour in a bilingual context by some and stigmatized by others; it was seen as having a variety of possible motivations and correspondingly varied linguistic forms.

In the next chapter, the possible categories, their linguistic manifestations, and the inter-relations between them will be considered in greater detail on the basis of transcriptions of natural conversations.

5

Conversational Analysis

I would propose . . . as a principle for sociolinguistics, that any analysis of speech behaviour will ultimately stand or fall on its success in coming to grips with audio recordings of what speakers actually say to each other in specific, naturally occurring settings.

(Stubbs 1983: 220)

i General Description: Data-Collection; Transcription; Distribution of Speakers

One of the most revealing methods of collecting data on code-switching is the recording, transcription, and analysis—not merely grammatical analysis—of spontaneous interactions. This method was used in the present study to complement the interviews and surveys; while it is arguably the most indispensable of the three techniques, it gains much by being used alongside them. Its usefulness is also largely dependent on an understanding of the context of and implications within each conversation.

Six separate conversations involving different sets of bilingual participants were recorded, each for approximately one hour. Following a method adopted by others (Milroy 1987), the tape recorder was left with the subjects, who agreed to record conversations involving themselves and members of their network at a suitable moment. This technique provides a way round the observer's paradox, particularly when the researcher is not a member of the community studied.

Three of the recordings selected for analysis were made in family contexts and three at places of work. Subjects were asked to record themselves and others in typical, everyday conversations in which both French and Alsatian were spoken, regardless of the proportion of one against the other. No mention was made of code-switching, and it was left to the subject in charge of the recording to decide whether or not the other speakers should be made aware of the tape recorder or not. In the six conversations reported here, one of the three families, the Schmitts,[1] were aware of the recording, as were three out of the six in the Beck household. As far as the work places are concerned, all the speakers were aware in one case (Accounts Office), and in both other cases certain speakers were or became aware of the recording while it was in progress. This awareness is, of course, significant and one would ideally hope to collect data

---

[1] All personal names have been changed.

without any such extraneous factors. However, there are both ethical and technical problems in doing this, and I would argue that data in which some subjects are aware of what is going on and others not is a reasonable compromise. First of all, the longer the recording, the more difficult it is to depart from one's normal patterns of speech, particularly if one is engaged in some everyday activity such as a family meal or conversations about work with colleagues; second, if some participants in the conversation are not aware of the recording, it is difficult for those who are aware to behave untypically without giving rise to comment or reactions of surprise, which would be apparent on the recording; third, those passages in the recordings where speakers are clearly 'playing to the microphone' in their linguistic behaviour can be revealing in themselves (such an incident is described below in Conversation A).

With thirty-one speakers and six conversations, one cannot of course offer a fully representative picture of Strasbourg bilingual speech (for an analysis see Fig. 5.1); but the aim of this analysis is not to give a quantitatively faithful picture of such interactions. It is rather to provide a basis for discussing the principal characteristics of such discourse, identifying major sub-types within it and exemplifying the numerous problems to which its analysis gives rise. Transcriptions were discussed afterwards with those participants in the conversations who were responsible for the recordings; cryptic allusions and implications could thereby be elucidated.

On the technical side, an infinite range of transcription styles and degrees of phonetic accuracy are, of course, possible; a balance was sought in this case between accuracy in relation to, on the one hand, pauses, interruptions, and self-interruptions and, on the other hand, readability: some recent transcriptions which attempt to show whenever two or more speakers are speaking simultaneously can become difficult to follow for the reader (Stubbs 1983: 11).

For the transcription of Alsatian, the system put forward in Matzen 1980: 171–200 (and used in his own poetry) is employed. Its purpose is to provide a standardized spelling system for the Strasbourg dialect; as mentioned in Chapter 2, Strasbourg is in various respects a linguistic island, characterized not only by the Franconian influence on the Alemannic base but also by the multiplicity of elements of French origin which the Strasbourg dialect has incorporated.

There are problems inherent in using a standard orthography to transcribe a variety which has no oral standard; for although the subjects whose speech is reported are all Strasbourgeois, some came originally from other parts of Alsace and still exhibit dialectal features of their region of origin which a standardized transcription glosses over, even more so than the variations within Strasbourg speech. This is, for example, the case with Annie (Conversation C) who says 'Mir asse jetz' and not 'Mir esse jetz' as the Strasbourg standard requires. The Matzen system is, however, used throughout so as not

	Total
A. Beck family	
men: Mr Beck, Mr Eder, Grandfather	3
women: Mrs Beck, Mrs Eder, Catherine	3
(Agnès, Hélène, Mother-in-law)	
B. Rick family	
men: René	I
women: Agnès, Marie	2
children: * Annie R.	I
C. Schmitt family	
men: Michel	I
women: Annie S.	I
children: * Émile, Claude	2
D. Administration office	
men: Conrad, Herr, Rick, Gress	4
(Nuss, Schott, Hemm)	
[Saleur]	
women: Klein, Durst, Meyer, Miller	4
(Jung)	
E. Accounts office	
men: Martin, Cedric, Georges, Gérard	4
women: Liliane, Denise	2
(Chantal, Andrée)	
F. Car park attendants	
men: Paul, Denis, René	3
(Frank)	
women: [Annie]	
	3I

(men: 16, women: 12, children: 3)

Key: ( ) = speaker taking the floor fewer than 10 times (not counted in totals)
     [ ] = monolingual speaker
     * = children under 10 years of age

FIG. 5.1. Conversational Analysis: Distribution of Speakers

to complicate matters for readers attempting to follow the original. Any system of orthography, in any case, is conventional and fails to represent variations between speakers. Matzen's system does not have as its sole aim to represent the Strasbourg dialect, although it is based on it; in many respects it harks back to Standard German (SG). Thus in many words the German 'ich-laut' is represented by 'sch' since the Strasbourgeois pronounce it [ʃ]

> SG **Bauch** = Stras. Büsch '**tummy**'
> SG **weich** = Stras. weisch '**soft**'

etc. but in order to distinguish between the personal pronoun **ich** and the verb **ist** in the third person singular, which in Strasbourg are both pronounced /iʃ/, the SG spelling 'ich' is used for the pronoun and only the verb is spelt 'isch'—a convention is thereby borrowed from a system where it is phonemically valid to one where it is morphemically useful. This spelling system, derived from German, would probably have a better chance of gaining acceptance than a more accurate phonetic one in Alsace, although it is not widely used: newspaper columns, cartoons, advertisements, etc. which are occasionally to be found in the dialect usually use their own idiosyncratic orthographies.

A problem did arise as to how to deal with more extreme forms of inter-dialectal variation, where one might consider there are two different words or grammatical forms involved. For example, at the end of Conversation C (Schmitt family) Michel, discussing the virtues of eating carrots, says, ''S isch au guet, wenn m'r nitt guet siegt' ' "It's also good when you can't see well"'; his use of the non-Strasbourg form **siegt** is immediately noticed by his son Émile, who says: 'Wenn m'r nitt guet sieht un nitt siegt' ' "When you can't see (sieht) well and can't see (siegt)"'. Had the two forms not been remarked upon, one could have let them pass as variation in pronunciation—an interesting example of the difficulty of keeping apart different aspects of linguistic description. Here the grosser variations have been represented in the transcription, and no attempt has been made as such to 'correct' the Alsatian, for example, by giving all nouns the same gender as they have in SG, as some Alsatian guardians of the language would advocate.

The Conversations

Purpose of the Descriptions and Typing Conventions of the Texts

Throughout this book it is assumed that code-switching cannot be analysed out of context, that even what appear to be 'purely' linguistic decisions (e.g. what is a loan and what is a switch) can only be taken with the fullest possible knowledge of the background, the context, the speakers, and their intentions. Therefore, in this chapter, the six conversations will be described fully and extensive samples of the transcriptions will be given (ideally, of course, copies of the original tapes—or, better still, video tapes—should be made accessible). In the next chapter some quantitative evaluations of the various phenomena identified will be undertaken; these are intended to complete the description of the conversations and to provide a basis for the discussion of analytical problems of code-switching which follows.

Whenever an extract or an example from the transcriptions is provided, the two languages are visually distinguished by the use of a different script, highlighting the switch points. This involved the making of a number of somewhat arbitrary decisions as to what should count as French and what should count as Alsatian. In particular, I discussed in Chapter 3 the vexed question of what constitutes a loan and what constitutes a switch, and argued that no hard and fast criterion exists; so a question repeatedly arose as to how to represent the doubtful cases in the examples given here. Even on a simpler level, words such as *Monsieur* or *Madame*, *merci*, *bonjour*, *salut*, etc., which are clearly part of Alsatian, as there is no alternative to them, posed a problem regarding their visual representation in one or the other script: within French segments of text they are French terms and within Alsatian ones they are Alsatian; but by their nature they are usually at the beginning or end of an utterance where one cannot necessarily tell. In fact, in a bilingual context the question of linguistic provenance of many such terms is irrelevant. Consequently, a decision was taken to proceed in an *ad hoc* manner and use whichever script seemed most appropriate in each case, fully conceding that this leads to inconsistencies. The two scripts should therefore only be taken as a rough visual guide and not as representing a principled decision in each case as to where a switch has occurred.

A. The Beck Family

This recording is divided into three parts, although it was all carried out on the same day, which was New Year's Eve. First we hear the Becks at home, having lunch and discussing plans for the evening when they expect guests, the Eders. Their three teenage daughters, Agnès, Hélène, and Catherine and Mrs Beck's aged father are all present.

Next we hear them in the evening of the same day when their guests, another middle-aged couple and the wife's mother, arrive; presents are distributed, they start their meal and listen to President Mitterrand's speech on television. The daughters are still there but the grandfather has gone to bed. Third, we hear the two couples, the Becks and the Eders and Mrs Eder's mother in conversation together after the meal.

Mr Beck is a self-employed plumber and his wife no longer works; she worked in the past in an administrative office, which is where she got to know Monsieur Eder; Mrs Eder does not work. Both couples are around fifty.

Mr and Mrs Beck generally speak Alsatian with the grandfather and French with their daughters, which leads to switching languages in accordance with changes in interlocutor, typical of many Alsatian families. They themselves belong to the so-called 'middle' generation, which was at school during the Occupation and which includes the most balanced bilinguals. When speaking to each other, they usually use Alsatian, sometimes French, and very often a mixture. Extract 1 below, shows Mr and Mrs Beck speaking Alsatian to each other and to the grandfather, then addressing their daughters in French. In the flow of French conversation, Mr Beck also speaks French to his wife [12]; the grandfather speaks French to his granddaughter [14].

EXTRACT 1

[1] MR BECK

Awwer hit morje isch kalt g'sinn, oh kalt!
But this morning it was cold, oh so cold!

[2] MRS BECK

's isch kalt, 's isch Winter!
It's cold, it's winter!

[3] MR BECK

A table, les enfants!
Lunch is ready, kids!

[4] MRS BECK

De Putzlumpe isch g'frore g'sinn! *Allez vite, maintenant!*
Allons!
The mop was frozen! *Come on, now! Quickly!*

[5] GRANDFATHER

Hit morje haw ich gelööjt, sinn's vier Grad g'sinn.
I had a look this morning, it was four degrees.

[6] MRS BECK

Ja, 's isch unter null g'sinn! 's isch g'frore g'sinn. *Des pommes de terre, qui veut des pommes de terre?*
Yes, it was below zero. It was frozen. *Potatoes, who wants some potatoes?*

[7] GRANDFATHER

Ich bin lätz dran.
I feel under the weather again.

[8] MRS BECK

Ja. *L'omelette? Hélène, passe-moi ton assiette!*
Yes. *The omelette? Hélène, pass me your plate!*

[9] HÉLÈNE

Hein?
Eh?

[10] MRS BECK

Passe-moi ton assiette!
Pass me your plate!

[11] HÉLÈNE

Attends!
Wait!

[12] MR BECK

Jesus! *Tu m'en a donné beaucoup là!*
Jesus! *You've given me a lot there!*

[13] MRS BECK

Oui, attends pour grand-père!
Yes, wait for grandfather!

[14] GRANDFATHER   *Pas beaucoup, Catherine!*
                    Not a lot, Catherine!

[15] CATHERINE   *Comme ça?*
                    Is that right?

The grandfather is over eighty and linguistically very dominant in Alsatian in spite of the words of French he says to his granddaughter; it is difficult to say to what extent the lack of a common language impedes or reduces the quantity of communication between them, but it must do to some extent: for it is only when Mr Beck asks his daughters to speak Alsatian (for the purposes of the recording) that the grandfather takes part momentarily in the general conversation.

EXTRACT 2

[1] MR BECK   Wenn'r nitt Elsässisch wöelle redde, redde Englisch!
                    If you won't speak Alsatian, speak English!

[*laughter*]

[2] MRS BECK   Noh kannsch dü's awwer nitt verstehn!
                    But then you [with emphasis] won't be able to understand!

[3] MR BECK   Joo na?
                    Oh yes?

[4] CATHERINE   *Oh, si il s'en sort, lui!*
                    Oh, yes, he'll manage!

[5] GRANDFATHER   D'r Germain Muller[2] het au g'saat, 'Ah, sie redde Elsässisch!'
                    Germain Muller also said, 'Ah, you speak Alsatian!'

Like many old people and due no doubt in part to his being hard of hearing, Grandfather, on the whole, carries on a separate conversation from the general conversation with Mrs Beck or with his son-in-law, on subjects which are of direct concern to him: his electric cushion, and later on the virtues of decaffeinated coffee.

The interest of this particular section lies also in the metalinguistic references due to the presence of the tape recorder, of which all except Grandfather are aware. Mr Beck tells his daughters to speak Alsatian [1] but they only giggle in return. Mr and Mrs Beck's use of Alsatian to each other is, however, not forced: this is what they usually speak, and anyway they do not wish to exclude Grandfather from the conversation by speaking French. Their

---

[2] Germain Muller is the best-known Alsatian song-writer and cabaret artist. His theatre is known as D'Barabli, from the French, *parapluie 'umbrella'*, this word being considered an archetypal borrowing of a French word into the dialect.

eldest daughter Catherine, for one, is not excluded by their use of Alsatian, as the next extract shows; they are discussing their guests for the evening.

EXTRACT 3

[1] MR BECK   Ja, ich denk, sie kumme nitt ze spot.
                   Yes, I think they won't come too late.

[2] MRS BECK   Am achte het's g'saat? Sie fahre's Patricia an d'*gare*.
                   Did she say at eight? They're taking Patricia to the *station*.

[3] CATHERINE   *Ah, bon?*
                   Ah, yes?

[4] MRS BECK   *Oui, elle va chez une copine à Obernai, elle est invitée.*
                   Yes, she's going to a friend's in Obernai, she's invited out.

Furthermore, they continue to speak French to the girls when they are not thinking about the recording. After the exchange of teasing in Extract 2 when Mr Beck asks his daughters to speak Alsatian [5], or if not then English (which they are learning at school) and Mrs Beck comments that he himself would not then understand what's going on, Catherine deliberately plunges into the 'game' and tries to speak Alsatian. Although she shows repeatedly that she understands it perfectly well, in trying to speak it she intersperses words of German, which she is also learning at school (these words are printed bold in the text).

EXTRACT 4

[1] CATHERINE   Ich will danze hit owe, danze un danze.
                   I want to dance this evening, dance and dance.

[2] MRS BECK   Mit wem?
                   With whom?

[3] MR BECK   Müesch zerscht e *cavalier* han!
                   You need to have an *escort* first!

[4] MRS BECK   Mit Paulette.
                   With Paulette.

[5] CATHERINE   Mit Mama, mit Babbe, **mit Grossvater**.
                   With Mummy, with Daddy, **with Grandfather**.

[6] AGNÈS   Mit mir.
                   With me.

[7] CATHERINE   **Mit meiner Schwester**.
                   With my sister.

Her confusion of Alsatian and German prompts her mother to correct her:

EXTRACT 5

[1] MRS BECK   Von morje ab därfsch alle Owe früej in's Bett, awwer hit owe
     müesch uf bliewe!
     From tomorrow you can go to bed early every evening, but
     this evening you must stay up!

[2] CATHERINE   **Danke**, Mamma!
     Thank you, Mummy!

[3] MRS BECK   Kannsch rewi *merci* saawe, brüsch nitt **Danke** saawe.
     You can say *merci* you know, you need not say **Danke**.

[4] CATHERINE   Dann, *merci!*
     Then, *merci!*

The conversation is increasingly interrupted by laughter, as Catherine plays at speaking Alsatian, employing what she sees as typical expressions (Jesus Maria! 'Jesus and Mary!'), getting into difficulties and having to switch to French.

EXTRACT 6

[1] MRS BECK   Uewwerhaupt kannsch doch nitt schlofe wenn se scheesse!
     Anyway you can't sleep when they're shooting (fireworks)!

[2] CATHERINE   Ich hab . . . *boules-quiès*.[3]
     I have . . . *ear-plugs*.

[3] MRS BECK   Na ja, dü hesch *boules-quiès* in de Ohre, awwer trotzdem!
     Höersch doch! Wenn de Babbe anfangt schiesse, do
     verwacht d'ganz Stross!
     Yes well, you may have *ear-plugs* in your ears, but still! You
     can still hear! When your father starts letting off fireworks,
     the whole street will wake up!

The Becks and their daughters are by now almost weeping with laughter at Catherine's tongue-in-cheek efforts to speak Alsatian. Only the Grandfather, unaware of the recording, remarks quite sincerely, 'D'Catherine lehrt allaan Elsässisch' '"Catherine is teaching herself Alsatian"'. 'It's high time for me to speak Alsatian', replies Catherine. 'It's taken you nearly twenty years', her mother returns between outbursts of laughter.

EXTRACT 7

[1] GRANDFATHER   D'Catherine lehrt allaan Elsässisch.
     Catherine is teaching herself Alsatian.

[2] MRS BECK   Ja, ja.
     Yes, yes.

---

[3] *Boules-quiès* is a competence-related switch for Catherine. It could be a loan in the speech of more fluent Alsatian speakers, although there is, in fact, an Alsatian equivalent, 'Ohrebolle'.

[3] CATHERINE	'S isch awwer Zit, dass i Elsässisch redde kann!
	It's high time for me to speak Alsatian!

[4] MRS BECK	Ja, 's isch wajer Zit. Hesch joo ball zwanzig Johr gebrüscht!
	Yes, it's high time indeed. It's taken you nearly twenty years!

[5] CATHERINE	*Sinon les cigognes vont s'en aller si plus personne parle alsacien en Alsace!*[4]
	Otherwise the storks will fly away if no one speaks Alsatian in Alsace any more!

[6] MRS BECK	*Elles ne s'y reconnaîtront plus.*
	They won't know where they are.

[7] CATHERINE	'S isch schlimm!
	That's bad!

[8] MRS BECK	Diss isch schlimm, ja. Noh hamm'r gar ken Elsass meh . . .
	That's bad, yes. Then we wouldn't have an Alsace at all any longer . . .

This passage is both revealing and a little pathetic; one is sorry for the Grandfather, who is genuinely pleased to hear his granddaughter speak Alsatian; and a little surprised, in spite of all the statistics, to see to what extent hilarity is provoked in a family where Alsatian is spoken every day, by a nineteen-year-old girl speaking it too.

The same evening, the Eders and Mrs Eder's mother arrive to spend New Year's Eve with the Becks. Like the Becks, the Eders are balanced bilinguals, and like the Grandfather, and many old people, Mrs Eder's aged mother speaks only Alsatian.

Mr Eder is an inveterate switcher (an utterance count reveals that he code-switches in almost 30 per cent of cases); he is also considered to be something of a wit and raconteur. The Becks said to me afterwards that his persistent mixing of the two languages was due to his years of work in the administration, where one is constantly exposed to people of varied linguistic competence and switching is therefore a way of ensuring that one is as intelligible as possible to the greatest number. His wife switches somewhat less—in this sample, in just over a fifth of her utterances. The Becks, for purposes of comparison, both switch in under 10 per cent of their utterances. The Eders, like the Becks, naturally address the Beck girls in French and they reply likewise. (At this stage, only Mr Beck is aware of the recording.)

They all sit down to listen to the President's New Year address to the nation,

---

4 Cf. cartoon, p. 16.

which largely centres around the economic crisis. Perhaps because of this French context, Mrs Eder's first comment at the end of the programme is in French. But Mr Eder, who always has a lot to say, goes back to Alsatian—with excursions into French:

EXTRACT 8

[1] MR BECK   Hoppla, *et oui*.
                 Hoppla, *there we are*.

[2] MRS EDER   *C'est pas rose, rose, hein!*
                 It's not too rosy, is it!

[3] MR EDER   M'r kann alles saawe. Er het e gueter Wille, awwer wie g'saat, s'isch international. S'isch international, s'geht alles eso. Ich hab diss letscht noch g'höert am Ditsche, Ditsche, die han *au point de vue entreprise* gell, e kleini Ding, Gschäfter, wie han sie denn e Üsdruck uf Ditsch . . . *enfin* sie mache *faillite, quoi*; Kursus?
                 You can say what you like. He has good intentions, but as he said, it's international. It's international, it's the same everywhere. I heard recently on the German radio, the Germans, they have *on the business front* you know, a thing, business, what is the expression in German . . . *well* they go *bankrupt, you know*; Kursus?

[4] MRS EDER   **Konkurs?**
                 Bankruptcy?

[5] MR EDER   **Konkurs**, ja. So han sie sich üsgedruckt, ja . . .
                 Bankruptcy, yes. That's what they called it, yes . . .

In this extract, Mr Beck speaks Alsatian until he comes to the word *entreprise* 'business'; this is not part of the traditional areas of dialect vocabulary and it must therefore be appropriated from somewhere else; a German expression would be felt as 'foreign', so a French word is used with partial phonological assimilation (*entreprise* is heavily stressed on the first syllable). This word 'triggers' a surrounding expression in ·French, in this case *au point de vue entreprise*. But the use of this French expression is not sufficient to make the whole utterance go over to French and Mr Eder goes back to Alsatian in spite of the fact that he is searching for an expression which he knows perfectly in French: *faire faillite 'to go bankrupt'*. It is an amusing passage to hear: Mr Eder is desperately seeking the German expression which he has heard on the radio in relation to German businesses: 'they go thing, whatsit, how do you say that?' he says in Alsatian; at last, so that the others could help him find the word, he adds as if in parentheses: '*enfin* sie mache *faillite, quoi*' [3]. There is no paradox, for him, in the fact that it is the French word which comes naturally, although he is using a German-based language: **Konkurs** is to him a foreign word whereas *faillite* is not. It is only our judgement as outsiders which says it is part of a 'different' language from the one he is using.

The Becks and the Eders then exchange New Year's gifts, and the switching is mainly related to changes in interlocutor, the girls being addressed in French. The use of *merci*, which is common to Alsatian and French, leads to some further triggering into French [5].

EXTRACT 9

[1] MR EDER   Jetz machsch dü's au emol so!
                     This is how you do it (open the package)!

[2] MR BECK   *Merci, oui.*
                     Thanks, yes.

[3] MR EDER   Mach dir ke Sorje!
                     Don't worry!

[4] GRANDMOTHER   E kleini *attention*.
                     A little *treat*.

[5] MRS BECK   *Merci, c'est gentil ça, merci beaucoup!*
                     Thank you, that's kind, thanks a lot!

[6] GRANDMOTHER   'S ich gern gschähn!
                     It's a pleasure!

[7] MRS BECK   Isch noch emol Wihnachte?
                     Is it Christmas all over again?

[8] MR EDER   Hesch au e Kleinigkeit! Un diss isch fur de Babbe, gell,
                     e bissel ebbs. Es isch e Malaga, diss wurd'r allewäj
                     vertraawe!
                     Here's a little present for you. And this is for
                     Grandfather, eh, a little something. It's Malaga, I'm sure
                     his stomach will take that.

[9] MRS BECK   Er isch eso böjfälli.
                     He's so fragile.

[10] GRANDMOTHER   Joo, 's isch au de Winter!
                     Yes, it is winter after all.

[11] MR EDER   [Giving out perfumed candles and sweets] *Alors là, y'a
                     differents goûts*, gell, hein, *vous n'avez qu'à vous arranger.*
                     Now, there are different flavours here, you see, *you need only
                     decide among yourselves.*

Mrs Beck also speaks French in describing preparations for the meal [3] (Fischer 1979):

EXTRACT 10

[1] MRS BECK   Haw i g'saat, awwer hit owe will i alles vorgerüescht han.
So I said, this evening I want to have everything prepared
ahead.

[2] MR EDER   Ah ja, dass m'r nitt numme's Schwänzele sieht.
Ah yes, so we don't only see your tail.

[3] MRS BECK   *Y'a du potage, et puis après y'a un buffet froid, dessert, tout est déjà*
prêt.
There's soup and then there's a cold buffet, dessert, everything is
already done.

[4] GRANDMOTHER   Ja, diss isch 's Beschte.
Yes, that's the best thing.

The Becks and the Eders then sit down for their meal and the discussion
turns to the purchase of the Beck's new house. The legal terms relating to the
purchase are all in French [1] and the use of one or the other French term gives
rise to triggering. However, some switching eludes explanation of this kind [5]
and one has to resort to a different speculative explanation which will be
discussed further below.

EXTRACT 11

[1] MRS BECK   E *promesse de vente* isch unterschriwwe, nitt, awwer de *contrat de*
vente nitt, denn . . . Der het's kauft vor zehn Johr, am
achtzehnte *janvier*; *s'il le revend avant*, hett'r e *plus-value*.
A *preliminary contract* has been signed, you see, but the *contract*
of sale hasn't, because . . . He bought it ten years ago, on the
eighteenth *of January*; *if he sells before* (*ten years are up*) he'll have
to pay *gains tax*.

[2] MR EDER   Ja, ja, er het e *plus-value*.
Yes, yes, he'll have to pay *gains tax*.

[3] MRS BECK   Jetz welle ihr's erscht end's Jänner, nitt, *le contrat de vente*
erscht end's Jänner.
So he wants it at the end of January, you see, *the sales contract*
only at the end of January.

[4] MR BECK   Diss versteht sich.
That's understandable.

[5] MRS BECK   *Naturellement.*
Of course.

[6] MRS EDER   *C'est normal. Vous n'êtes pas à quelques semaines près.*
Naturally, a few week's won't make the difference to you.

[7] MRS BECK   B'sundersch bi dem Wetter, kannsch nitt grossartischi *travaux*
                 mache.
                 Especially with this weather, you can't undertake any major
                 works.

Here, for instance, within a few seconds Mrs Beck mentions one date in a
mixture of French and Alsatian [1] and another in Alsatian [3]. It is important
to differentiate such seemingly arbitrary switching from that which has a clear
sociolinguistic or plausible psycholinguistic reason (e.g. terminological or
triggered switching); this is the kind which Scotton (1986*a*) has termed
switching as an unmarked choice and which raises some of the most interesting
questions.

As the meal continues, Alsatian predominates except where the Beck's
daughters are addressed, or the table as a whole (e.g. *Prenez du pain*), or where
set expressions are used (e.g. *Mettez-vous à l'aise . . . Bon appétit!*). Only Mr Eder
continues to switch frequently in an apparently arbitrary manner, provoking
others to reply in kind.

EXTRACT 12

[1] MR EDER   Darf i grad de Pullover e bissel üszeje?
                     May I just take my jumper off?

[2] MR AND MRS BECK Ja, ja.
                     Yes, yes.

[3] MR EDER   Nämlisch, sunscht haw i e bissel ze warm, weisch . . .
                     Awwer ich höer dann uf, nitt . . . Ich mach nitt witersch
                     eso.
                     Because, otherwise I'm a bit too warm, you know . . .
                     But then I'll stop, OK . . . I won't take any more off.

[4] MRS BECK   *Mettez-vous à l'aise. Bon appétit!*
                     Make yourself comfortable. Bon appétit!

[5] MR EDER   *Alors le papa il va pas, il va pas bien* im Ding . . .
                     So your Dad is not so, not so well, in his whatsit . . .

[6] MRS BECK   *C'était pas terrible*. Mir han'm schunn am End ebbs
                     g'saat g'het devun eso, awwer noch nix . . .
                     It wasn't too great. In the end we had to tell him
                     something about it (i.e. the planned move), but we
                     haven't yet . . .

[7] MR EDER   Ja, ja.
                     Yes, yes.

There is also switching in both directions for tags, interjections, and other
phatic expressions (Alsatian: gell, hoppla 'don't you see, right'; French: *enfin*,
écoute, *effectivement*, *ah voilà*, *ah oui* '*well, listen, yes indeed, ah I see, ah yes*'). This

well-attested form of switching was also noted in the Insurance Office and will be discussed further in the overall quantification of the results.

In the last part of the recording, the Eders and the Becks are conversing after dinner; Mrs Eder's mother is there, but the Beck girls have gone to bed. The tape recorder is switched on in the middle of a discussion as to how butchers in Alsace prepare meat badly; Mr Eder, switching freely, is holding forth on the subject, the others echoing and reinforcing what he says. The predominant language throughout is Alsatian.

EXTRACT 13

[1] MR EDER   Dü bekommsch do e Fätze . . . *Je sais pas dans quelle graisse, avec quoi, avec de*, de, de, de, de, was weiss denn de Teifel . . .
What you get from this is scraps . . . *In I don't know what fat, with what, with* . . . Goodness knows what . . .

[2] MRS BECK   Nitt operiere.
They don't clean it up properly.

[3] MR EDER   Noh geh i anne un putz diss Ding, *parce que lorsque tu as un morceau de viande* im, im Teller, un noochär hesch eso . . . gschnuddels un muesch abschniede diss ganze Ding, gell, oder e so hoch Fett uf'm Ding, diss haw i halt schliesslich a nitt gäre, gell?
And then I go and clean the thing up, *because when you have a piece of meat* in, in your plate, and then you have a . . . mess and have to cut the whole lot off, you know, or this much fat on the thing, I really don't like that, you know?

[4] MRS BECK   Ja, ja.
Yes, yes.

[5] MR EDER   Natirlich, d'Metzjer saawe sich: mir han s' Viej so verkauft bekomme, mir welle ken, mir welle ken *perte* han, nitt? Sie bekomme's an de Hoke g'hängt un so un so viel macht's. Noh muen se einfach so abschnide, dass se widder uf ihri Rechnung kumme.
Of course, the butchers say to themselves: we got the beast like that, when we bought it, we don't want to make a *loss*, you know? They get it hanging on a great hook and it weighs so and so much. They then just have to cut it in such a way as to balance the books.

[6] MR BECK   Ja, so isch's.
Yes, that's how it is.

[7] MR EDER   Wenn sie doch vorhäre diss Ding . . . zamme ketzere, un eso *et seulement y'a une manière de couper que . . . dans . . . dans d'autres départements*, wo m'r 's Fleisch wunderbar so sieht.

If they'd only assemble the thing . . . properly before, like, *but there is a way of cutting which . . . in . . . in other départements*, where one sees the meat all looking wonderful.

[8] MR BECK   Im Innere,[5] gell?
                In l'Intérieur, you mean?

[9] MR EDER   Do siesch diss nitt. Bi uns siesch diss nitt.
                Here you don't see that. Over here you don't see that.

[10] MR BECK   Im Innere, gell, im Innere, diss het mini *grand-mère* immer g'saat.
                In l'Intérieur, yes, in l'Intérieur, that's what my *grandmother* always said.

Mr Eder's switch to French in [7] seems very likely to have been provoked by the fact that he is thinking of l'Intérieur at that moment.

A similar phenomenon can be observed in the next extract. Mrs Eder quotes a friend's comments (in French, the language the friend actually used) and Mr Eder continues with a more elaborate description of a visit to a market in Royan:

EXTRACT 14

[1] MRS EDER   *Charcuterie*, der Bordelais wo als kommt, der Kamerad vom Paul, saat immer: '*La charcuterie, c'est splendide à voir chez vous, vraiment, j'ai du plaisir à voir la charcuterie, mais . . .*'
                Charcuterie, the chap from Bordeaux who always comes, Paul's mate, he always says: '*Charcuterie is a pleasure to see over here, really, I find it a pleasure to see the charcuterie, but . . .*'

[2] MR EDER   Mir han jo wunderbari *charcuterie*.
                We do have wonderful *charcuterie*.

[3] MRS EDER   . . . *la boucherie, c'est pas ca!* . . .
                . . . *as far as butchery is concerned, you haven't got it there!*

[4] MR EDER   Un wenn mir als schunn emol in Royan sinn g'sinn, gell, noh het'r mi mitgenomme uf de Märik, *un marché, mais alors formidable. Vous rentrez la-dedans, hein, mais incroyable, tellement c'est bien presenté. Mais . . . mais, que ce soit le boucher, que ce soit l'épicier, que ce soit n'importe quoi, quoi, tout est bien bien présenté, tu vois . . .* Un unseri mache d'r e Fätze do, noh gehsch haam, wenn d's ufmachsch, oh, verklammi, noh hesch do e so Hampfel, awwer e richtigi Hampfel, wo de kannsch nemme, wo de Dreck ewwegg g'schnitte hesch.
                And when we were in Royan once, you see, he took me to the market, *a market which was quite fantastic. You go in there, and it's*

---

[5] 'Innere' or 'l'Intérieur' refers to the rest of France apart from Alsace.

incredible, it's so well presented. But . . . but, be it the butcher, the grocer,
whatever, whatever it may be, everything's beautifully presented, you see
. . . And ours just reduce it to rags, you go home, and when
you open it, oh, 'struth, you get a handful, a real handful you
can pick up, of all the muck you've cut away.

After this remarkable excursion into 'evocative' switching, the Becks and the
Eders discuss other food shops and in particular one case where the local
residents complained about the smells from a delicatessen, a minor drama
which was reported in the local newspaper. The mention of newspapers sets off
the following discussion which typifies a certain type of Strasbourgeois code-
switching, unselfconscious and, again, largely arbitrary. It is to such examples
that one should look for the best approximation of mixed discourse in the
Strasbourg context.

EXTRACT 15

[1] MRS BECK   Ja, ich läs als d'Zitung, ich läs d'Iwwerschrifte, *en diagonale*.
                  Yes, I always read the paper, I read the headlines, *diagonally*.

[2] MR EDER   *Enfin écoute, à vrai dire, le journal*, üsser wenn de jetz de
                  Express, de Point, odder so Dings eso hesch, gell, *où vraiment*
                  c'est, là vraiment on peut dire que c'est des journalistes qui t'écrivent
                  sur un sujet X, ne. Awwer, wenn d'so e Zitung hesch *comme les*
                  Dernières Nouvelles, alles was in de erschte vier, finef Site
                  steht, hesch schunn an de *télé* g'höert.
                  Well, you know, to be honest, newspapers, unless you have the
                  Express, the Point, or such things, you know, *where you really,*
                  you can really say you've got journalists writing on topic X, you
                  know. But when you have a newspaper *like the Dernières*
                  Nouvelles, everything that's in the first four or five pages
                  you've already heard on the *TV*.

[3] MRS EDER   Ja, *les gros titres dans tout les cas*.
                  Yes, *the headlines in any case*.

[4] MR EDER   *Les gros titres*, un hinte dann, noochhär, na *bon*, do hesch e
                  Portion *annonces, et puis après c'est les régionales*.
                  The headlines, and then afterwards, *OK*, you have a section of
                  adverts, and *then you're on to the regional news*.

[5] MRS BECK   Ja, 's isch . . .
                  Yes, it's . . .

[6] MR EDER   Noh höersch emol e bissel von Gunderschhoffe . . .
                  You hear a bit about Gunderschhoffe . . .

[7] MRS BECK   *C'est quand même une feuille de choux, hein?*
                  It's really a bit of a local rag, isn't it?

[8] MR EDER   Von Gumbrechtshoffe, un Haawenau un so Gedings, noh
klappt's, net. *D'accord* . . .
About Gumbrechtshoffe, and Haguenau and such like, then
that's it. *OK* . . .

[9] MRS EDER   *Y'a pas grand-chose dedans.*
There's not much in it.

[10] MRS BECK   *Non, y'a pas grand-chose.* 'S isch nitt vil drinne.
No, there isn't much. There's not much in it.

[11] MR EDER   *Non, c'est, c'est,* 's isch nitt ass se dini ganze Dings . . . de . . .
No, it's, it's, it's not as if the whole thing . . . the . . .

[12] MRS EDER   *C'est plutôt régional, et puis alors, en gros,* was m'r an de *télé*
höert . . .
It's regional on the whole, plus, roughly, what you hear on the
TV . . .

[13] MR EDER   *N'empêche,* wenn de awwer d'Zitung nitt hesch, fählt se
einem.
All the same, if you don't have the paper, you do miss it.

Above all, such a passage contrasts strongly with those, such as we saw earlier, where switching is strongly correlated with the addressing of interlocutors of varying bilingual competence. One can talk in such a case of a mixed form of discourse: its mixedness is clearly important in distinguishing it from the way these same speakers would talk in other circumstances. Who speaks French, who speaks Alsatian, and the exact proportion of each in the conversation are probably much less significant.

B. The Rick Family

This conversation takes place round the table where Mr and Mrs Rick (René and Agnès), Marie, Agnès's mother, and Annie, their eight-year-old daughter, are having lunch. A schoolfriend of Annie's is briefly present at the beginning but she soon leaves and the conversation is held principally between the three adults, interrupted by some comments on Annie's behalf and exchanges with one or other of the adults.

Mr Rick is a company coach driver; Mrs Rick used to work as a secretary but since having Annie has instead minded a couple of children at home while their parents work. The parents are in their thirties.

Generally speaking, language choices in the family are as follows: Agnès speaks French almost exclusively with her daughter, but speaks both languages with her mother and her husband (mainly Alsatian with her mother, more French, and a lot of switching with her husband). René speaks mainly Alsatian and invariably does so with his mother-in-law, Marie. The couple's linguistic choices are not reciprocal when speaking to each other: he speaks mainly Alsatian and switches a lot, whereas she sticks to French in most cases. Unusually, René sometimes addresses his daughter Annie in Alsatian; as is the case with most children of her age in Strasbourg, she is basically a French speaker, although she shows that she understands Alsatian. Finally, Marie, the grandmother, speaks Alsatian in most cases to her daughter and son-in-law, though she occasionally uses French or switches. With her granddaughter she speaks French most of the time, which clearly involves some effort on her behalf.

Annie's friend Cathy leaves shortly after the recording starts and the family sits down to eat. The same kind of speaker and interlocutor-related switching as at the beginning of Conversation A is evident.

EXTRACT I

[1] RENÉ   Diss do will ich.
I want that there [*pointing at food*].

[2] AGNÈS   *Ouais.*
Yeah.

[3] ANNIE   *Hum, mama, brr, j'ai mouillé mon chemisier!*
Hey, Mum, brr, I've wet my blouse!

[4] AGNÈS   *Ça ne m'étonne pas!*
I'm not surprised!

[5] MARIE   Was het's?
What's the matter with her?

[6] AGNÈS   *Elle a mouillé son chemisier.*
She's wet her blouse.

[7] RENÉ   Oh je, oh je, gibsch mir e Wasserglas?
Oh dear, oh dear, can you give me a water glass?

As we have remarked before, it is the bilingual 'middle' generation's choices which are the most unpredictable and it is they who are most likely to switch in an apparently arbitrary fashion, as is the case here with Agnès:

EXTRACT 2

[1] AGNÈS   *Comment tu trouves la viande, René? Non, mais t'aimes pas? Écoute, c'est la première fois depuis qu'on est marié que j'en fais.*
How do you like the meat, René? You don't like it? Listen, this is the first time since we've been married that I've made it.

[2] RENÉ   *C'est bien ça!*
That's good!

[3] AGNÈS   *Alors tu peux pas râler,* fur emol wie ich mach!
So you can't complain, for once that I've made it!

At the same time many language choices are deliberate and very much part
of the message the speaker wishes to convey; thus René shows his impatience
with his daughter by addressing her in Alsatian: 'He, mach doch ken so
Spektakel!' '"Hey, stop making such a scene!"' By using a language in which
she theoretically cannot reply to him, he negates the possibility of dialogue and
reinforces the peremptoriness of his order. Annie, who has some passive
knowledge of Alsatian, puts that knowledge to active use when it suits her, as
below:

EXTRACT 3

[1] MARIE   Ich find jetz nitt dass es . . .
            I don't think that it . . .

[2] ANNIE   *Maman, j'en veux pas de la salade, parce que ça . . .*
            Mummy, I don't want any salad, because it . . .

[3] AGNÈS   *Oui, mais c'est bon, tu l'as au moins déjà dit deux fois!*
            Yes, OK, OK, you've said it at least twice already!

[4] MARIE   Was het's?
            What's the matter with her?

[5] ANNIE   *Parce que ça* griwelt!
            Because it prickles!

When she finds her use of the Alsatian griwelt 'prickles' amuses the adults, she
repeats the same comment: '*J'en avais déjà goûte la dernière fois, ça* griwelt *de trop!*'
'"*I tried it last time already, it* prickles *too much!*"'. On various occasions Annie
also shows her understanding of the dialect:

EXTRACT 4

[*Marie is describing a coach trip on which certain passengers felt sick.*]

[1] AGNÈS   Ah, 's isch ire so schlecht g'sinn?
            Oh, did they feel as sick as that?

[2] MARIE   Ah, joo, un wie!
            Oh, yes, and how!

[3] ANNIE   *Vous devez* [*sic*] *vous arrêter parfois?*
            Did you have to stop sometimes?

and then again, shortly after:

EXTRACT 5

[1] RENÉ   Ich hab e Stüeck im Hals stecke.
            I've got a piece stuck in my throat.

[2] ANNIE   *Ben, bois.*
            Well, drink.

It is in fact repeatedly obvious that father and daughter use language choice as a means of taunting one another: when she calls him a pig for taking too many chips, he uses Alsatian to tell her off (Halt's Mül, un ess! 'Hold your tongue and eat!') whereas Agnès always addresses her daughter in French, even if she is telling her off (*T'as failli attraper une claque maintenant, c'était pas loin* 'You almost got a slap there, it wasn't far off ').

A new topic is then introduced, that of a school skiing trip in which Annie is at first reluctant to take part.

EXTRACT 6

[1] MARIE   *Tu sais, c'est bien quand on peut faire ça.*
                You know, it's nice when you can do that.

[2] RENÉ   Ja, ja, dü, noh kriejsch e scheener anorak un noh kriejsch scheeni Hosse.
                Yes, yes, you, you'll get a smart anorak and you'll get smart trousers.

[3] AGNÈS   *Ouais, t'auras de belles choses.*
                Yes, you'll have some lovely things.

[4] RENÉ   Un noh kriejsch *chaussures.*
                And you'll get *shoes.*

[5] ANNIE   Un scheeni *skis.*
                And smart *skis.*

[6] AGNÈS   Naan, *skis* sinn dert.
                No, *skis* are there.

[7] RENÉ   Un e *passe-montagne?*
                And a *balaclava?*

[8] ANNIE   *Oh, qu'est ce que c'est que ça?*
                Oh, what's that?

[9] MARIE   Was isch diss, e *passe-montagne?*
                What's that, a *balaclava?*

[10] AGNÈS   *Une cagoule.*
                A hood.

[11] RENÉ   E Kopf schoner.
                A head protector.

[12] MARIE   *Ah oui.*
                Oh yes.

Although they speak some Alsatian to Annie, all the vocabulary is French and there is therefore no difficulty of comprehension; Annie herself joins in [5]. A moment later, when René tells a story of a little girl who, seeing bras displayed in a shop window, thinks they are huge driving goggles (e auto-brill)—a story which, if told in French, would no doubt have captured Annie's attention—he speaks rapidly and fluently and Annie does not follow. She talks of something else and then goes off to watch TV.

The adults continue to discuss Marie's excursion to Mulhouse and particularly her tour of a famous car museum. The conversation is entirely in Alsatian, with the exception of a few loans (*parrain* 'godfather', *auto* 'car', *monsieur* 'gentleman', *musée* 'museum') and/or switches (*excursion* 'excursion', *chance* 'luck') and other expressions (*disons, ben* 'let's say, well') or short exclamations by Agnès (*à tes souhaits* 'bless you', *ils sont marrants* 'it's all right for them').

Then Annie returns to eat her pudding and René goes off to carry out some household repair. The conversation therefore returns to French, since it is mainly between Agnès and Annie: with her mother, Agnès continues to speak Alsatian. Because of this split into two dyads and perhaps also because of slight deafness, as was the case with the Beck Grandfather, Marie finds it easier to ask Agnès what Annie is saying, rather than address her granddaughter directly. But when Annie throws a rotten nut on the floor, she tells her off in Alsatian: 'Jo, *écoute*, was machsch denn?' '"Yes, *listen*, what are you doing there?"' Annie then exploits the normal scheme of communication to avoid answering the question and instead turns round and explains to her mother: '*C'est caca, cette noix, mamman, regarde!*' '"*It's pooey, this nut, Mummy look!*"' When René returns for coffee, the balance is re-established as he and Marie speak to each other in the dialect; but gradually Agnès introduces more French, and it becomes apparent that this is because she wishes René, rather than her mother, to take particular note of her remarks. She wants to visit the museum which Marie has been describing, but knows that René is likely to be difficult.

EXTRACT 7

[1] AGNÈS   *Ça doit être beau.*
            It must be beautiful.

[2] RENÉ   Jo, *ben*, de Philippe saat, 's sinn, noch vil *autos* wo nitt . . .
            Yes, *well*, Philippe says there, there are still a lot of *cars* which aren't . . .

[3] AGNÈS   *Quoi?*
            What?

[4] RENÉ   *Qui ne sont pas restaurées*, weiss du . . .
            Which aren't restored, you know . . .

[5] AGNÈS   *Elles peuvent quand même être jolies*, jo . . .
            They may still be attractive, you know . . .

The conversation deviates for a moment on to the question of the Schlumpf brothers, whose collection of cars is housed by the museum; this section is marked more by legal and car-related terminological switching.

EXTRACT 8

[1] MARIE   Ja, existiere die noch, die Schlumpf?
                Yes, do they still exist, the Schlumpf brothers?

[2] AGNÈS   Ja, sie sinn awwer nimmi do, sie sinn ab in d'Schwiz, sie sinn
                condamnés worre, ich weiss jo nitt für was . . .
                Yes, but they're not here any more, they were *convicted*, I don't
                know what for . . .

[3] RENÉ   Ja, weil's Ding, weil's . . .
                Yes, because thing, because . . .

[4] AGNÈS   *Ils ont fait faillite, c'est ça?*
                They went bankrupt, didn't they?

[5] RENÉ   Nee, *on leur reproche d'avoir pris les, l'argent* vum Betrieb, *pour acheter
                ces trucs là*, wäje dem han se *faillite* gemacht . . .
                No, *they're criticized for having taken the money* from the Company *to
                buy those things*, that's why they went *bankrupt* . . .

[6] MARIE   Diss muess m'r g'sähn han, die *autos*, die *autos*, alles wunderbar,
                gel, glänzt, sie han sogar e Dings g'hett, e *carosserie*, uf'm Schlitte
                It's really a must to see the *cars*, all marvellous, you know,
                shining, they even had a what do you call it, a *car body* on a sledge

They then return to the possibility of going to the museum; René says he doesn't know where it is, but with Marie's help he works it out; Agnès keeps emphasizing that she wants to go, though she has some doubts about Annie being prepared to spend all day there. René mumbles eventually that they could go along with their friends, the Riebs, but at that point Agnès loses her temper—in Alsatian, perhaps in order to enlist her mother's support for her point of view.

EXTRACT 9

[1] AGNÈS.   Mit's Riebs, gell? Ja, ja, mit 's Riebs, du wursch wie de Charles,
                du kannsch nix meh mache ohne 's Riebs, un 's Riebs kenne nix
                meh mache ohne 's Ricks, 's Ricks un 's Riebs, diss isch so e
                Ding, so zwei Klette, so zwei *aimants*, noh sinn se als manchmol
                üssenander un noh, plaf, alle Sunndaa . . .

                With the Riebs, you say? Yes, yes, with the Riebs, you're
                becoming like Charles, you can no longer do anything without
                the Riebs, and the Riebs can no longer do anything without the
                Ricks, the Ricks and the Riebs, this really is something, like two
                magnets, like two *magnets*, they come apart sometimes and then,
                bang, every Sunday . . .

This tirade confirms yet again that there is more to language choice than the simple interplay of varying linguistic competences, although it is necessary to understand those competences in order to distinguish, in Scotton's terms, which of the choices are 'marked'.

C. The Schmitt Family

This recording was carried out in the Schmitt family, with Annie and Michel Schmitt (in their early thirties), their son Émile (aged 8), and their godson Claude, who is also a cousin (aged 10). Michel is an accountant and Annie works as a secretary. Unusually for young dialect-speakers, Annie and Michel speak Alsatian to their son; their cousin Claude also speaks the dialect, so although the average age is much lower here than in the other family recordings, the different generations are in this case equally bilingual.

In the first part of the recording, Claude and Émile are playing noisily together before lunch. Annie is cooking and she pops in from time to time to see what they are doing, as does Michel who is recording them secretly.

The general language of communication is Alsatian, mixed with a number of loans or lexical switches. Some of these are in fact words common to the two languages, such as *pull* 'jumper' or *orange*, the colour 'orange'; others are names: *parrain* 'godfather', *bateau-pirate* 'pirate boat'; others still may be the only form known and used by these speakers, although Alsatian equivalents do exist: *toupie* 'spinning top', *coffre à jouets* 'toy chest'. In any actual example of speech, theoretical distinctions such as that between switches and loans will be of doubtful validity: what may appear to be a plausible demarcation line when talking about a group phenomenon will always have to be reviewed with reference to individuals.

EXTRACT 1

[1] CLAUDE   *Parrain*, wenn asse mir dann? Ich hab Hunger
            Godfather, when are we going to eat? I'm hungry.

[2] MICHEL   Wenn 's gekocht isch.
             When it's cooked.

[3] ÉMILE   *On range*, noh mach ich grad zu. Was mache mir jetz?
             Let's put it away, I'm just closing up. What shall we do now?

[4] CLAUDE   Ich weiss nitt, mir spiele.
             I don't know, let's play.

[5] ÉMILE   Ja was, mit *parfum?* E schöens Hiisele!
             OK what, with *perfume?* A beautiful little house!

[6] CLAUDE   Mir mache's. Mir nemme de Radio, gell? Émile, uf's Bett!
             We'll make that. Let's take the radio, OK? Émile, on the bed!

[7]	ANNIE	Hesch jetz de *toupie jaune?*
		Do you have the *yellow top* now?
[8]	CLAUDE	Nein.
		No.
[9]	ANNIE	Wo han ihr se anne?
		Where've you put it?
[10]	CLAUDE	Weiss ich au nitt.
		I don't know.
[11]	ANNIE	Luej mol in de playmobil Lad, han ihr schunn geluejt?
		Have a look in the playmobil box, have you already looked?
[12]	CLAUDE	Villicht han mir se nitt g'funde.
		Perhaps we didn't find it.
[13]	ANNIE	'S isch grad numme so gäls *toupie*.
		There's a yellow *top*.
[14]	CLAUDE	Nitt gäl, *orange*.
		Not yellow, *orange*.

As usual, the use of such terms can have a triggering effect, either prospective or retrospective, as in the example below where Claude could clearly have used the Alsatian word for 'look':

EXTRACT 2
CLAUDE   *Parrain*, kumm, ich zaij dir ebbs! *Regarde parrain, parrain* kumm emol!
Godfather, come, I'll show you something! *Look godfather, godfather* have a look!

or in Extract 1 [7], de *toupie jaune* 'the *yellow top*'. It seems likely that *jaune* is here 'triggered' by *toupie*, since in [13] Annie repeats the expression with the adjective in Alsatian—gäls *toupie*; interestingly, the noun–adjective order follows the French rule when the adjective is in French and the Alsatian rule when the adjective is in Alsatian, which appears to suggest that a loan-type noun like *toupie* is felt to have an intermediate status between French and Alsatian and does not therefore dictate a particular word-order, whereas a truly one-off switch like *jaune* does.

Michel alternates between participating in the children's make-believe, which he does in French, and reassuming a controlling parental role, for which he switches to Alsatian, the language he normally speaks to Émile.

EXTRACT 3
[1] MICHEL   *Fais voir, ton trésor!*
Let's see your treasure!

[2] CLAUDE   *Il est super, ton trésor, mieux que le mien, eh!*
              It's super, your treasure, better than mine!

[3] MICHEL   *Oh! Qu'est-ce que vous vouliez en faire?*
              Oh! What did you want to do with it?

[4] CLAUDE   *Si t'as un trésor comme ça, qu'est-ce que tu dirais?*
              If you've got a treasure like this, what would you say?

[5] MICHEL   *Je le garderais bien . . .* [*Singing and playing in the background.*]
              I'd hang on to it . . .

[6] CLAUDE   *Émile, carton!*
              Émile, the box!

[7] MICHEL   Naan, denne machsch jetz nitt an, Émile, schunscht mach i 's üs!
              No, you're not to put that on, Émile, or I'll put it off again!

Annie switches frequently, within sentences or between two propositions:

EXAMPLE 1
Mir esse jetz sowieso! *Mais c'est dommage.*
We're eating now anyhow! *But it's a shame.*

EXAMPLE 2
Oui, oui, moi j'crois aussi, denn ihr han nix andersch hüsse g'het das . . .
Yes, yes, I think so too, because you haven't had anything else out that . . .

EXAMPLE 3
Noh koenne se jo s'Spiel nitt mache, wenn sie d'*toupie* nitt han. *Vous avez regardé sous le lit, au moins?* Luej noch emol.
You won't be able to play the game if you don't have the *top. Have you looked under the bed, at least?* Have another look.

The children—but not Michel—also switch between clauses, but less frequently.

CLAUDE   Ich weiss es joo, *alors tu ouvres* . . .
          I know that, *so you open* . . .

The tendency to switch within an utterance does not appear to be simply a function of the situation in which speakers find themselves, although a relaxed atmosphere, like here, seems to provide a fertile ground. As with Mr Eder in Conversation A, there appears to be a strong personal factor, which means that here Annie does this much more than, say, her husband.

As they all sit down to lunch, the two boys notice that Michel has installed the tape recorder near the table. They don't seem particularly bothered by it, although the explanation they receive is somewhat meagre:

EXTRACT 4

[1] CLAUDE   *Pourquoi est-ce que tu enregistres?*
               Why are you recording?

[2] MICHEL   *C'est pour le professeur d'anglais.*[6]
               It's for the English teacher.

[3] ÉMILE   *C'est Pénélope!*
               It's Penelope!

[4] CLAUDE   *C'est un anglais?*
               Is he English?

[5] MICHEL   *C'est une anglaise!*
               She's English!

[6] ÉMILE   *Elle s'appèle* Penelope *en anglais et Pénélope en français, voilà.*
               She's called Penelope *in English and Pénélope in French, you see.*

There seems no particular change in the language patterns described so far as a result of this 'exposure' of the recording. During the meal numerous culinary terms are in French, as is very usual in Strasbourg: (*potée de carottes* 'carrot purée', *porc roulé* 'rolled pork', *raisins* 'grapes', *oignons* 'onions', etc.) and when a conversation develops on how to prepare carrot purée, this is held in French, until Annie tires of the children's questions and various noises made by Émile and returns to Alsatian, or rather to her own mixed brand:

EXTRACT 5

[1] ANNIE   *Pourquoi? Ta maman met plus de pommes de terre et moins de carottes,*
               odder . . .
               Why? Does your Mummy put in more potato and less carrot, or . . .

[2] CLAUDE   *Et toi le contraire.*
               And you do the opposite.

[3] ANNIE   *Je fais pas le contraire, c'est exactement la même chose.*
               I don't do the opposite, it's exactly the same.

[4] CLAUDE   *Tu mets plus de* Grumbeere.
               You put in more potato.

[5] ANNIE   *Émile, non!* Sovil Grumbeere un sovil *carottes. C'est pas de la purée,*
               c'est de la purée de carottes. Dass es nooch *carottes* schmeckt, nooch
               Grumbeere, noh brüchsch ken *purée de carottes* mache. Émile,
               halt jetz 's Mül un ess! Witt noch e bissel *sauce* uf's Ding? Joo,
               Émile, *regarde moi ça!*
               Émile, no! This much potato and this much *carrot. It's not mashed
               potato, it's carrot purée.* So that it tastes of *carrots*, of potatoes, you
               don't need to make a *carrot purée.* Émile, shut up now and eat!

---

[6] At the time of this recording, Michel was in a class of English for adults which I was teaching.

Do you want a bit more *sauce* on the thing? Oh, Émile, *look at
that!*

In passages such as the last, one could justifiably ask whether there is a base
language with some admixture from the other language or whether it is
meaningless to think in such terms; for we must always remember that to speak
at all of switching is to emphasize the external relationship—this group versus
other language groups—rather than the inner structure of the discourse.
Arguably, the grammatical 'cement' here is still in Alsatian, and the whole
sentence in French, *C'est pas de la purée, c'est de la purée de carottes* [5], is due to
expressions *purée* and *purée de carottes*; by saying the whole sentence in French,
one avoids switching too often within the sentence. As for the interjection:
regarde moi ça! (final line), it may be in French so as to mark the change of
interlocutor and give added emphasis.

Certain very common words (potatoes, carrots) are used by Annie sometimes
in one language and sometimes in the other. Her choice does not seem to
depend on the language of the sentence, since she says: Dass es nooch *carottes*
schmeckt 'So that it tastes of *carrots*'. On the other hand, Annie does tend to
follow the language just used by the other speaker: when Claude first asks
Annie, in French, about the ingredients of her purée she replies, listing the
ingredients in French also. A bit lower down, Claude refers to potatoes in
Alsatian and she replies: 'Sovil Grumbeere un sovil *carottes*' [5]. Finally, a bit
later again, following Michel's example this time, she says carrots in Alsatian
too!

EXTRACT 6

[1] CLAUDE   Diss will i nitt!
             I don't want this!

[2] ÉMILE   Ich will einfach *purée*.
             I just want *purée*.

[3] MICHEL   Gälleruewegemues.
             Carrots.

[4] ANNIE   Gälleruewegemues, e bissele.
             A bit of carrot.

While the rather simplistic explanation sometimes given for code-switching
(even by speakers themselves), that it is due to 'laziness' is clearly inadequate,
one can perhaps identify an inertia factor in examples such as these where both
terms are equally accessible and the speaker just uses whichever has just been
offered to her.

Annie also uses switching in a more deliberate manner, to tell off Émile more
emphatically:

Émile, jetz haltsch 's Mül un esch schöen. *Coupe ta viande et tais-toi*.
Émile, now you shut up and eat. *Cut your meat and be quiet*.

She does not shy away from very dense switching, as in the following examples, where the main verb's infinitival complement is in French and the rest of the sentence in Alsatian:

EXAMPLE 1

Noh köenne ihr *choisir* ob ihr Spätzle woëlle, *potée de carottes ou porc roulé.*
Now you can *choose* whether you want Spätzle, *carrot purée or rolled pork.*

EXAMPLE 2
Witt du es *goûter* diss do, dezue?
Do you want to *taste* this here with it?

The phonology of the verb 'choisir' in Example 1 is particularly interesting (/ʃwɑˈzeːrə/) since it is at least partially integrated with Alsatian. Native speakers with whom I discussed the question said that (*a*) they had not come across this usage before and the term was therefore likely to be particular to Annie or members of her network, and (*b*) that it could well be filling a lexical gap since the nearest Alsatian equivalent, üswähle, has a slightly different shade of meaning.

Michel, Annie's husband, does not provide us with any such dense examples of switching, although one out of three of his utterances is in French. The children also switch within utterances and within sentences, both in talking to the parents and to each other, although their excited, playful interruptions and changes of direction make it somewhat difficult to decide what is a sentence and what is not:

EXAMPLE 1
ÉMILE   *Incroyable, mais vrai, ah, ça vient!* Villicht isch's . . .
         Unbelievable, but true, ah, it's coming! Perhaps it's . . .

EXAMPLE 2
CLAUDE   *Non, Émile, Émile, non, éteins ça! Parrain*, loss es an, de Émile macht nix
         meh, loss se!
         No, Émile, Émile, no, turn that off! Godfather, leave it on, Émile won't do
         that anymore, leave it!

EXAMPLE 3
ÉMILE   Babbe, kumm emol, do isch se nitt, *d'toupie.*
         Daddy, come here, it isn't there, the *top.*

EXAMPLE 4
CLAUDE   *Hé, parrain*, isch's wohr, dass mir aller Krach . . . De klein . . . Do
         hinte im *magnéto* . . . Wo muesch ne hewwe . . . Ich weiss es joo, *alors
         tu ouvres* . . .

Hey, godfather, is it true, that we'll all get . . . the small . . . behind
there in the *tape recorder*. . . Where must you . . . Oh, yes, I know, *so
you open up* . . .

Once again, this recording is notable for the considerable individual differences
in language use one can identify, on close inspection, within a single bilingual
family and a single interactive context. Such differences need to be borne in mind
when analysing the speech patterns of a large number of subjects in a quantitative
paradigm.

D. Administrative Office

Conversation D takes place in a local government office, the tape recorder
being placed on the desk of one of the employees, Mr Conrad, who was in
charge of the recording. He speaks to a total of seven men and five women in
various different configurations.

We cannot know to what extent Conrad's own frequent use of the dialect
influences his colleagues to speak Alsatian in his presence. He himself assured
me that he had not spoken Alsatian any more than usual during the recording.
Of the others, only one, Saleur, does not speak Alsatian, but even he
understands it. Conrad is in his early forties and speaks both languages
fluently, his French being marked by a light Alsatian accent. The predominant
use of Alsatian—and uninhibited switching—by all the speakers except Saleur
is related to the familiar register of the conversation, to the relaxed atmosphere
which prevails among this group of colleagues as they chat about their pets, the
restaurants where they have lunch, the purchase of crib figures for the
Christmas tree, and occasionally, of course, about their work.

At the beginning Conrad and Herr are wondering if someone should be sent
off to buy milk, as Nuss, who has been asked to, is thought likely to forget. Both
Conrad and Herr switch languages [4], [5] in opposite directions during this
short passage.

EXTRACT I

[1] CONRAD   Kann mir sich uf de Nuss verlonn? Dü weisch jo, 's letscht
Mol, wie der 's uns renne het lonn. Er het versproche, drej
Woche lang het er 's versproche, un jedes Mol het er nimm
dran gedenkt.
Can we really rely on Nuss? You know last time how he let us
down. He promised, he promised it for three weeks and each
time he forgot.

[2] HERR   . . . *Oui, mais il n'arrivera pas maintenant, il va arriver vers dix heures et
demie, hein* . . .
. . . *Yes, but he won't be coming now, he'll be coming around ten thirty,
you know* . . .

[3] CONRAD   Ja, wart! Ich geh zeerscht do nüs, ich hol e bissel, ich hol e
                  bissel Pulver.
                  Now wait! I'll just go out, I'll get some, I'll get some cash.

[4] HERR   Wo?
                  Where?

[5] CONRAD   Ah, am *distribanque*, do hüewwe. Mir muen e bissel Milich han,
                  ich will nitt warte, bis de Nuss kummt . . . *Attendez, je sors avec*
                  vous, hein, ich geh do nüewwer . . .
                  Oh, the *cash dispenser*, over there. We must have a bit of milk, I
                  don't want to wait until Nuss comes . . . *wait, I'll go out with you,*
                  eh, I'm going over there . . .

Rick then comes in to discuss a work-related matter with Conrad. Like Conrad, he is a fluent dialect speaker, but since they are discussing work and constantly come up against French vocabulary, he switches to French [1] in certain sentences in order to avoid constant intra-clause switching (here with the words *commis* 'employee' and *rédacteur* 'editor'). Moreover, Rick would appear to be an idiosyncratic switcher, since he switches to French for an expression like *jeune homme* 'young man'—for no very apparent reason.

EXTRACT 2

[1] RICK   . . . Sinn alli do . . .! Höere se . . . Guete morje, *monsieur Conrad*.
                 Euh . . . Wenn se im *jeune homme* wöelle saawe, er soll mir zwei
                 photocopies . . . S'Catherine müess sich widder frisch inschriwe
                 lonn, *et elle a intérêt de le faire pour le commis parce que pour le rédacteur,*
                 même si elle réussit, elle risque d'attendre deux ou trois ans . . .
                 . . . They're all here . . .! Listen . . . Good morning, *Mr Conrad*. Er
                 . . . If you could kindly tell the *young man* to do me two *photocopies*
                 . . . Catherine must register again, *and it's in her interest to do it for the*
                 employee because with the editor, even if she succeeds, she may wait two or
                 three years . . .

[2] CONRAD   Ja.
                 Yes.

[3] RICK   Natirli, es will hit un morje, noch nitt schaffe . . .
                 Of course, she won't be working today and tomorrow . . .

Further 'grammatical' switching (preposition and article) is triggered by his use of French figures:

EXTRACT 3

[1] RICK   Höere se, *dans les trois cent, trois cent vingt-sept*, un noh sinn noch
                 emol fufzehn dezüg 'kumme, *trois cent quarante deux francs* . . .
                 Listen, *about three hundred, three hundred and twenty-seven*, and then

another fifteen were added to that, *three hundred and forty-two
francs . . .*

Conrad's next interlocutor is Madame Klein, who like him speaks mainly
Alsatian, but uses a large number of French words and expressions, from the
professional domain as such: *bulletin de commande 'order form'; accompte 'deposit';
contrôle financier pour mandatement 'financial control for the payment order'*. From a
broader field which one could term the world of French: *volets roulants 'roller
shutters'; courrier 'mail'; exemplaires 'copies'; gymnastique 'gymnastic';* and also for
phatic expressions: *voilà, merci! 'there we are, thanks!'; d'accord 'OK'; entendu
'OK'.*

There appears to be a constant 'balancing of the books' between the two
languages; as soon as French has been used for a while, Alsatian rears its head,
however bizarre the resulting sentence, as in the last part of the example below.
In such a passage one can argue that there is a base language, Alsatian, and that
the surprising switch 'bezahle' is in fact a switch back to the base language
which happens to coincide with the end of that utterance.

EXTRACT 4

[1] CONRAD　*Au fond*, ihr köennte aans mache hinte nooch, was ich als mach
im so ne Fall. Ich mach ne e klaani *note*, e ganz klanni *note* im
*contrôle financier . . . Euh . . . Engagement soldé par mégarde sur fac-
ture antérieure, prière bien vouloir* bezahle!
In fact, you could do one thing afterwards, what I always do in
such a case. I write a little *note*, just a very little *note* to *Financial
Control . . . er . . . Order issued in error on previous invoice, kindly* pay .

Alsatian continues to be the cement language in Conrad's subsequent
conversation with Madame Durst, an ex-colleague who arrives to pay a social
call. They are discussing the health of their respective dogs; medical terms are
in French.

EXTRACT 5

[1] DURST　Un . . . Ding . . . mir han awwer Ding . . . eu . . . *homéopathique*,
mit'm *traitement homéopathique*. Noh het er noch *levure* wie d'r
nemme muess.
And . . . thing . . . we have a whatsit . . . er . . . *homeopathic*, with
a *homeopathic treatment*. And he has *yeast* to take.

[2] CONRAD　*Ultra-levure.*
Dietary yeast.

[3] DURST　Ja, awwer in . . . 's isch Ding . . . *diététique*, wissen'r . . . *ultra-
levure* . . . d'glaane Ladele.
Yes, but in . . . the thing . . . *health food*, you know, *dietary yeast*
. . . the little shop.

So are quotations:

EXTRACT 6

DURST   Un . . . ich find, er isch radikaler ass de Meyer, denn er het schunn
g'saat g'hett, 'Joo *on le pique!*'
And . . . I think he's more radical than Meyer, because he's already
said, 'OK *we'll give him a jab!*'

and certain short expressions:

EXTRACT 7

[1] CONRAD   Was macht de Hund?
How's the dog?

[2] DURST   *On a des emmerdes!*
Have we got problems!

We also encounter the usual conversational expressions which ensure that
French is symbolically present in an Alsatian conversation (*non* 'no'; *ah bon* '*I
see*'; *à propos* '*by the way*'; *au fond* '*really*'; etc.) but also sentences where the
switching is grammatically more intricate, for example:

DURST   *Bon, on a un tas de problèmes* wiriklisch demit, ne!
All in all, we have a heap of problems really with him, you know!

where the switch occurs between the direct object and the adverb. Sometimes
it occurs between the auxiliary and the verb:

DURST   De Larouge het ne aa schunn *soigné*
Larouge has already *looked after* him

When the conversation moves on to another topic, that of common acquaintances and the firm where Conrad and Madame Durst used to work, the same
basic scheme continues and the same basic categories of switching are to be
found:

(i) specific terminology, be it in the form of loans or lexical switches:

résidence secondaire	'*holiday home*'
chauffeur	'*chauffeur*'
informatique	'*word processing*'
portes ouvertes	'*open day*'
gouverneur militaire	'*military governor*'
cabinet	'*lavatory*'
guide	'*guide*'
visites guidées	'*guided tours*'
groupement alsatique	'*Alsatian co-operative*'
secrétaire	'*secretary*'

(ii) expressions which do not affect the grammar of the sentence but which symbolically introduce French into the conversation:

paraît-il	'*it seems*'
d'ailleurs	'*anyhow*'
ah bon	'*I see*'
Sacré Matt	'*good old Matt*'

(iii) short idiomatic sentences:

ça c'est intéressant	'*that's interesting*'
celui-là mettait les	'*that one dotted all*
points sur les i	*the i's*'

Throughout the discussion, the base language remains Alsatian and all the examples therefore concern the importation of French elements.

The conversation between Conrad and Madam Durst is interrupted by various colleagues of Conrad. Mr Rick comes up to tell Mr Saleur, the only monolingual French speaker in the office, that salaries are going up and that he will get a rise. Although they all address Saleur in French, Conrad and Durst continue to make odd remarks in Alsatian as Saleur does understand the dialect.

Conrad and Durst continue their chat, touching on topics ranging from the economic situation to the sky, which promises snow and reminds them of an exceptionally hard winter they had when they worked in their old firm; such relaxed exchanges provide a fertile ground for switching, as in the following anecdote, accompanied by much hilarity:

EXTRACT 8

[1] CONRAD   Schaffe han mir gelehrt, dunderwetter!
              We learnt what work is, my goodness!

[2] DURST   Nundebuckel noch emol!
              You can say that again!

[3] CONRAD   Die hans uns dressiert!
              They really had us trained!

[4] DURST   Ja, ja.
              Yes, yes.

[5] CONRAD   Von d's—morjes vom achte bis am zwei, un von zwei bis
              sechs . . .
              From—in the morning from eight to two, and from two to
              six . . .

[6] DURST   Ja, ja . . . Jo, Jo . . .
              Yes, yes . . . Yeah, yeah . . .

[7] CONRAD   Mir han emol e *période* g'hett, wie de Kleinmann g'fröjt het,
                 wenn aaner uf d'*toilette* gemüent het, ob's notwendig isch!
                 We once had a *period*, when Kleinmann would ask, if someone
                 needed to go to the *toilet*, whether it was necessary!

[8] DURST   ... Ja.
                 ... Yes.

[9] CONRAD   ... Noh het ... Mich het er emol g'fröjt ... Noh het ... Noh
                 het'm de Mey ... De Kleinmann het mi g'fröjt, schon widder?
                 ... Ich bin zwei Mol drüsse g'sinn, ob's ... '*Vous pensez que c'est
                 nécessaire?*' ... Noh het de Mey g'saat, '*Écoutez, Monsieur
                 Kleinmann*, wenn er doch de Durichfall het, muess er doch
                 nüss uf's *cabinet!*'
                 ... Then ... he asked me once ... then ... then Mey ...
                 Kleinmann asked me again? ... I'd been out twice, whether ...
                 '*Do you think it's necessary?*' ... Then Mey said, '*Listen, Mr
                 Kleinmann*, if he has diarrhoea then he surely has to go to the
                 lavatory!'

[10] DURST   *Celui-là mettait les points sur les i!*
                 That one dotted all the i's!

[11] CONRAD   Ha, ha, der isch ningetappt! Ha, ha!
                 Ha, ha, he fell right into it! Ha, ha!

The same apparently arbitrary switching pattern continues as they talk of
borrowing and being in debt, or indeed of the weather:

EXTRACT 9

[1] DURST   Die han so nix, denne krieje se sowieso! *Mais c'est vrai!*
                 They have nothing, so that's what they get! *But it's true!*

[2] CONRAD   Stimmt!
                 That's right!

[3] DURST   Un wer het ken Schulde hitzedaas, in denne *sociétés*, un diss
                 ganze Gedings?
                 And who does not have debts these days, in those *companies* and
                 all that sort of thing?

[4] CONRAD   Jeses Naa! Ja, wer het ken Schulde?
                 Jesus no! Yes, who has no debts?

[5] DURST   *Moi, je vois, là où travaille mon mari, hein, les petites sociétés hein!*
                 I see it where my husband works, eh, small companies, eh!

[6] CONRAD   Ja.
                 Yes.

[7] DURST   Nunde Buckel noch emol! Denne duen se d'Kravatt züdräje, so
             guet as se 's kenne!
             Lordy me, I say! They're tightening up the noose around their
             necks for all they're worth!

The only 'reason' one can find for many of these switches—and it must remain
an extremely hypothetical one—is that, possibly, one word in the utterance or
sentence comes to mind in French (*sociétés* [5]) and triggers a little bout of
French surrounding the word; but there are flagrant inconsistencies: why does
the same not occur with *sociétés* [3]?

The relative, though not total arbitrariness of switch points in skilled
bilingual discourse is again illustrated. Madame Meyer, a secretary, then
comes to chat with Conrad and almost immediately remarks on the tape
recorder. Conrad says he is recording for an English lady who is learning
Alsatian and wants to adapt to the Alsatian environment. Reassured by
Conrad's tactful version of the truth, Madame Meyer continues, as she has
started, in Alsatian, using only some French lexical elements (e.g. *générateur*
'generator', *gonarthrose* 'gonarthrosis') and some idiomatic expressions, though
even those can have internal switching (e.g. nix *spécial* 'nothing *special*').

A tripartite conversation then starts with Saleur, Conrad, and Madame
Durst trying to persuade him to join them for lunch, Saleur protesting that he is
too broke, but not wishing to be paid for once again (*Vous m'avez déjà invité pour
la pizza* 'You already paid for the pizza'). Conrad and Meyer insist, saying that if
he eats shepherd's pie (*hachis parmentier*) two or three times like a good old
Alsatian, he too will speak the dialect!

On the whole, Saleur and Meyer manage to continue speaking Alsatian in
spite of speaking to Saleur who understands but does not speak the dialect, by
ostensibly addressing to each other remarks which are in fact directed at him—
the converse of interlocutor-related switching. His replies show that he
understands the tactics:

EXTRACT 10

[1] CONRAD   Ja, er het's awwer . . . Er het's awwer villicht nitt gern!
             Yes, he may not . . . He may not like it!

[2] MEYER   Was het er nitt gern?
             What doesn't he like?

[3] CONRAD   *Hachis parmentier!*
             Hachis parmentier!

[4] SALEUR   *Non, moi je mange n'importe quoi.*
             No, I'll eat anything.

However, Saleur's presence does lead Conrad and Meyer to exchange a few
words in French:

[5] CONRAD *Il* koch guet, do hüewwe!
           He cooks well, over there!

[6] MEYER *Au oui, il* koch guet!
           Oh yes, he cooks well!

[7] CONRAD *Si, si . . . Ah si, si . . .*
           Yes, yes . . . Ah yes, yes . . .

[8] MEYER *Si, ah, c'est un bon cuistot!*
           Yes, ah, he's a good cook!

[9] CONRAD Ah doch!
           Oh yes!

It is noteworthy that Meyer has no hestitation in repeating the somewhat unusual switch provided by Conrad in [5], between pronoun subject and verb.

In the last part of the recording, Conrad is again talking with Rick about a variety of points of common interest: about a colleague and how old he is compared with Rick; Rick's new garden fence; the dishonest builder who installed it; their wish to hear a reading of a text in good clear Alsatian; and finally the Christmas garland in their office and how to maintain it. The dominant language continues to be Alsatian, with unremarkable terminological and idiomatic expression exceptions. Rick occasionally starts sentences in French, then interrupts himself or allows Conrad to interrupt him and continue in Alsatian:

EXAMPLE 1
CONRAD   *Enfin*, ich müess zügenn, in de leschte Zit han sich mini
           Beziehungen mit ihm vil gebessert.
           Well, I must admit my relations with him have improved a lot lately.

RICK   *Ah, il est . . .*
           Oh, he's . . .

CONRAD   Er isch nämlich stüür . . .
           He's very obstinate . . .

EXAMPLE 2
RICK   *Voilà, Monsieur Conrad*, jetz . . . Heu . . . Wenn mir morje owe . . .
           Wenn nitt am Mondaa . . . Sie kenne awwer au bi mir . . . *Je veux bien*
           . . . Selbscht e ganzi Stund, *Monsieur Conrad* . . .
           There we are, Mr Conrad, now . . . er . . . if tomorrow evening we . . . If
           not on Monday . . . But you can also come over to me . . . *I'd be very*
           happy . . . Even a whole hour, *Mr Conrad* . . .

EXAMPLE 3
RICK   Awwer wenn sie's do . . . Also ich . . . *Moi je* . . . Ich hab am Oweds
           . . . Bin ich rüejisch . . .

But if you . . . Well I . . . *I myself* . . . In the evening I have . . . I keep quiet . . .

His disjointed manner of speech appears to facilitate code-switching (see 'disjointed switching' in the next chapter) as it avoids the whole problem of intra-clause switching. Finally, we hear Conrad talking to Madame Miller and Monsieur Hemm about Madame Miller's plans to buy a Christmas tree and crib figures (*santons*). Conrad and Hemm use mainly Alsatian, but Madame Miller, like Madame Durst earlier, seems to use either language more or less indifferently and to switch with equal nonchalance:

EXTRACT 11

[1] HEMM　Ja, was machsch denn? Du machsch jo alles verrecke . . . wenn de . . .
　　　　　What do you get up to? You make everything break . . . If the

[2] MILLER　Ja, ich hab se hien gemacht.
　　　　　Yes, I smashed them up.

[3] HEMM　Machsch alles verecke!
　　　　　You make everything break!

[4] MILLER　*Non, non, je les ai cassés quand j'étais petite fille . . .*
　　　　　No, no, I broke them when I was a little girl . . .

[5] CONRAD　Ja.
　　　　　Yes.

[6] HEMM　*Ah bon!*
　　　　　Oh I see!

[7] MILLER　*Je les ai sortis, j'ai joué avec . . .*
　　　　　I got them out and played with them . . .

[8] CONRAD　Ja, ja, natirli, noh sinn see fütti![7]
　　　　　Yes, yes, of course, so they're all spoiled!

[9] MILLER　Nur sinn se zamme gebäppt . . . sie sinn noch Ding . . . Sie sinn awwer gebäppt . . . Awwer . . . *j'ai joué avec quand j'étais gosse, alors maintenant ils sont . . .*
　　　　　They've collapsed . . . they're still what do you call it . . . but they've collapsed . . . But . . . *I played with them when I was a kid, so now they're . . .*

Once the topic of crib-figures, which are a French tradition, is introduced into the conversation, attendant French terms creep even into the speech of Hemm who does not do much switching:

---

[7] Fütti is from French *foutu* (in this sense: wrecked).

EXTRACT 13

[1] MILLER   *D'vierge*, un de Joseph, un de *petit Jésus* sinn ganz, un de *âne* un
de *bœuf* sinn aa noch ganz, numme was hüsse g'stande isch, isch
alles e bissel . . .
The *virgin*, the Joseph, and the *baby Jesus* are whole, and the
donkey and the *ox* are also OK, but everything that stood outside
is all a bit . . .

[2] HEMM   Wenn de *âne* odder de *bœuf* nimm ganz wärt g'sinn, wärt i
kumme wärt drunter gelaje, an de Wihnachte!
If the *donkey* or the *ox* hadn't been whole, I would have come
and lain under there at Christmastime!

To conclude, Conrad's fairly consistent use of Alsatian with speakers of
varying competence configurations does not preclude the most varied of
switching and selection patterns among his interlocutors. Although we cannot
guess in what ways their performance here would have been different if Conrad
had made a heavier use of French, it is at least clear that he was being his
normal self and that his use of the dialect is what everyone expects. Since the
recording took place in a local government office, it is interesting to note the
contrast between the language choices 'behind the counter' and those
presented to the public, since the administration is normally considered in
Alsace to be a bastion of French.

E. Hospital Accounts Office

This recording took place in the accounts office of a large Strasbourg hospital
where eight employees work, four men and four women, all aged between
twenty-five and thirty-five. Their main language of communication is
Alsatian—in spite of their age, the fact that they work in an office in town, and,
indeed, in an institution where French medical and administrative language is
present at every corner.

To begin with, Martin (who is in charge of the recording), Cédric, Denise,
and Chantal are observing with interest the Sony Walkman tape recorder,
thanks to which they are being recorded, comparing the microphone to an
electric razor, then to an ice-cream cone. Their remarks about the recording
alternate with brief exchanges concerning work questions and remarks about a
colleague who had an accident. Whichever the topic, the Alsatian base is
punctuated with French.

EXTRACT 1

[1] MARTIN   'S isch Ding do, luej doch, Sony.
It's what do you call it, have a look, Sony.

[2] DENISE   Mmh, Sony.
             Mmh, Sony.

[3] CÉDRIC   Prima!
             Great!

[4] MARTIN   G'fällt er dir? Wottsch au so aaner? Kaufsch de aaner?
             Do you like it? Would you like one too? Will you be buying
             one?

[5] DENISE   *Eh, il cause là.*
             Hey, it's talking.

[6] MARTIN   Ah, jo!
             Oh yes!

[7] DENISE   Gar nitt gewisst!
             I didn't know!

[8] CÉDRIC   Ich hab 's g'sähn!
             I saw it!

[9] DENISE   Er isch an, *tiens*, 's geht e Licht an.
             It's on, *look*, the light's going on.

[10] MARTIN Ja, 's derf nitt do drüewwer, *enfin*, 's isch wie an alle *magnétos*
             nitt.
             Yes, it shouldn't go over there, *well*, it's like on all *tape-
             recorders*.

There is a good mixture of 'symbolic' switches (French expressions such as
enfin, *bon*, *tiens* 'well, OK, hey'), loan-words (*accidents, mandat* 'accidents, postal
order'), lexical switches (*débiles, temps morts* 'mentally retarded, (cassette) blanks'),
but also whole clause switches without any obvious motivation.

EXAMPLE 1
CÉDRIC   *Mais il s'est cassé la gueule.* Isch er nitt mi'm Motorrad kejt?
         But he's had an accident. Didn't he fall off his motorbike?

EXAMPLE 2
CEDRIC   *Regarde, c'est simple!* Abalo,[8] wart emol, diss machsch eso, e *trombone*
         machsch dran.
         Look, it's simple! Abalo, just a minute, you do it like this, you put a
         paper-clip on.

DENISE   Hoppla, *voilà, c'est tout ce que je voulais savoir*, Bosser,[9] hoer, ich
         mach's. Hoppla, *merci* Cédric.

---

[8] Abalo is the name of a file on which they are working.
[9] Bosser is the name of a file on which they are working.

Good, *there we are, that's all I wanted to know*, Bosser, listen, I'll do it.
OK, *thanks* Cédric.

There are also several examples of switching at the junction of appositional
structures which appear to be particularly frequently used in bilingual
discourse in order to avoid intra-clause switching:

EXAMPLE 1
DENISE   *La cassette*, wie lang ass se geht?
          The cassette, how long does it run for?

EXAMPLE 2
CHANTAL   *Hé, t'as vu*, der aant, *il marche mal*, der wie 's *accident* het g'hett.
          Hey, did you see, that chap, *he can't walk properly*, the one who had the
          accident.

EXAMPLE 3
MARTIN   Ah ja, 's geht als an, *la lumière*.
          Oh yes, it always comes on, *the light*.

The next part of the recording is repeatedly interrupted by the tape recorder
being turned on and off so as not to record long silences while everyone
worked. The resulting conversational fragments which are recorded are nevertheless probably reasonably representative of the situation in question:

EXTRACT 2
[1] DENISE   Isch Zit schunn?
              Is it time yet (to eat)?

[2] MARTIN   Zehn bis . . . So bis . . . Jo, Cédric . . .
              Ten to . . . So until . . . Yes, Cédric . . .

[3] CÉDRIC   Hesch de *CCP*[10] odder hesch ne schunn fertig?
              Have you got the *CCP* or have you already got it ready?

[4] MARTIN.   Do haw i ne grad annegeläjt, bis dü kummsch . . . [*picking up the
              microphone*] Sottsch 's so in d'Höh köenne hänge, *ce serait plus
              pratique*.
              I just put it on there until you come . . . You ought to be able to
              hang it up high like this, *that would be more practical*.

[5] DENISE   Walkman.
              Walkman.

[6] MARTIN   Jetz dräjt's.
              Now it's on.

---

[10] *Compte Crédit Postal* (Post Office Account).

This extract does not so much illustrate an aspect of linguistic choice, which is unremarkable (the one switch into French probably being ascribable to emphasis); it illustrates the way in which speakers rapidly jump from one subject to another—lunch, a bill to pay, the placing of the tape recorder—with many interruptions and self-interruptions. Such a format, which is, of course, very common, facilitates switching since there is no reason why some of these segments should not be in the other language. Commas and other punctuation marks in the transcription are no more than a conventionalized representation of pauses and interruptions which in fact have a range of possible reasons.

One of these reasons is quite simply that, owing to the inherent redundancy of the language, it is perfectly possible to stop an utterance after a few words and without completing a single clause, and still be understood. The better speakers know each other the easier this is, and the easier it is also to switch repeatedly between segments.

Amongst the switches recorded at this stage in the conversation, there are also numerous examples of the frequently found repetitive switching, that is a change of language which coincides with a repetition or near-repetition of what immediately precedes so as to reinforce the message:

EXAMPLE 1
MARTIN   *Maintenant, ça tourne, mais avant ça ne tournait pas*, jetz dräjts awwer.
          Now it's turning, but before it wasn't turning, but now it's turning.

EXAMPLE 2
DENISE   Machsch's üs jetz, *maintenant on arrête! La suite au prochain numéro*.
          Turn it off now, *we're stopping now! Watch out for the next episode*.

EXAMPLE 3
DENISE   Jo, ich find . . . *ça allait. Le raisin n'était pas bon. Moi, j'ai trouvé qu'il
          n'était pas bon du tout*. Mir het er gar nitt g'schmeckt.
          Yes, I think . . . *it was OK. The grapes weren't any good. I found they
          weren't any good at all*. I didn't like them at all.

A little later, Cédric, Martin, Georges, and Gérard are discussing the behaviour of a driving instructor whom they know. This section provides examples of intensive switching; this can to some extent be traced to triggering attendant on the use of car terms (*auto-école* 'driving school', *panne d'essence* 'empty tank', *faire le plein* 'to fill up with petrol', *avoir le permis* 'to have your licence') but the speed and fluency with which the two languages are manipulated suggest that the speakers have fallen into a form of mixed discourse where the reasons for each switch are secondary to the choice of this mode; transcription was difficult due to the amount of overlapping speech and the number of interruptions.

EXTRACT 3

[1] GEORGES   Ja, mir han dreimol in de selb Stund Zigarettle muen hole, mol holt er Wecke, mol holt er diss, mol holt er zäll, *moi je ne trouve pas ça normal*, dass es emol passiert alles bezitte. *Tu sais la meilleure, il est tombé en panne d'essence* mit'm Waawe *auto-école!*
Yes, we had to stop for cigarettes three times in the same hour, once he fetched bread rolls, once he fetched this, once he fetched that, *I don't think* its *right* to do all this at the same time. *You know the best story, he ran out of petrol* with the *driving-school* car!

[2] MARTIN   Wenn isch's denn . . .
Who is it then . . .

[3] GEORGES   Aaner bi uns, ich weiss nitt wie der heisst, het e Ding gemacht, isch er g'fahre, üewwer aanmol, paf, *panne d'essence. Tu te rends compte pour une auto-école* . . . Het e *bidon* hinte drinne, noh derfsch widder nin . . . *Mais c'est quand même pas normal!*
One we had, I don't know his name, did it, he was driving and suddenly, bang, *no more petrol. Just think of it for a driving-school* . . . He had a *tank* behind in the boot, so he could . . . *But it really shouldn't happen!*

[4] MARTIN   Diss hätt nitt solle passiere!
That shouldn't have happened!

[5] GEORGES   Ah ja, noh het er getankt, *mais il devrait donc faire son plein le soir* . . . Es tät doch lange e *plein* im Daa.
Oh yes, so he filled up, *but he should really fill up in the evening* . . . One *full tank* should be enough for the day.

[6] MARTIN   Ja, diss wurd nitt druf gehn, nemm i an.
Yes, I don't suppose any more would go in.

[7] GEORGES   Sogar wenn er üewwer Middaa noch emol hole muess, awwer diss soll . . . *Ça c'est une faute grave*, wenn dir diss passiert *au moment de faire le permis*, zuem Beispil . . .
Even if he needs to get some more over lunchtime, but this should . . . *That's a serious fault*, if it happens to you *when you're taking the test*, for instance . . .

[8] MARTIN   Doh kannsch dü awwer nix defur, nitt . . .
But there's nothing you can do about it, you know . . .

[9] GEORGES   Awwer *disons*, ja, wenn 's dir awwer doch passiert, *si ça t'arrive* wenn d'grad, *que tu as le permis, c'est une faute grave, je trouve.*

Théoriquement, soll's nitt passiere.
But *let's say*, yes, if it happens to you, *if it happens to you* just when you, *when you have your test, it's a serious fault, I think. In theory*, it shouldn't happen.

[10] MARTIN   Normal soll's nitt passiere.
Normally it shouldn't happen.

[11] GEORGES   *Raison de plus* . . .
All the more reason . . .

[12] MARTIN   Mir isch's au schunn passiert, emol oder zwei.
It's happened to me, too, once or twice.

[13] GEORGES   Awwer dass es in de *auto-école* passiert . . .
But for it to happen in the *driving-school* . . .

[14] CÉDRIC   Noch schlimmer, wenn de *client recalé* wurd am *permis* weje de *panne d'essence*.
Even worse, if the *client* is *failed* on the *test* because of the *empty tank*.

[15] GEORGES   Ja na, *je pense, c'est pas le client qui est fautif*.
No, no, *I don't think it's the client who is at fault*.

[16] MARTIN   Do kann der nix defur, diss kann er nitt mache.
He can't help it, he can't do that.

[17] GEORGES   *Non, si, éventuellement* de *inspecteur* koennt ihm saawe . . .
No, yes, conceivably the *examiner* could say to him . . .

Even in such dense switching as this, intra-clause switches are relatively rare. Cases where this does unambiguously occur are to be found in [1], [7], [9], [14], and [17] (see the next chapter for a discussion as to how to distinguish the different categories).

Let us look briefly at one of these examples in 'slow motion' in [9]:

Awwer *disons*, ja, wenn 's dir awwer doch passiert, *si ça t'arrive* wenn d'grad, *que tu as le permis, c'est une faute grave, je trouve*.
But *let's say*, yes, if it happens to you, *if it happens to you* just when you, *when you have your test, it's a serious fault, I think*.

We begin with an example of repetitive switching (wenn 's dir awwer doch passiert, *si ça t'arrive* . . .) which appears to have no deeper significance than being an oratorical device to 'fill out' what he has to say. Hardly has he gone back to Alsatian (wenn d'grad) than he must anticipatorily realize that he is going to have to use a French word, *permis*; even though it is a loan, it clearly retains enough Frenchness about it to trigger a surrounding expression in French (*que tu as le permis* . . .). But rather like a motorist who hits a mile-post on the side of the road because he is concentrating on avoiding a pedestrian, Georges has decided to switch to French too hastily to avoid all damage. The last part of his sentence is clumsy, the Alsatian wenn 'when' and the French *que* '*that*' do not tally. To avoid the problem, he could have said: Wenn d'grad de *permis* hesch, or else: *lorsque tu es juste en train de prendre le permis*. The unusualness of examples such as this underline the skill with which bilinguals generally manage to avoid such conflict, while switching abundantly.

After this, Martin and Cédric discuss health shops and herbalism. The switching continues but is less intense: the Alsatian is peppered with a large number of French terms (*céréales* 'cereals', *raisins* 'raisins', *articles de bureau* '*office articles*', *quartier* '*part of town*', *chemise* '*shirt*', etc.) but mixed clauses are rarer, though we have one example of a relatively unusual switch, between main verb and auxiliary: Tee hett er als zamme *mélangé* 'He's always *mixed* teas together'. This may in fact be an even more unusual intra-word switch, since Alsatian has a word, zammemische 'to mix together'.

In the last part of the recording, Martin, Gérard, and Cédric discuss video clubs and electronic games. The switching, which is again denser, seems linked to the greater degree of excitement they feel towards this subject than towards health food. One can sense the connection between the excitement of the speaker and the lack of regard for linguistic homogeneity in the following description.

EXTRACT 4

GÉRARD Wenn d'mit drüewwer witt, *alors il cogne, alors la moto se renverse, puis il faut la remettre sur pied. Moi, je suis arrivé à 80.* 'S isch e *truc*, wenn 's e paarmol gemacht hesch, hesch's hüsse, *après il y a des difficultés*, kannsch e *programme deux* mache, noh muesch, *pour pouvoir traverser*, isch dann d'*distance entre le début et la fin de l'obstacle*, un vorhär hesch e so grosser Platz g'hett, *disons*. Noh geht's allaan enab, *quand la machine est en haut* un geht widder erab, *distance* wie sovil hesch, Platz fur drüewwer hüpse, noh muesch do erabgehn, dass drüewwer kummsch.

If you want to get across with it, *then he knocks, and then the motorbike turns over and you have to right it again. I got up to 80.* 'thing is, when you've done it a couple of times, *then there are difficulties*, then you can put on *programme two*, then you must, *in order to cross*, there's the *distance between the beginning and the end of the obstacle*, and before that you've had, say, this much space, *let's say*. Then it goes down on its own, *when the machine is at the top* and goes down again, you have so much distance, room to jump over, then you must go down in order to get over it.

In spite of the frequency of switches in this passage, most of them are single words or expressions or else whole clauses. Yet the overall impression one gains is that this is mixed discourse, the latter being defined not so much by the grammatical density of the switching as by its frequency and apparent arbitrariness.

Overall, this recording is somewhat bitty as there are several short exchanges, often with comments about the tape recorder itself, which no doubt betray some inhibitions about it; however, it also contains some very interesting passages of mixed discourse. In spite of the frequency of switches in these passages, intra-clause switching remains relatively rare and cases where switching leads to syntactic infelicities even more so.

F. Car Park Attendants

The conversation recorded here is between three young men, René, Paul, and Denis, aged between twenty and twenty-five, who work as car park attendants or doormen for a large Strasbourg company. The recording was carried out in their cubicle at the car park entrance and their conversation is repeatedly interrupted to greet people going in and out of the building.

A fourth employee, Frank, joins them towards the end of the recording but rapidly disappears on noticing the tape recorder: Uf einmol saat er nix meh, weil er diss g'sähn het 'All of a sudden he won't say a word because he's seen this', remarks Paul. The other three are probably all aware of the tape recorder even before Frank arrives (Paul is actually in charge of the recording), but uninhibitedly discuss cars, football, girls, and colleagues. As with the other work place conversations, work does not figure very much as a topic of conversation; in this case, the only strictly work-related speech are the greetings mentioned above.

A female employee, Annie, also comes to speak to them for a few minutes, during which time they converse entirely in French. When questioned, Paul said he did not know whether or not Annie spoke Alsatian, although she is Alsatian, her husband speaks Alsatian, and she herself lets out a 'ja, ja' during the conversation. Confirming one of the commonly found differences between the sexes in linguistic matters, Paul remarked to me later that girls he knew generally did not use the dialect, even if they were capable of it.

At the beginning of the recording, Paul, Denis, and René are all discussing René's new car, a Renault 18. The principal language used is Alsatian, but there is much terminological switching which adds itself to various car-related loans: *R 18* (said in French), *turbo*, *vitesse de pointe* 'top speed', *autoroute* 'motorway', *pneus* 'tyres', *taille basse* 'low-profile tyres', etc. to which one must also add various figures, all said in French (*dix mille quatre cents, cent quatre vingt-cinq*). Figures would tend to be in French for speakers of this generation since they all had their schooling in French. As usual, the use of such terms can lead to further triggered switching (e.g. [11] below).

EXTRACT 1

[1] DENIS   Er isch zufridde mit sin *R 18*, de René?
              Is he satisfied with his *R 18*, René?

[2] PAUL   Ho, 's isch diner, e *turbo*. Lauft's guet?
             Aha, it's yours, a *turbo*. Good runner?

[3] RENÉ   Ja, guet, prima ich bin zufridde demit.
             Yes, good, excellent, I'm satisfied with it.

[4] PAUL   *Bonsoir Madame . . . Vitesse de pointe . . .?*
             Goodnight madam . . . Top speed . . .?

[5] DENIS   Hesch-ne schunn prowiert?
             Have you already tried it out?

[6] RENÉ   *Cent quatre vingt cinq.*
             A hundred and eighty five.

[7] PAUL   *Cent quatre vingt cinq.*
             A hundred and eighty five.

[8] RENÉ   Uf de ditsch Autobahn.
             On the German motorway.

[9] PAUL   Wievil Kilometer hesch drowwe?
             How many kilometres are on the clock?

[10] RENÉ   Jetz haw i *dix mille quatre cents, même pas*.
             Now I have *ten thousand four hundred, not even*.

[11] PAUL   Stabill uf de Stross . . .?
             Stable on the road . . .?

[12] RENÉ   Er hebbt.
             It lifts.

[13] PAUL   *En général, les Renault, ça . . .*
             In general, Renaults . . .

[14] RENÉ   Ja.
             Yes.

[15] DENIS   *Ça* schwimmt.
             They swim.

[16] RENÉ   *Oui, c'est ça*, sie schwimme.
             Yes, that's it, they swim.

Utterances [13] to [16] are of particular interest: Paul starts a sentence in French (perhaps because he is using a French name, Renault?). The verb which appears to be 'missing' (from the point of view of a written transcription) at the end of utterance [13] is almost certainly replaced by a gesture of the hand to indicate the movement he is talking about, since René immediately replies Ja. The next clause *Ça* schwimmt is an unusual example of switching between a pronoun subject and the verb; when René picks this up in the next line, he unifies that part of the sentence although the first part of his sentence is in French [16].

The switching here is rapid and fluent; in the last four utterances, consisting of fourteen words, there is a change of language at each turn and two more within turns. The passage illustrates well how quickly and naturally bilinguals can adapt to language changes when these are part of an accepted mode of speech for them; and second it highlights the fact that there is important work to be done on switches between turns as well as within them (Valdès-Fallis 1977).

René then leaves and the conversation continues between Paul and Denis in Alsatian, after a short interlude where they discuss a colleague in French (they may thus be marking the difference between work- and leisure-related conversation topics). There is a lot of switching to and fro, sometimes several times within one utterance, as they discuss squash:

EXTRACT 2

[1] DENIS   Ja, *j'ai joué la semaine dernière*, verdeckel dü! *Deux jours, hein, courbaturé!* Ich maan, ich bin verschlawe worre!
Yes, *I played last week*, blimey! *Two days, you know, stiff as a poker!* I felt as though I had been beaten!

[2] PAUL   *Tu m'étonnes, hé*, wenn d' so lang spielsch . . .
You surprise me, eh, when you've been playing for so long . . .

The swear-word comes to mind in Alsatian and the medical term *courbaturé* '*stiff*' in French, but this does not provide sufficient explanation of the switching in this context. Why, for example, does Denis say: *J'ai joué la semaine dernière* in French when a few seconds earlier he had asked: Hesch squash g'spielt? showing the Alsatian expression was perfectly accessible to him? Nor can it be the expression: *la semaine dernière*, which triggers the use of French, since moments later he says in Alsatian: Ich hab g'spielt d'letscht Wuch. Ich spiel alle Wuch 'I played last week. I play every week'.

One is left once again with the hypothesis that in some cases such as this, bilinguals switch for the sake of switching. It matters little whether the bilingual effect is achieved through dense intra-clause switching or by alternative choices, as is the case here; the choice of tactics probably depends as much as anything on the style of conversation; where utterances are short and each consists of a single clause, one may easily change between utterances rather than within them. A correlation has already been shown, unsurprisingly, between the length of utterances and the number of switches (Woolford 1983: 529). Appositional structures such as the one below render it further unnecessary to switch within clauses.

EXTRACT 3

DENIS *Enfin*, d'meischte wie drinne spiele, *ils sont costauds*, verdeckel dü.
Well, most of those who play there, *they're tough*, blimey.

Annie, another employee, stops for a moment on her way out to talk to Denis
and Paul. The conversation, which lasts several minutes, takes place entirely in
French with the exception of one 'Ja, ja' from Annie. The situation here is
different from what happens with Saleur in the Administrative Office or the
mother-in-law in the Beck family, who are also monolinguals, in a bilingual
setting. Here the presence of Annie (who is probably not monolingual in fact)
imposes the use of French. It is not a bilingual conversation where a
monolingual is present, but a monolingual conversation in which two of the
participants are, incidentally, bilingual. It is fairly clear how this type of
situation can, in conjunction with the prestige factor, bring about a change in
the linguistic language habits of a social or professional group.

EXTRACT 4

(Paul and Denis have been discussing whether or not to go to a moto-cross
race.)

[1] PAUL Ja, ich hab . . . Ich weiss awwer nitt, ich bin noh nitt b'stimmt
dass ich mach.
Yes, I have . . . I don't really know, I'm not yet sure that I'll do it.

[2] DENIS *Bonsoir.*
Good evening.

[3] PAUL *Salut, Annie! J'suis pas encore sûr.*
Hi, Annie! I'm not yet sure.

[4] ANNIE *Ha! C'est Paul!*
Oh! It's Paul!

[5] PAUL *Ça va?*
How are you?

[6] ANNIE *Oui.*
Yes.

[7] PAUL *Tu vas aux fraises?*
You going to the strawberries?

[8] ANNIE *Hein?*
Eh?

[9] PAUL *Tu vas aux fraises? Tu es allée aux fraises?*
You going to the strawberries? Have you been to the strawberries?

[10] ANNIE *Dix-neuf kilos aujourd'hui . . .* [*Their conversation continues in French.*]
Nineteen kilos today . . .

As soon as Annie takes her leave, they go back to their switched mode, although they are still talking about strawberry-picking, which they were discussing with her:

EXTRACT 5

[1] DENIS   Ja, dü, Achtung! *C'est fatigant, hein*.
            Watch out you know! *It's tiring, eh*.

[2] PAUL   Ja, in . . . Ja, Kaltehüse, *aussi Stotzheim, j'ai lu aujourd'hui, Stotzheim
            aussi*.
            Yes in . . . yes, Kaltenhausen, *and also Stotzheim, I read today,
            Stotzheim also*.

[3] DENIS   *Bonsoir, messieurs-dames*.
            Evening, ladies and gentlemen.

[4] PAUL   Ja, wie lejt denn diss?
            Yes, where is that then?

[5] DENIS   *J'ai lu ça*, ho, in de Zitung, Stotzheim, ja, *attends, c'est entre Saint-
            Pierre et Benfeld, près de Barr*, nooch dem *plan, sept francs le kilo*.
            I read that, uh, in the newspaper, Stotzheim, yes, *hang on, it's
            between Saint-Pierre and Benfeld, near Barr*, according to the *map*,
            seven francs a kilo.

[6] PAUL   Siwwe Franke, jo, *ça va*.
            Seven francs, ya, *that's OK*.

We have examples here of switching within clauses, before the place complementizer [5], between a preposition and its complement [5], and shortly afterwards between demonstrative subject and verb (or, rather, in this case, a filler which replaces the verb (*Ça* Ding [1] below) and between article and noun (gibt e *gâchis* [1] below).

EXTRACT 6

[1] DENIS   *En cueillette libre*, noh, manchi awwer do, *ça* Ding, gibt e *gâchis, les
            gens quand ils cueillent, tu sais, c'est pas toujours dit* . . .
            In pick your own, but some in that case, *they* do thing, there's a
            waste, when people pick you know, they don't always . . .

[2] PAUL   Ja, awwer die wisse's jo, diss wisse se jo, weisch.
            Yes, but they know that, they know that, you know.

[3] DENIS   Jo, *ça fait partie du risque, hein, je suppose y a quand même quelqu'un qui
            supervise un petit peu ça*.
            Ya, *that's part of the risk, eh, I suppose there must be someone supervising it
            all a bit*.

[4] PAUL   Ja, ich glab, 's isch niemand do, jeder derf hole vun . . . Sie gehn
            Pfadle un . . .

Yes, I think there's no one there, everyone may help themselves
... they go up little paths and ...

[5] DENIS Un so un so vil.
And so and so much.

[6] PAUL Un so un so vil, do, un do hab, hole se, en messe, es müess
richtich geputzt sinn, *plus ou moins*.
And so and so much, there, and they have, they pick and weigh, it
has to be properly cleaned up, *more or less*.

[7] DENIS *Ah voilà*, nitt dass se do *cueillir*, un gehn dann uf d'ander Sit.
Ah that's it, they're not supposed to *pick* there, and then go to the
other side.

[8] PAUL *Voilà*, diss isch so.
That's it, that's how it is.

Paul appears to use a lot of French expressions and to switch between clauses,
but Denis does not recoil before the densest of switches, as [7]: *Ah voilà*, nitt
dass se do *cueillir*, un gehn dann uf d'ander Sit. This example represents an
interesting infringement of *both* grammatical systems, as the verb '*cueillir*'
should be in the third person plural to be grammatical in either French or
Alsatian. There are two possible explanations for this aberration: either there is
a kind of separation between the two halves of the sentence—there *is* a very
brief pause before '*cueillir*'; or the '*ir*' ending of the verb allows it to
masquerade temporarily—for it is not at present a loan word—as an Alsatian
verb ending in '-iere' (like *choisir* /ʃwɑˈzeːrə/ in Conversation C); the third
person plural of such a verb would indeed be '-iere' (/eːrə/ although no [ə] is
audible at the end of the word on this occasion). The resourcefulness of skilled
bilingual speakers at exploiting any similarity between their two languages
would then again be demonstrated, in spite of the slightly pidgin-like sound of
this sentence! A short while later the conversation ends, on a typical and
amusing note:

EXTRACT 7

[1] DENIS *De toute façon*, kannsch widdersch lueje hit owe, gell, *il y a la
retransmission du match*.
In any case, you can have another look this evening you know,
they're showing the match again.

[2] PAUL Ja.
Yes.

[3] DENIS *Oui, à vingt-heures trente, sur Antenne 2*. Odder uf'm Ditsche, denn
sie sinn ganz verruckt uf Fuessball.
Yes, at eight-thirty, on Channel 2. Or on German TV, because they're
quite crazy about football.

[4] PAUL   Ja, d'Ditsche, ja, hopp- . . .
            Yes, the Germans, yes, hopp- . . .
[5] DENIS   . . . -la, *c'est bien!*
             . . . -la, that's good!

Hoppla!—the most typical of Alsatian expressions, with a range of meanings from 'there we are' to 'sorry', is actually split between the two speakers, without any perceptible pause. This shows the close understanding between the two colleagues and the fact that one immediately understands what the other means. The sharing of a word is symptomatic of the same closeness between speakers which also legitimizes the most intense forms of switching.

The predominant use of Alsatian by these three young men may well constitute a form of escapism with respect to their work, which officially takes place in the French-speaking environment of a large Strasbourg company. It is also characteristic of the speech of young, solidary males to employ a very informal vernacular style, and this may well go some way towards explaining the amount of switching we have witnessed.

This switching is, however, almost certainly also related to questions of competence: it would be rare to meet Strasbourgeois of this age who were *able* to speak a very 'pure' form of the dialect. But contrary to situations where there are several generations present and where switching can be linked up with interlocutor changes, code-switching here is characteristic of a particular kind of bilingual speech with its own connotations.

ii Conclusion

Several common patterns of language selection and switching emerge from the study of such recordings. These provide a useful additional angle to the information which can be gleaned from surveys, since we have information here on language choices in an interactive context, whereas surveys can usually only provide data on the language patterns of individuals. As regards language selection, we have some confirmation here of expected patterns related to speaker age: the oldest tend to speak more Alsatian, the youngest French. Those who are neither very old nor very young may speak either; but considering that I by no means sought out people who would speak mainly Alsatian, but merely bilinguals, overall a remarkable amount of Alsatian is spoken in these six conversations. There was only one long passage of pure French, that with Annie in Conversation F. This may be chance, but it is probably related also to the informality which characterizes even the work-place conversations. Far more French was spoken, for example, in the Insurance Office survey, as soon as clients were addressed by employees.

As regards switching, as one lady said to me in the Cité des Chasseurs interviews, everyone does it, more or less: the old to fit in with the young, and vice versa, the middle generations when they are talking to the old and the young, to fit in with them, and to each other because they themselves can often use the two languages more or less indifferently. In the last case, switches would tend to be triggered by particular topics or expressions rather than being interlocutor-related.

But even within couples or among friends or colleagues who are in close and frequent interaction with each other, and whose basic linguistic background is broadly comparable, strong individual differences emerge. In particular as regards dense intra-clause switching, some speakers seem to have a particular predilection for, or lack of inhibition about it: compare Annie with her husband Michel in Conversation C, or Mr Eder with his wife or the Becks in Conversation A. Naturally, there may be factors in their personal history which lead them to switch a lot and which we may or may not be able to pin-point and comprehend; but there also appear to be differences relating to personality (e.g. talkativeness) and social role (adults often go in for longer, more complex stretches of discourse than children because they see it as their role to explain and direct the children's actions; this affects not only what they talk about, but which language they use and how much they talk overall). There are almost certainly also differences concerning how acceptable different people find switching (Romaine 1989) and therefore how much and when they will allow themselves to do it.

Such differences related to personality and attitude are lost if one contents oneself with large-scale quantitative studies of switches divorced from their context. They point to the need to develop a theory linking individual and community-wide language use, such as that which underlies Le Page's concept of 'projection' (1978).

In the next chapter I shall nevertheless be counting up some of the phenomena which have emerged *from these conversations* as being significant sub-units of language choice and switching, in the hope that the categories chosen are true to the kind of speech and the kind of speakers who were recorded. There is still an uneasy compromise to be reached in sociolinguistics beween case-studies and quantification, which seems preferable to the exclusion of either method.

6

Quantification

In this Chapter, aspects of the code-switched conversations described in Chapter 5 are broken down and quantified. The classification of the linguistic phenomena which make up code-switching is of fundamental importance, and some of the difficulties arising in such an analysis have already been mentioned in Chapter 3; a further discussion of this issue will be found in the final chapter.

Loans v. Switches

In an attempt to quantify code-switching, the question will arise as to whether all single lexical items from variety A, embedded in a text in variety B, should be counted as switches, or whether some of them should not be treated differently because they lack the *ad hoc* quality characteristic of code-switching. In this analysis single words originating in A but commonly and widely used, even by monolinguals in B, were classed as loans and left out of the subsequent analysis of switching. In order to determine which these were, all single lexical items which stood out as switches in the transcriptions were listed, and three bilingual Strasbourgeois judges were asked to assign these items to one of three categories: loans, switches, or in-between (loans in some speakers' repertoires but code-switches in others'). There were, unsurprisingly, far more single items of French origin in Alsatian segments than vice versa, reflecting the cultural dominance of French in Alsace (see below). But more significantly—and largely due to the heavy use the judges made of the intermediate category—the degree of agreement between the three judges was only 37 per cent (that is to say, all three placed the items in the same category in only just over a third of cases).

Because of this lack of general agreement, which appears to reflect rapid change in progress in the linguistic situation, no attempt was made to alter the rough-and-ready classification adopted in the examples transcribed in the first part of Chapter 5, where French items are printed in italic.

Street names (*rue des Orfèvres*, *boulevard d'Anvers*) were unanimously considered as loans, although some streets maintain a dialect appellation as well (*rue de la Papèterie* 'd'Papierfawrikstross'). Such a decision is supported by cases where words are pronounced the French way when part of a street name, but the Alsatian way otherwise (e.g. the village of La Wantzenau which is pronounced /vɑ̃tzəˈno/ in *route de la Wantzenau* but /ˈvɑntsənaʊ/ otherwise (by dialect speakers). Judges would occasionally fluctuate between ascribing words which came up several times to one or another category (e.g. *gymnastique*, hoppla) and for certain other words which are present in the same written form in both systems the judges remarked that one had to know the pronunciation in order to ascribe them (e.g. *président* 'president', *plan* 'plan').

In order not to overestimate the amount of code-switching, only words which were classed as switches by two out of the three judges were counted as such. The 'intermediate' category, for words in the process of becoming loans, was amalgamated with the loans category (one word, *piscine*, was placed in the intermediate category by all three judges), as loans were not the focus of attention here. It should be noted, however, that such categorizations are extremely problematic in a situation such as that obtaining in Strasbourg, where there is utterance-internal switching in numerous everyday situations. To categorize some words as loans and some as code-switches presupposes that there are two clearly distinguishable languages, whereas numerous lexical elements in Alsace could be said to belong to one *or* the other code.

Single-Word Switching

Having eliminated those elements which at least two judges considered to be loans, single-word switches, in which one lexical item or short idiomatic expression appears in a different language from the surrounding part of the sentence, were counted up for each conversation. Table 6.1 shows the distribution of single-word switches in the various conversations (at this stage French and Alsatian single-word switches are not distinguished).

Single-word switches are much more frequent at work than in families. This cannot be entirely due to the fact that work contexts demand a more specialized vocabulary, as in work places work is often not the main topic of conversation. The difference in frequency is due to other factors which distinguish the work context from home.

In Table 6.2 French switches are distinguished from Alsatian switches and a grammatical breakdown of the single-word switches is made. Recurrences of the same word are only counted again if they appear in a different conversation (which explains why the absolute total here is slightly lower than in Table 6.1); the nature of those elements which are switched repeatedly is discussed below. Neither proper nouns, nor street names, nor figures (sums of money, etc.) are counted. No single-word switches were recorded in grammatical categories outside those on this list (e.g. no prepositions).

Nouns

By far the most frequent category of single-word switches is French nouns in Alsatian utterances (58 out of 117). These nouns can be grouped along semantic lines (Fischer 1979); as the examples in Table 6.3 show, they frequently come

TABLE 6.1. Breakdown of Single-Word Switching by Context

	No. of switches	Average no. of switches per transcribed page
Beck family	30	2.1
Rick family	35	1.6
Schmitt family	9	1.5
Subtotal	(74)	(1.7)
Administration office	71	2.8
Accounts office	47	3.4
Car park attendants	18	2.6
Subtotal	(136)	(2.9)
TOTAL	210	2.4

TABLE 6.2. Breakdown of Single-Word Switches by Language and Grammatical Category

	French in an Alsatian utterance	Alsatian in a French utterance
Nouns	58	2
Verbs	9	2
Adjectives	6	0
Adverbs	13	1
Conjunctions	4	3
Greetings, interjections, tags, phatic markers, and other expressions	27	17
TOTAL	117	25

from the same semantic categories as other words which the judges classified as loans.

The two classes did not appear to be treated differently at a morphological or phonological level and the fact that they come from the same semantic areas suggests that gradually the words which are classed as switches will move over into the category of loans. This seems all the more likely in cases where the same switch is found in more than one of the conversations (e.g. *oignons* 'onions', *faillite* 'bankruptcy'). It is, of course, less surprising to find repetitive loan words (e.g. *radio* and *chauffeur*).

TABLE 6.3. Single-Word Switches and Loans by Semantic Category

	Loans	Single-word switches
Cooking/Food	*purée, sauce, chocolat* 'purée, sauce, chocolate'	*pruneaux, moutarde* 'plums, mustard' *civet* 'game casserole' *carottes* 'carrots'
Professions	*moniteur, patron* 'guide, boss'	*poissonier, espion* 'fishmonger, spy'
Technical field	*pneus, auto, micro, etc.* 'tyres, car, microphone, etc.'	*générateur, contact* 'generator, connection'
House/building	*cabinet, balcon* 'lavatory, balcony'	*clôtures* 'fences' *volets roulants* 'roll-up shutters'
Office work	*bureau, stock* 'office, stock' *abonnement, budget* 'subscription, budget' *photocopies, secrétaire* 'photocopies, secretary' *caissier, enveloppes, etc.* 'cashier, envelopes, etc.'	*exemplaires* 'copies' *mandatement* 'transmission' *bulletin de commande* 'order form' *chemise, rotation* 'file, rotation' *engagement* 'commitment' *articles de bureau* 'office articles' *contrôle financier* 'financial control'

Furthermore, the two examples of single-noun switches going in the opposite direction (Füschthändschi 'gloves', and Grumbeere 'potatoes') also come from areas already on our list, clothes and food: it is possible that in such language-contact situations, certain areas are 'permeable' in either direction depending on the speaker's linguistic dominance. Other switches do not have any equivalents among the loans or among the Alsatian elements, though they may still reflect the cultural influence of French. Some of these are expressions connected with commerce (e.g. *perte* 'loss' (as opposed to profit), *gâchis* 'waste', *choix* 'choice') or ready-made idiomatic expressions (*bataille de boules de neige* 'snowball fight', *plaque de verglas* 'patch of black ice') which may in themselves be mixtures (e *effort* mache 'to make an *effort*'); there are also examples of more abstract terms with no particular contextual associations (e kleini *attention* 'a kind *thought*'; er het d'*hantise* 'he has a *dread*').

As far as loans are concerned, as has been mentioned already, street names and many proper nouns are in French, as are names designating members of the family (grandfather, cousin, niece, godfather) and corresponding nicknames (e.g. *tata* for 'auntie'). Some of these are in free variation with the Alsatian version (even totally French-speaking children in Alsace will often call their grandmother mamama and their mother mama). Figures may be in either language and the choice may be significant (see remarks above on we code/they code) for some bilinguals, but for many younger people they are always in French and so should probably be considered loans.

Lastly, as concerns nouns, there are a small number of cases where the article is in the language of the noun rather than in that of the surrounding sentence, e.g.: *La cassette*, wie lang ass se geht? '*The cassette*, how long does it run for?' . . . diss haw i jetz zufallig g'sähn, *le remboursement* '. . . I just happened to see that, *the repayment*'; . . .'s geht als an, *la lumière*, es kummt uf de Ton an . . . 'it always comes on, *the light* . . .'. The article being in French tends to confirm the fact that these are switches rather than loans. Such examples constitute a transitional step between single-word switching and multiple switching (see below).

Expressions, Exclamations, Connectors

In order of frequency, after nouns there comes a set which include invariable expressions of various kinds, ranging from 'yes' and 'no' to tags. Greetings (*bonjour*, *au revoir*), titles (*Monsieur*, *Madame*), and politeness formulas (*s'il vous plaît*, *merci*) were all considered by the judges to be loans.

It is in this category that one finds the most symmetrical relationship between French and Alsatian: there were 27 French expressions in an Alsatian base and 17 Alsatian expressions in French. Each expression was only counted once per conversation and such expressions as gell? ('isn't that so?') were repeated very frequently, so numerically the two are quite comparable. In Table 6.4 these expressions, difficult to classify in a grammatical analysis, are classified according to their pragmatic function. The typically Alsatian Hoppla caused the judges some confusion as they wanted to know its meaning in context, in order to decide whether it was a loan or a switch.

Overall, the parallelism highlighted by Table 6.4—such expressions are clearly available in both languages and so there is no lexical need to switch— underlines that this type of switching is of a symbolic nature, serving to maintain the presence of both languages in the conversation.

Table 6.4. Switched French and Alsatian Expressions by Function

Function	Alsatian	French
Expressing agreement/ disagreement	ja, nee 'yes, no'	*oui, bon, d'accord* 'yes, good, okay' *entendu, ouais, non* 'sure, yep, no'
Expressing surprise	ah joo 'o really'	*ah bon* 'o really'
Drawing attention/ linking	so, also 'so, well then'	*donc* 'well' *à propos* 'while we're on that' *écoute, bien, attends* 'listen, well, hang on'
Seeking confirmation (symbolic)	gell, nitt 'eh, don't you think'	*non, quoi* 'eh, don't you think'
Softening the message	glauw'i, weisch dü 'I think, you know'	*disons, n'empêche* 'let's say, all the same'
Swearing	Jesus, verdeckel dü (swear-words)	*Jésus Marie Joseph, merde* (swear-words)

Verbs

There were nine French verbs in an Alsatian base among the single-word switches, of which seven past participles attached to main verbs in Alsatian, e.g.: (i) Noch schlimmer, wenn de *client recalé* wurd am permis 'Even worse, if the *client* is *failed* on the test' (Conv. E); (ii) Sie sin *condamnés* worre 'They were *convicted*' (Conv. B); and one infinitive complementizer of an Alsatian main verb; Witt du es *goûter?* 'Do you want to *taste* it? (Conv. C).

In examples (i) and (ii) the syntax of the Alsatian sentences, into which the French verbs are slotted, is at variance with that of the equivalent French sentences (which, in the above cases, exactly parallels the English). Such a pattern is therefore at odds with the 'equivalence constraint' (Poplack 1979). The relatively rare examples of switching within the word all concern verbs, as in: Tee het er als zamme *mélangé* [*lit.*: tea has he always *together mixed*] 'He's always *mixed* teas together', where the second half of the Alsatian verb zammemische 'to mix up, mix together' is in French. Another example is the verb /kœjirə/ (*cueillir* (F.) + iere (Als.)) which is commented upon further below. The form used, the infinitive, stands out as ungrammatical in either language as it occurs in the sentence: nitt dass se do *cueillir*, un gehn dann uf d'ander Sit 'they're not supposed to *pick* there and then go to the other side' (Conv. F).

The presence of switching of this kind, which is ungrammatical in either language, has been attested elsewhere (Maters 1979) and raises an interesting question as to the conflicting strategies at work behind code-switched productions (see also p. 137 for another example of a switched second conjugation verb).

It is noteworthy that all the verbal switches encountered concern forms—past participle and infinitive—which are invariable at an auditory level (the -e of the feminine and the -s of the plural forms being silent). The Alsatian verbs in a French base do not show a very great interpenetration of the two languages, e.g.: (i) *prière bien vouloir* bezahle '*kindly* pay!' (Conv. D). The whole expression *prière bien vouloir* has a formulaic quality and after this expression the speaker is in a sense merely returning to the original language, Alsatian. (ii) *Parce que ça* griwelt '*Because it* prickles'; *Ça* griwelt *de trop* '*It* prickles *too much*'; *Ça* griwelt *plus* '*It isn't* prickling *any more*' (Conv. B). The repeated verb griwelt is culturally specific; it comes from the name of a kind of lettuce, 'Griwele-Salat', which has just been referred to.

One can also mention here the cases where the switch takes place between a pronoun subject and a verb, e.g.: (i) *il* koch guet '*he* cooks well' (Conv. D); (ii) *ça* schwimmt [*lit.*: *it*'s swimming] '*it*'s fuzzy, moving'; and even (iii) *ça* ding '*it* thing(s)' in which the verb is replaced by a filler-word. Leaving aside this last slightly odd case, the switches in (i) and (ii) are fluent and unhesitating and thus demonstrate that this is one of the possible, though unusual, switch points in a sentence in this context.

Adjectives

As with other switches, some of the adjectives which appear in French in an Alsatian context are due to the cultural dominance of French in certain spheres, e.g. medicine: (i) 's isch Ding ... *diététique*, wissen'r ... 'the thing ... *health food* [adj.], you know' (Conv. D); (ii) sinn nix as eso *produits* g'sinn, *biologiques*, *diététiques* 'there were nothing but *products*, there, *organic*, *health food*' (Conv. E).

These adjective switches are marked off by pauses which are visually interpreted as commas here but which arguably cut off the switch grammatically from the rest of the clause (see dislocated switching below).

In other cases, however, the adjectives switched are everyday terms with no particular technical connotations and the fact of switching in no way interrupts the flow of the sentence:

(i) Ja, *capable* isch se.
   Yes, she's *capable* all right (Conv. D);

(ii) D'*carrosserie* isch hoch g'sinn un de Schlitte, jo ung 'fähr so hoch,
wunderbar, also alles *impeccable*, was ich g'sähn hab.
The *car body* was raised and the sledge, about so high, wonderful, yes all
impeccable, what I saw (Conv. B).

Adverbs

The majority of adverbs or adverbial expressions switched in these conversations are placed at the beginning or end of clauses and some are separated by a
short pause (comma) from the rest, making it syntactically as easy to switch
them as other expressions (cf. above), e.g.: (i) Noch 'm Sainte-Anne, fufzig
Meter *à peu près* 'After Sainte-Anne, fifty metres *approximately*' (Conv. A); (ii)
Théoriquement soll's nitt *passiere* '*In theory* it shouldn't happen' (Conv. E); (iii) *A
l'époque*, 's isch nitt wild g'sinn '*At the time*, it wasn't so hot' (Conv. E). In example (ii) the inversion of the subject dictated by the adverb placement in Alsatian
is observed but in example (iii) it is not. There are also some examples where
the adverbs are fully integrated into the structure of the sentence: jetz muen ihr
diss nochemol ändere, do *plus* un do *moins* mache 'now you have to change this
once again, make *more* here and *less* here' (Conv. E).

There was only one similar example of an Alsatian adverb in a French
sentence, no different in form from the opposite situation: *Il y a des mouettes dans
les maisons*, üewweral '*There are gulls in the houses*, everywhere' (Conv. D).
Another highly elliptical sentence is symptomatic of the difficulties of assigning
linguistic elements to one or the other language: *Tata, raisins* nochhär! '*Auntie,
grapes* afterwards!' (Conv. C). Although two words out of three are in French,
the sentence should arguably be considered to be an Alsatian one with one loan
(*tata*) and one switch (*raisins*), since the adverb, nochhär, carries the structural
weight due to the lack of verb; in fact of course, such a 'sentence', typical of the
spoken language, shows up the meaninglessness of such a categorization.
Finally, only one French adverb, *vis-à-vis*, was considered to be a loan by the
judges.

Conjunctions

There are several examples of the use of *parce que* '*because*' in Alsatian
utterances, e.g. 'Un noh isch de Kleinmann nunter, *parce que* ich hab mi dort
muen melde 'And now Kleinmann is downstairs, because I've had to register
myself there' (Conv. D); and several uses of odder 'or' in French sentences,
e.g.: *Et lui qui n'est là que 3 mois* odder *2 mois* odder *4 mois* '*And with him only being
there 3 months* or *2 months* or *4 months*' (Conv. E).

Clyne (1967) found conjunctions were frequently the subject of switching
either in anticipation of the language used in the rest of the clause, or when
sandwiched between two nouns, the language of which they follow. This
provides a plausible explanation for the fact that *ou* is in French in an example

like the following: . . . ob ihr Spätzle wöelle, *potée de carottes ou porc roulé* '. . . whether you want Spätzle, *carrot purée or rolled pork*' (Conv. C). In other cases, the object of switching for a conjunction such as 'because' or 'or' would seem to be rather to highlight the structural relationship which that conjunction marks between the two clauses.

Multiple Switches

Multiple switches, which are those involving more than one word at a time, were subdivided into four groups according to the degree of independence of the two languages in the sentence:

1. *Switches between independent clauses*: switches between the two main clauses separated by a pause represented by a full stop, semi-colon, hesitation marks, or a conjunction.
2. *Switches between dependent clauses*: switches between a main and a subordinate clause or two subordinate clauses, whether both are dependent on the same main clause or one subordinate clause is dependent on the other.
3. *Switches within clauses*: switches within a clause including switches within incomplete or elliptical clauses but excluding switches only affecting one word (or short idiomatic expression) which were covered under 'single-word switching'.
4. *Disjointed switching*: switches marked by a pause, hesitation, or interruption which coincides with a grammatical break in the utterance.

Three of these categories are defined along grammatical lines, the fourth being defined by the lack of grammatical relations between the different language segments which are represented ('disjointed switching'). Let us recall that we are only considering utterance-internal switching, the utterance being defined here as a segment of speech addressed to one person or group of people.

Table 6.5 shows that multiple switches, like single word-switches, are much more frequent in the work context than in families (more than twice as frequent when measured against the total number of words). Certain contexts, or perhaps certain types of interlocutor relationships, clearly call forth more switching than others within the same overall sociolinguistic context—in the accounts office the average number of switches per page is 6.1.

Switches between Independent Clauses

Switches between two independent clauses represent half the total number of cases of multiple switches in families and almost half in the work context. Out of 108 instances (33 in families and 75 at work), six concern quoted speech which is reported in the language originally used, e.g.: (i) denn er het schunn

TABLE 6.5. Multiple Switches by Context and Grammatical Relation of Switched Segments

	Switches between independent clauses	Switches between dependent clauses	Intra-clause switching	Disjointed switching	Total multiple switches	Average no. of switches per transcribed page
Beck family	16	4	9	3	32	2.3
Rick family	7	6	5	0	18	0.8
Schmitt family	10	5	1	0	16	2.7
Families total (%)	33 (50.0%)	15 (22.7%)	15 (22.7%)	3 (4.6%)	66	(1.3)
Administration office	22	10	6	12	50	2.0
Accounts office	45	29	5	7	86	6.1
Car park attendants	8	5	3	9	25	3.8
WORK TOTAL (%)	75 (46.6%)	44 (27.3%)	14 (8.7%)	28 (17.4%)	161	(4.0)

g'saat g'hett: 'Joo *on le pique!*' 'because he's already said, "OK *we'll give him a jab!*"' (Conv. D); (ii) der Kamerad vom Paul, saat immer, '*La charcuterie, c'est splendide à voir chez vous . . .*' 'Paul's mate, he always says, "*Charcuterie is a pleasure to see over here . . .*"' (Conv. A).

Eighteen examples concern more or less exact repetitions of what has just been said in the other language. This is a much attested form of switching, the purpose of which appears to be to add emphasis, highlight, or 'frame' to what is being said, e.g.: 'S tät e bissel witt gehn, *je trouve ça irait un peu loin*. 'That would be going a bit far, *I think that would be going a bit far*' (Conv. E).

Switches between independent clauses may be triggered by one or several switched words at the end of the preceding clause, e.g.: Sovil Grumbeere un sovil *carottes.* →[1] *C'est pas de la purée, c'est de la purée de carottes*. 'This much potato and this much *carrot. It's not mashed potato it's carrot purée*' (Conv. C).

In one case this occurred after an expression the judges had considered a loan (*panne d'essence* 'empty tank'), showing once again the psychological tenuousness of the distinction between loans and switches: üewwer aanmol, paf, *panne d'essence.* → *Tu te rends compte pour une auto-école . . .* 'suddenly, bang, *no more petrol.* → *Just think of it for a driving school . . .*' (Conv. E).

Quotations, repetitions, and triggered switches can, of course, like other kinds of switching, contribute to a balanced use of the two languages within an utterance or within the whole conversation. Thus a somewhat mechanical 'explanation' of why a switch has taken place—such as triggering—does not preclude the necessity for a more sociolinguistic or psychologically orientated explanation of code-switching over a longer stretch of discourse.

Switching between Dependent Clauses

Switching between dependent clauses occurs in these data in a wide variety of grammatical positions, of which the following represent only a few examples:

(i) between main clause and subordinate clause which is its direct object: Ich mach's selte, *vérifier les niveaux* 'I do it seldom, *checking the gauges*' (Conv. E);

(ii) between main clause and conditional clause: *s'il le revend avant*, hett'r e plus-value '*if he sells on before*, he'll have to pay *gains tax*' (Conv. A);

(iii) between main clause and subordinates of time, place, reason, etc.:

(a) *Seulement y'a une manière de couper que . . . dans . . . dans d'autres départements*, wo m'r's Fleisch wunderbar do sieht '*But there is a way of cutting which . . . in . . . in other départements*, where one sees the meat all looking wonderful' (Conv. A);

(b) Er nimmt's nitt, *parce qu'il l'a ramené de là-bas* 'He won't take it, *because he brought it back from over there*' (Conv. E);

[1] → = trigger point.

(iv) between main clause and relative clause: Diss isch ken *palette* g'sinn, s'isch e anders Stüeck, Ding, *porc* → *qu'il emballe et qu'il vend* 'That wasn't *palette*, it's another piece, thing, *pork* → *which he wraps up and sells*' (Conv. B);

(v) between two subordinates dependent on the same clause: m'r fröjt . . . ob alles diss . . . au wertvoll isch genau, un üssgedenkt isch, *et si ça va aboutir*, nitt 'one wonders . . . whether all this . . . is really valuable, and thought out, *and whether it will succeed*, you know' (Conv. D);

(vi) between two subordinates of which one completes the other: *Ça c'est une faute grave*, wenn dir diss passiert *au moment de faire le permis* '*That's a serious fault*, if it happens to you *when you're taking the test*' (Conv. E.);

(vii) between main clause or subordinate clause and another subordinate clause or phrase in apposition to the first:

    (a) der aant, *il marche mal*, der wie 's *accident* het g'hett 'that chap, *he can't walk properly*, the one who had the *accident*' (Conv. E);

    (b) d'meischte wie drinne spiele, *ils sont costauds*, verdeckel dü 'most of those who play there, *they're tough*, blimey' (Conv. F);

    (c) noh het'r mi mitgenomme uf de Märik, *un marché, mais alors formidable* 'he took me to the market, *a market which was quite fantastic*' (Conv. A).

Appositional structures such as those above lend themselves particularly well to switching; the inbuilt break which characterizes them 'legalizes' the grammatical rupture which a change of language can provoke.

Switches, like intonation, can also highlight grammatical relations and transitions in discourse, for example by indicating which part of the sentence is in metaphorical brackets, e.g.: Noh han mir e andere Winter g'hett, *d'ailleurs c'était marrant aussi*, han mir emol e so *période* g'hett . . . 'Then we had another winter, *that was funny also*, we had a *period* once during which . . .' (Conv. D).

In spite of the variety which they exhibit, switches between dependent clauses appear to be less frequent in our data than switches between independent clauses (Table 6.5). In order to establish whether this is really so, one would need to compare the number of switched occurrences with the absolute number of occurrences of each type of clause in these and comparable speech samples. But even this might be misleading as there may well be more independent clauses in mixed discourse than in monolingual discourse. To the extent that switching fulfils a particular psychological or sociolinguistic need, speakers will be motivated to adapt their discourse structure to make it easier to switch.

Intra-Clause Switches

Intra-clause switches are as frequent as switches between dependent clauses in the family context but proportionately much less frequent at work (14 cases only out of 161). On the other hand, in the work context there are a large number of cases of disjointed switches which do not occur much in families. Intra-clause switches occur in these data:

(i) between subject and verb: *La sauce* isch wie *palette* . . . '*The sauce* is like a *palette* . . .' (Conv. B);

(ii) between verb and direct object: Sie mache *faillite, quoi* 'They go *bankrupt, you know*' (Conv. A);

(iii) between article and noun: Hesch jetz de *toupie jaune?* 'Do you have the *yellow top* now?' (Conv. C);

(iv) between verb and prepositional phrase: *Il avait commencé* näwe 'm Prisunic '*He started up* next door to Prisunic' (Conv. E);

(v) between co-ordinating conjunction and the clause it introduces: *C'est vachement riche les raisins, aussi* ich ess als gern von denne '*They're very rich are grapes, and* I always like eating them' (Conv. E);

(vi) between two subjects which are both attributes of the same verb: *C'était un militaire en retraite*, glaww i, odder e Polizist '*He was a retired military man*, I think, or a policeman' (Conv. E);

(vii) before a time expression: *Bah, tout va de travers* hit morje '*Bah, everything is going wrong* this morning' (Conv. D);

(viii) between direct object and adverb: *On a un tas de problèmes* wiriklisch demit, ne '*We have a heap of problems* really with him, you know' (Conv. D);

and so on.

Because of the variety of positions where switches can occur, it would require a far bigger corpus to gather together a large number of examples of switches occurring in the same grammatical units. However, from a theoretical point of view, the fact that switches can occur at these various junctions is more significant than the absolute number of switches found there.

Secondly, it is important to stress that there is often a certain arbitrariness in assigning switches to the 'multiple switches' category as many may in fact more plausibly be considered 'repeated single switches' (that is a single switch followed by another single switch) or switches arising from a rather limited form of triggering. Let us consider some of the borderline cases between one-word and multiple switches—two examples already quoted: *il* koch guet and *ça* schwimmt, which are complete utterances, could just as well be considered intra-clause switches rather than single switches occurring between the pronoun subject of the sentence and the verb. Example (iii) above, Hesch jetz de *toupie jaune?* can be considered not as a multiple switch as it was above, but as a single-word switch where the adjective has through simple triggering followed the language of the noun; this is supported by the fact that the same speaker says de gäls *toupie*, with the adjective in Alsatian a few moments later. Example (ii) above, Sie mache *faillite, quoi*, may be considered as a single-word switch on the word *faillite* '*bankruptcy*', followed by another single switch in the form of the tag, *quoi* at the end of the sentence. Example (vi) can be considered rather than a switch between two subject attributes of the same verb, as a sentence interrupted by a conversational filler (glaww i 'I think'), which itself triggers a change of language affecting the rest of the sentence.

Such different interpretations of various switches are not contradictory but complementary; their simultaneous validity only underlines the poverty of a grammatical analysis such as this faced with the complexity of actual discourse.

Disjointed Switching

I mentioned above the strong likelihood that certain types of sentence structure which render switching easier, such as independent clauses without subordination and appositional structures, may be more frequent in bilingual than in monolingual discourse.

It also appears from these data that switches often coincide with ruptures in the flow of speech marked by self-interruptions and hesitations of various kinds. For this reason, a further category of multiple switching was included in the analysis, called 'disjointed switching': this covers those cases in which the grammatical relationship between the two parts of the utterance is discontinuous or non-existent; it is not the same as the 'flagged switching' identified in certain contexts by Poplack (1988) which is often accompanied by metalinguistic comment, or where the pause/hesitation serves as a metalinguistic comment.

It is important to note that some grammatical analyses of code-switched speech (e.g. Bentahila and Davies; Poplack) consider that such instances do not represent proper code-switching. This exclusion represents a crucial question to which I shall return in the final chapter; it is a direct extension of the fact that linguists working on monolingual speech within a universalist framework deliberately discount data which they consider to represent 'performance errors'.

Disjointed switches are much rarer in the family settings (4.5 per cent of switches) than in the work settings, where they represent 17.4 per cent of switches. It is interesting that they are considerably more common in the contexts where switches overall are more frequent. It may be that the type of conversations which take place in, for example, office settings, are more broken up and interrupted than family conversations, even in a monolingual environment; in a bilingual context these interruptions are exploited to facilitate changes of language.

A revealing example is provided in Conversation D (Administration Office). Conrad is describing his ex-boss, who was such a stickler for work that he would interrogate the employees when they went to the toilet:

(i) Ich bin zwei Mol drüsse g'sinn, ob's ... *'Vous pensez que c'est nécessaire?'*
'I'd been out twice, whether ... *"Do you think its necessary?"'*

Conrad has already pronounced the words ob's 'whether it' when he realizes that what he is saying is a quotation. Since quotations of people's speech are usually in the original language used, Conrad must switch to French as well as making his story more lively by quoting what the boss said directly. The self-interruption after ob's therefore coincides with a switch.

Earlier on in the same context, Conrad uses a self-interruption and a switch to draw attention to himself, so that his colleagues do not go out without him:

(ii) ich will nitt warte, bis de Nuss kommt . . . *Attendez, je sors avec vous, hein*, ich geh do nüewwer . . .
'I don't want to wait until Nuss comes . . . *Wait, I'll go out with you, eh*, I'm going over there . . .'.

The second switch in this example is marked by the expression 'hein', which serves the same purpose as the first pause.

A third transitional technique consists in the repetition of one or two words in the other language which facilitate a new departure:

(iii) *Non, c'est c'est* 's isch nitt ass se dini ganze Dings . . . de . . .
'*No, it's it's* it's not as if the whole thing . . . the . . .' (Conv. A).

The 'repetition' in question may be only approximate and the semantic link between the two halves of the sentence takes the place of a grammatical link; in the next example, the idea of obligation (soll) in the first part is taken up by the idea of a fault (failing in your obligations) in the second part:

(iv) awwer diss soll . . . *ça c'est une faute grave!*
'but this should . . . *that's a serious fault!*' (Conv. E).

Sometimes the link between the two parts of the utterance is almost impossible to guess, but this can arise in monolingual as well as in bilingual discourse:

(v) . . . ich geh immer noch in Begleitung, nitt, ich bin . . . *Les dames* . . .
'. . . I still always go with company, you know, I'm . . . *Ladies* . . .'. (Conv. D).

Madame Meyer is perhaps on the point of saying that ladies never go out alone, thus completing the first part of the utterance where she says she is always accompanied. But Conrad, who is on the telephone while talking to her suddenly says something to his interlocutor, and interrupts Madame Meyer, whose precise intentions are therefore not revealed.

Just like other kinds of switching, disjointed switching can have various kinds of reason. In example (ii) the reason might be that to switch languages draws attention more effectively to what is said in the switched segment; in example (iv) it may be anticipatory triggering provoked by the expression *faute grave*; in example (v) the refinement associated with the expression *les dames* may have provoked this recourse to French, language of good manners.

The proportionate increase in disjointed switching in contexts where switching in general is more frequent suggests that this form of switching is better accepted when the mixing is intense enough to constitute a form of mixed language and inhibitions relating to how one 'should' speak (in one language at a time, in full sentences) are dropped. Far from being excluded from an analysis of bilingual discourse, disjointed switching may constitute one of its most revealing features.

Other Cross-Linguistic Markers

The data described in this chapter also provide considerable material for the analysis of other cross-linguistic markers apart from code-switches. The presence and status of loan-words for one has already been mentioned; phono-logical aspects of code-switching are also worthy of study (Grosjean and Soares 1986). The grammatical and stylistic influence of one language on another with which it is in contact (Jadin 1985) can also be studied in the context of switched discourse. In these data, there are a number of examples of calques in both directions:

(i) French → Alsatian: achtung mache (← *faire attention*) 'to look out'; es saat mir nix (← *ça ne me dit rien*) 'I don't think much of it'; es hett jo nimmi gedräjt (← *ça n'a pas tourné*) 'it hasn't been turning'.

(ii) Alsatian → French: *toujours il était bon* (Alsatian word order) '*it was always good*'; *Vous aurez le droit de rester plus longtemps debout* '*You'll be allowed to stay up longer*' (in French: *rester reveillés*; the Alsatian ufbliewe, which means 'to stay up' both literally and metaphorically is translated literally into French).

There are instances of Alsatian nouns adopting the gender of their French equivalents (denne Dach, denne Musée) and of an expression made up of a switch and a loan from French, placed in the Alsatian word order ('e *moutarde* sauce'). Such examples could be multiplied but this is not really the aim; the important point about the other cross-linguistic markers is that there is continuity between them and code-switches.

This continuity is particularly well illustrated by the numerous French verbs 'Alsatianized', thanks to the ending -iere. Although some of these are well-integrated loans, others are clear instances of off-the-cuff intra-lexical switching. Many of those which are loans have for a long time been borrowed by German also (camoufliere 'to camouflage'; engagiert 'taken on (as employee)'; confirmiere 'to confirm'; dressiert 'trained'; arrangiert 'arranged'; forciert 'forced'; etc.) whereas others are spontaneous Alsatian creations (demenagiere 'to move house'; enregistriere 'to record'; and, remarkably, choisire 'to choose', to which the only alteration was the adding of a [ə]. The existence of many well-established French loans in German, some of which were common, especially in Southern Germany, as far back as the nineteenth century appears to give a licence for the creation of new words according to the same principle, of which some may be adopted as fully fledged loans, whereas others just serve an *ad hoc* purpose. This provides a further illustration of the continuity between the processes of borrowing and of switching.

Patterns of Choice and Switching

In the last part of this chapter, I shall attempt to identify the main groups of factors which appear to be important in order to understand patterns of language choice and switching in these six conversations, thereby bringing together both the general descriptions in the previous chapter and the linguistic analysis of this one. These factors will be compared with those identified in three other analyses of code-switching, Gumperz (1982), Saville-Troike (1982), and Valdès-Fallis (1977) with a view to establishing points of convergence or divergence between their results and these.

First, two preliminary remarks: No direct relationship should be sought between the factors below and speaker motivations. Each time a speaker chooses to speak a language—and consequently each time s/he changes—his/her motivations may be multiple and it would be an illusion to think that one can establish any simple correspondence between each choice and its motivation. We may even be mistaken as to which of those changes are psychologically significant for him/her.

Let us take the example of Agnès Rick, who, in Conversation B, loses her temper with her husband René because he proposes that they go for an excursion together with their friends, the Riebs, whereas Agnès would like them for once to do something on their own. Agnès speaks French to René most of the time but when she gets angry she does so in Alsatian. Why?

(i) Because when she is really angry, her real mother tongue takes over?
(ii) Because René is himself a dominant Alsatian speaker and her reproach therefore gets through to him more effectively in the dialect?
(iii) Because, consciously or otherwise, she wants to engage the support of her mother, Marie, in this discussion, and Marie will participate far more in a conversation held in Alsatian?

These different reasons, and others, may all pertain at the same time and there are many examples of similar complexity to this. Moreover, the different forms which switching can take are almost as varied as the motivation underlying them, ranging from the insertion of specialized vocabulary from Language A into a base in Language B, to practically systematic switching by whole sentences or clauses.

It is tempting to hypothesize that each clearly identifiable language pattern corresponds to a distinct set of motivations. Lexical switches, for example, could be either the result of lacunae in the speaker's vocabulary or of the sociolinguistic influence exercised by one language on another in a given domain of use. But in reality different motivations for switching and different linguistic patterns overlap and are difficult to separate from each other: for example, in these six conversations single-word lexical switching is at its most frequent in the *same* situations as multiple switching.

One can, however, group together the main factors which determine the frequency and type of code-switching in these six conversations (Table 6.6):

1. Factors relating to the speaker's linguistic competence.
2. Factors relating to the speakers' perceptions of each other (including of their respective competence).
3. Factors relating to the characteristics of the particular conversation.
4. Factors relating to the characteristics of the spoken language.
5. Factors deriving from 'deeper' reasons: individual characteristics, language change, ethnic compromise, and social behaviour.

Below is an explanation of what is intended by these various factors in relation to the six conversations described. At the same time, I attempt to show to what extent these categories resemble those proposed by three other authors, Gumperz (1982), Saville-Troike (1982), and Valdès-Fallis (1977), who have attempted similar classifications. Note that whereas this classification is in terms of significant 'factors', Gumperz and Saville-Troike talk in terms of 'functions of code-switching', and Valdès-Fallis of its principal 'patterns'. However, as the table shows, there are numerous resemblances between the contents of the different lists; I shall also try to show how these contents could be further systematized.

Factors Relating to the Speaker's Linguistic Competence

The speaker's linguistic competence is a factor which must come before his motivations, for you can only exercise a choice to the extent that you can speak both varieties sufficiently to have an alternative.

Switching due to a competence problem does not figure as such in the other lists, although Saville-Troike and Valdès-Fallis both have a factor which they term 'lexical need'. In fact, one needs to distinguish between a need arising from the speaker's lack of competence (Hamers and Blanc 1989) and a need arising because the language itself does not contain a term for the precise nuance of meaning which is sought (Poplack (1988), calls this 'mot juste' switching). Switching which is due to a competence problem need not only be lexical, and the interplay of competences even helps determine who speaks to whom: for example, in both of the family conversations where a grandparent (mainly dialect-speaking) and a child (mainly French-speaking) are present, communication between these two generations tends to take place via the

Table 6.6. Functions/Patterns/Principal Factors in Selection and Switching

Gumperz (1982)	Saville-Troike (1982)	Valdès-Fallis (1977)	Gardner-Chloros
A. Quotations	A. Softening or strengthening of request or command	(i) *Switching patterns which occur in response to external factors*	(1) *Speaker's competence* (Saville-Troike E, Gumperz B, Valdès-Fallis G)
B. Addressee specification	B. Intensification/elmination of ambiguity (repetition)	A. Situational switches	(2) *Perception of the interlocutor* (Gumperz B, Saville-Troike F, Valdès-Fallis M)
C. Interjections	C. Humorous effect/direct quotation/imitation	B. Contextual switches	
D. Reiteration	D. Ideological statement	C. Identity markers	(3) *Characteristics of the particular conversation* (Gumperz F, Saville-Troike C, D, G, H)
E. Message qualification	E. Lexical need	D. Proper nouns	
F. Personalization v. objectivization	F. Exclusion of other people within hearing	E. Quotations and paraphrases	(4) *Characteristics of spoken language* (Gumperz A, C, D, E, Saville-Troike A, B, C, G, Valdès-Fallis H, J, L)
	G. Avoidance strategy	(ii) *Switching patterns occurring in response to internal factors*	
	H. Repair strategy	F. Random switches of high-frequency items	(5) *Deeper reasons*
		G. Switches which reflect lexical need	(i) Individual characteristics (Valdès I);
		H. Triggered switches	(ii) language change;
		I. Preformulations	(iii) ethnic compromise (Valdès F);
		J. Discourse markers	(iv) social behaviour (Valdès N).
		K. Quotations and paraphrases	
		L. Metaphorical switches	
		M. Sequential switches	
		N. Associative responses	

middle generation, the parents. This factor therefore partially covers factor B ('addressee specification') in Gumperz's list and possibly also G ('avoidance strategy') in Saville-Troike's.

A clear example of switching due to lexical need is contained in Mr Eder's utterance (Conversation A): . . . wie han sie denn e Üsdruck uf Ditsch . . . *enfin* sie mache *faillite, quoi* 'what is the expression in German . . . *well* they go *bankrupt, you know*'.

It should be stressed that in a context where the majority of speakers is capable of speaking both languages, the role of competence in their various choices is in practice very difficult to evaluate. In so far as possible, as Lüdi showed in German-speaking Switzerland (1984a: 14), speakers actively contribute to the definition of situations in which they find themselves and maintain as much freedom as possible even when external factors exercise a powerful influence on their choice.

Factors Relating to the Speakers' Perceptions of Each Other

Gumperz's function which he terms 'addressee specification' is relevant under this heading, since, as we have seen, language changes often coincide with changes of interlocutor. The characteristics of the person you are speaking to are, in fact, naturally one of the major factors in language choice and amongst these characteristics is their presumed linguistic competence. For this reason, the more speakers there are, the more language choice is likely to be unstable, and this is one possible reason why switching is more common at work than in families. For although only switches within a single utterance, addressed to one person, have been counted as such, changing languages often in order to address different people introduces into the conversation the possibility of changing rapidly from one language to another, and this possibility can then be extended to use within a single utterance for communicative purposes.

One can either adapt to one's interlocutor's language choices (Valdès-Fallis (M)) or use language choice as an avoidance strategy (as in the case of Annie Rick, who continued to speak French when her grandmother told her off in Alsatian—function F in Saville-Troike's list). One can of course also switch in order not to be understood or in order to score a point at the expense of one's interlocutor.

As to the effect exercised by the presence of a monolingual in a bilingual conversation, this can vary from the imposition of the monolingual's language on the other bilinguals (as with Annie in Conversation F) to slight modification in the form of discourse which takes account of the monolingual without completely adapting to him (as with Saleur in Conversation D).

Factors Relating to the Characteristics of the Particular Conversation

This very broad category covers factors which help determine language choice but which are themselves independent of the speaker's competence and of the interlocutor's perceived characteristics.

This category would therefore even include Gumperz's 'situational switches', that is, switches provoked by or linked to changes in physical/social context. These are covered by Valdès-Fallis's categories A and B, but they do not appear on Gumperz's list since this only covers his 'conversational' switches. Factors relating directly to the conversation itself, its topic, setting, register, purpose, etc. are grouped together in the list because:

(i) they are clearly distinguishable from the other sets of factors;
(ii) because all such factors have to be mediated or perceived by speakers to be meaningful to them, before giving rise to a linguistic 'reaction' such as a switch. Social constraints (such as those associated with a diglossic-type distribution) and connotations of particular subject-matter are also included), as are:

   (a) Gumperz's function F (personalization or objectivization of the switched segment);
   (b) switching employed for humorous effect (Saville-Troike (C));
   (c) the use of a language to symbolize a particular ideology (Saville-Troike (D));
   (d) the use of language as a repair strategy, that is when one realizes that the language spoken before was inappropriate (unless this is due to a realization about one's interlocutor, in which case it would come under (2));
   (e) the use of a language as an avoidance strategy, e.g. to avoid having to make a distinction which would be necessary in the other language, such as a *tu/vous* distinction;
   (f) the use of one language (here usually Alsatian) as an affective language and the other as a more dispassionate, distancing vehicle (we code/they code);
   (g) the use of proper nouns and names in one language rather than the other to the extent that this is connected with questions of identity (Valdès-Fallis (C)).

Any such list of factors involves simplifications and even the distinction between competence-related factors and conversation-dependent factors is not cut and dried, as there is an overlap in the area of register. A speaker may be able to manipulate the more formal registers of a language, but not the informal, slangy ones. Now in certain circumstances it is the register which best frames one's communicative intention which may determine the language spoken. An example of this occurs in Conversation E, in which Denise uses two expressions in slangy French (*Eh, il cause, là!* '*Hey, he's talking now*' [i.e. *the tape recorder is on now*] and *C'est râté* '*It's failed, it's no use*') although the rest of the time her colleagues and she quite consistently speak Alsatian. It is the slanginess itself which seems to provide the key: she uses these expressions because she knows them in French and wants to use that particular register of which they are part.

Factors Relating to the Characteristics of the Spoken Language

As it has been mentioned, certain characteristic aspects of the spoken language, in particular its discontinuous character, are exploited in bilingual discourse; the switches which coincide with breaks in speech, such as pauses, hesitations, interruptions, and self-interruptions, pass almost unnoticed at one level, but like switches at major grammatical boundaries, can serve to mark discourse movement; quotations, emphasis, backgrounding, contrasting, etc.

Gumperz (D) and Saville-Troike (B) both identify a function of code-switching which depends on message repetition (also found in the Alsatian data). The quotation function also appears on all three lists (Gumperz (A); Saville-Troike (C); Valdès-Fallis (K)). Gumperz (E) and Saville-Troike (A) identify a possible function which they term message-qualification; Valdès-Fallis (J) identifies cases, as I did, where the structuring expressions themselves are the subject of switching and others where switching serves an emphatic or contrastive purpose (L). Gumperz (C) also pin-points an 'interjection' function, another instance of switching used to get attention.

To these one must add the phenomenon of triggering, which also seems to be typical of conversational speech with its shorter planning time than the written language (Valdès-Fallis (G)). Jacobson (1978: 23) considers that triggered segments are often in a sense deliberate, since they allow the speaker 'to achieve unilinguality within the boundaries of a given syntactic unit'. In other words, by switching for a whole clause or phrase rather than a single word, one avoids switching straight back again into the matrix language. Depending on how one 'counts switches', triggering may therefore allow one to limit the number of switches in a sentence.

Factors Deriving from 'Deeper' Reasons

Like Russian dolls each fitting one within the other, each layer of explanation of switching calls for another deeper reason, each time getting closer to answering the question: 'Why change languages?'. For example, to say, as above, that there are characteristics of ordinary conversation which lend themselves particularly well to switching, begs the question: why do some participants switch more than others when they are all involved in the same conversation?

Code-switching is undoubtedly connected with individual factors which concern people's linguistic histories as well as their personalities. For example, Mr Eder in Conversation A, who loves chatting and telling stories, has far more *opportunities* to switch languages than someone who only says the minimum needed for survival. He also has more opportunity to use a number of ready-made formulas which can be encoded in either one language or the other (Valdès-Fallis (I)).

A second deeper factor is the relationship between the code-switches observed in a set of data such as this and language shift in Strasbourg. As far as single switches are concerned, we noted an indicative imbalance, French terms being used in place of Alsatian ones more often than the reverse. Many of these will, no doubt, become loans, but even when this is not so, the penetration of French into Alsatian territory in Strasbourg is striking.

Thirdly, code-switching can and does often represent a compromise between the exclusive use of one language and of the other, each with their respective cultural connotations; there are occasions, for example, when it seems too snobbish to speak French but too rustic to speak Alsatian and code-switching provides the solution. This compromise-seeking no doubt explains the very frequent use of conversational fillers in the opposite language to that of the sentence (Valdès-Fallis (F)). It may also underlie certain cases of apparently quite arbitrary switching.

Finally, when switching is very frequent indeed, one should view it as a particular kind of socially conditioned behaviour (Valdès-Fallis (N)). In the bilingual families I recorded, where each member could speak Alsatian or French according to their own preferences, switching of all types was less frequent than in work places. I have already discussed the likely origins of this situation, which are connected with the type of conversations which occur in such settings and the number of interlocutors of varying competence who interact here. Alsatian is used at work in order to create solidarity bonds between colleagues who know each other, although obviously less well than members of a family. It is used in spite of lacunae in the competence of some— especially younger—speakers and in spite of its lack of appropriate specialized vocabulary relevant to many professional fields. This desire to use Alsatian combined with an impossibility to use it to everyone and for all communicative purposes leads to frequent switching or indeed, as in conversations D and E, to mixed discourse.

In the final chapter, I shall attempt to integrate some of the factors identified here as important in switching with the results of the surveys and interviews described in earlier chapters; I shall also indicate which I feel are the most promising lines for future research.

7

Conclusions

The study of code-switching involves a constant refocusing of one's point of view from very broad to very detailed issues. Any intelligent layman can be made to understand within a couple of minutes what code-switching is and almost any bilingual would admit to practising it; many also have firmly held attitudes regarding its acceptability (Chana and Romaine 1984). The reason for its existence is simple: there is more than one variety of language in the world and those different varieties are not kept in hermetically sealed boxes. Their mutual spill over and influence is one of the major keys to understanding how languages develop, change, and die.

For the linguist, the results of language contact provide an endlessly intricate field of study; code-switching itself has developed from being considered just one among many bilingual phenomena (Haugen 1956)—and indeed something of an aberration among these (Weinreich 1953)—to being seen as central to the concerns of sociolinguists:

Code-switching, it appears, is one of the phenomena most central to the interests of sociolinguistics, as we are faced with a situation where the choice of different codes belonging to the linguistic repertoire of a speaker or speech community is determined primarily by social factors. (Mühlhäusler 1972: 172)

Alongside these social factors, many linguists today are concerned with questions of identity (Le Page and Tabouret-Keller 1985) and code-switching is rightly studied in numerous immigrant contexts where the issue of identity arises with particular poignancy (Dabène and Billiez 1986). Linguists of differing tendencies are anxious to take up the challenge which code-switching provides, as was the case with pidgins and creoles when their importance was first realized.

There are three main points I want to make at the conclusion of this study of code-switching in Strasbourg. Firstly, as this study has confirmed, code-switching is part of a complex network of symptoms or manifestations of bilingualism. The idea (Skutnabb-Kangas and Toukomaa 1976; Skutnabb-Kangas 1984) that the bilingual can in any sense be described as the sum of two monolinguals or with reference to a 'container' view of linguistic competence has been rejected both at a sociolinguistic (Martin-Jones and Romaine 1985) and a psycholinguistic level (Grosjean 1985b). It is increasingly being realized and demonstrated that bilinguals adopt strategies peculiar to themselves to manipulate and keep separate their two languages (Hamers and Blanc 1989) and that they are capable of developing third systems, codes which are not simply explicable in terms of the rule systems of the two-or-more original languages (Agnihotri 1987). Code-switching in Strasbourg varies from a limited alternation which *can* be described in terms of 'French and Alsatian' to a mixed code, some of whose social/situational characteristics have already emerged from this study but whose detailed linguistic characteristics require further investigation. It is a code used among peers who know each other well (e.g. colleagues at work or friends) rather than in families or between generations. It does not appear to be much constrained by topic, but it is strongly associated with an informal, chatty register. Its description is heavily complicated by the fact that in actual situations it coexists with, and merges into, other less intense forms of mixed language. What this means is that while one can draw the type of theoretical distinctions which I have above, actual examples which illustrate them perfectly are extreme cases and therefore difficult to come by.

Secondly, the way in which one chooses to analyse code-switching is all-important for the conclusions which one reaches. Obvious as this may seem, it is crucial to remember that code-switching is not there, like a physical object, to be put on a table or under a microscope; it is a construct, and people may reasonably differ as to its definition and scope.

In this study a choice was made to consider as code-switching only those changes of variety which occur within a single utterance or turn of speech (Chapters 4, 5, 6). Other studies (e.g. Valdès-Fallis 1977) have on the contrary concentrated on changes of variety which coincide with changes of speaker, thus highlighting the way in which language choice reflects relationships and reactions of the speakers to each other. My choice was due to a desire to concentrate on language changes connected as closely as possible to a linguistic train of thought, and as far as possible uninfluenced by any 'prompting' by the environment; this type of switching, I felt, was more likely to occur in an uninterrupted flow of speech than it was when there was a change of speaker, which might be accompanied by hints and influences difficult to detect on a recording. It is clear, however, that the distinction between Valdès-Fallis's approach and this one is ultimately artificial. Either of these approaches is likely to make distinctions between phenomena which should not be distinguished. A mid-utterance switch can perfectly well occur in response to some hint from, or realization about, one's interlocutor—and fail to make distinctions between phenomena which are in fact differently motivated: two different switches within the same utterance might be thought to be both due to lacunae in competence, or to footing, for example, a desire to highlight part of the utterance, when in fact one of them might be due to these factors and the other to a desire to be better understood, prompted by, perhaps, a slightly puzzled expression on behalf of the interlocutor. We are a long way from being able to capture the variety of motivations in such an analysis (Chapter 5), and it would be pointless to set oneself such an unattainable goal.

Another example of the arbitrariness of these analytical procedures is to be found in the distinction between single-word and multiple switches (Chapter 6). In order for this distinction—which has been adopted by numerous researchers into code-switching—to be valid, there should be some psychologically significant distinction accompanying the distinction between single-word and multiple switches. But is there? Again one is almost certainly drawing lines where there should be none and failing to draw any where they are needed. Some multiple switches are loans or set expressions, brought in to fill a gap in the matrix language or in the speaker's competence and with no negotiating or 'marked' function, whereas some single-word switches are entirely one-off, spontaneous, and highly marked in terms of the connotational meaning which they impart to the conversation—that is, the opposite of what one might superficially expect.

Equally, some apparent multiple switches are better viewed from a psychological or a pragmatic point of view as concatenations of single switches (Chapter 6), and some single switches as multiple switches which were interrupted after the first word. What is important and interesting is *why* people switch, and it is all too easy to make facile associations between a particular, linguistically defined switch type and its presumed motivations. Yet if you do not categorize individual examples correctly, then there is little point in making elaborate quantitative evaluations based on those categories. I believe that this is the problem which occurs when Poplack and others interested in showing that universal rules or constraints underlie code-switching eliminate from their analyses instances of language alternation which do not fit their proposed scheme. Since this leaves only those instances which do conform to the model, their argument is circular and cannot be disproved. The reality is not quite so tidy. Even the 'errors' and stumblings of spontaneous conversations are clearly significant and an analysis of code-switching which ignores them is ignoring half the story:

Much recent work in conversational analysis has shown that the structure of conversation including hesitations, repairs, repetitions and use of 'fillers' . . . is highly systematic and serves a range of clear communicative functions . . . These characteristics are frequently described as 'errors'; yet, since they have a clear function in spoken language, they are errors only if conversation is judged from the normative standpoint of written language. (Milroy and Milroy 1985: 141–2)

In sociolinguistics, as in other disciplines, we must be vigilant regarding the distortions which can be brought about by our method of observation and our analytical tools (Cheshire 1987). It is highly likely that grammatical analysis is an inadequate tool with which to approach code-switching and that, as in the case of child language, our efforts should be directed far more towards developing a speech act-discourse analysis-based approach (Gardner-Chloros, forthcoming).

The third point is partly, but only partly, derived from the first. If code-switching is a construct, an intellectually based way of selecting and delimiting a portion of the real world, and if people differ as to what they wish to include under that heading, then it is important to know along what dimensions they differ. I would propose that there are two such dimensions: the first is the extent to which code-switching should be considered as a synchronic or a diachronic issue, and the second is the extent to which it should be viewed as the property of a community rather than an individual, where the community can be everything from a small, close-knit immigrant group to humanity as a whole.

Synchrony/Diachrony

When languages disappear and other languages emerge, there is bound to be a transitional period, shorter or longer, during which some form of bilingualism prevails. Depending on the speed with which the change is taking place—which itself does not depend on linguistic factors—that bilingualism, at community level, can take at least two forms:

(i) there may be a large number of bilinguals within the community, and each new generation may shift its competence and its preferences slightly in favour of the new language, until the old language dies out;

(ii) there may be bilinguals only in the middle age group, the older people being monolingual in A and the younger generation monolingual in B.

There is at least one other possibility: that users of A progressively modify their A in the direction of B, and users of B modify B in the direction of A, so that eventually a convergence takes place and C emerges; but this I consider unlikely to occur in any thoroughgoing manner (Bickel-Kauffmann 1985) in Alsace.

In Alsace the situation at present is more like (i) unless one considers the very extreme age groups, say people over 80 and under 8, in which case the situation is more like (ii); the two cases described in (i) and (ii) are of course the two extreme ends of a continuum. In any of these situations one can reckon with there being some code-switching; in (i) there will be more intra-utterance and perhaps intra-clause switching than in (ii) where the code-switching will be more speaker and interlocutor-related and therefore more likely to coincide with changes of turn.

Now why does this raise a question as to whether code-switching should be viewed as a synchronic or a diachronic phenomenon? Of course it is always there to be observed, photographed at a particular moment in the history of the linguistic community. But at the same time we should always bear in mind that it is part of a diachronic process, often part of ongoing language shift and therefore that we need to consider differences between speakers and between types of switching in a dynamic manner. Both Scotton (1986) and Poplack (1987) have considered how different types of community produce different patterns of code-switching; Romaine (1989) has also discussed the likely outcome of contact between more or less typologically similar languages. All these approaches are important, but in future we should also concentrate on the different patterns present in the same community (e.g. age- or gender-related)—a synchronic view of diachronic facts (Trudgill 1988*a*).

Approaches to code-switching which attempt to extract universally applicable rules from code-switching data (Di Sciullo, Muysken, and Singh 1986) run a serious risk of ignoring the function of code-switching in language shift. What they ought to be looking at is not what is common to all bilingual speakers' code-switches at a particular moment in time, but what, if anything, is common to the type of switching which arises in the early stages of contact and the type which one finds when one of the two languages is well on the road to disappearance.

They should be looking, if they are really searching for universality, at what is common to a spontaneous importation which breaks all the proposed constraints because it is entirely new and unregulated by any norms or judgements, and well-established loans which have been adapted to fit the patterns of the receiving language—for universality cuts across time as well as space. But universal grammatical rules do not provide a suitable framework for investigating the gradual adaptation by individuals of one set of patterns to another. Fascinating work has been done in relation to the question as to which forms disappear first and which remain last in a moribund language (Dorian 1981; 1988); code-switching provides the further challenge of understanding why parts of one system are preferred to parts of another. Because it is a type of speech unregulated by overt prescriptive norms, it provides each succeeding generation with a golden opportunity to rewrite the rules followed by its elders without the latter having any firm basis from which to condemn these new variations on a mixing theme.

What we should certainly not do if we are to understand this process is to eliminate from our field of study the apparent aberrations—what Poplack has called 'incomplete acquisition and language loss' (1988) and what Bentahila and Davies (1983) on much the same basis rejected as 'performance errors'—for these variations in the general pattern provide the key to understanding the role of code-switching in language change; it is a mistake to think that linguistic descriptions must resemble photographic film shown in slow motion, that is, consist in a series of static images.

Individual, Group, Community: The Locus of Code-Switching

There is a second important reason, apart from understanding the role of code-switching in language change and shift, why we should now turn our attention to intra-group comparisons of code-switching patterns. This is because making such comparisons will help us to understand at what level code-switching behaviour is generated and the extent to which it is tied up with communication needs, discourse strategies, and people's basic identifications.

Both in Chapter 4 and Chapter 5 it emerged clearly that people's motivations for code-switching are often complex, made up of several different layers which one has to try to disentangle. For example, in the Department Stores survey, people appeared to switch abundantly in environments which were socially quite different from each other; accommodating the linguistic environment appeared to be an inadequate explanation of many cases of switching; and switching by various age-groups when addressing their own and other age-groups was clearly determined by factors other than speaker and perceived interlocutor competence only. This complexity of motivations was also apparent in Chapter 5, for example in the discussion of Agnès Rick's language choice when arguing with her husband in Conversation B. The role of personality, or if one prefers idiolect, was illustrated with respect to Mr Eder's switching in Conversation A.

To paraphrase Le Page (1978), people switch in such a way as to resemble the members of groups with which they wish, from time to time, to be identified—to the extent, as Le Page adds, that they have an opportunity to master the required forms and have access to the groups which they wish to imitate. The process of identification through switching patterns which characterizes bilingual societies is of course part of a more general process of conformism/non-conformism in language, clearly illustrated when people express approval or disapproval for particular types of switching (Chapter 2). We are constrained in our own usage by the linguistic patterns which we hear round about us, but the question is how much? It is a well-recognized danger of the sociolinguistic approach that it disguises important intra-individual variation in seeking to provide a picture of the group. This danger should make us particularly wary of very broad concepts—the classic example being diglossia, which for many years was thought to hold great explanatory power, and is now seen if anything as disguising the subtlety of linguistic hierarchies even in the most archetypal communities (Chapter 3).

Like many other linguistic concepts, diglossia is doubtless best viewed as an extreme case or as one end of a continuum. The same can be said of the concept of marked and unmarked choices: 'Markedness is a gradient, not a categorical, concept. One choice is more unmarked than others and, among marked choices, some are more marked than others' (Scotton 1987*a*). I have argued above and elsewhere that there is also a gradient relationship between code-switching and borrowing (Gardner-Chloros 1987*a*). Indeed in trying to distinguish between all kinds of variables (phonological, morphological, syntactic), a continuum seems more appropriate than trying to draw clear-cut distinctions. Cheshire (1987: 263–4) makes this point and goes on to say: 'We would do better to acknowledge the gradience and indeterminacy that exists and to look for ways of incorporating these into our analyses, rather than try to construct an intellectually "tidy" but unilluminating typology of clearcut categories, into which we then try to force our data.' The incompatibility of such clear-cut categories in sociolinguistics with a view of science based on falsifiability has recently been highlighted by Janicki (1990).

But although an increasing number of linguistic concepts which were previously thought to be categorical *are* now being seen as fuzzy-edged, there is none the less a systematicity in mixed codes, as in other forms of language, which makes acquisition possible and which remains to be elucidated (Romaine 1984). The onus is on those who reject universalist grammatical approaches to continue finding viable alternative ways to describe that shifting systematicity.

What, finally, of language in Strasbourg? A lot more could be done, at a sociolinguistic level, to describe the situation, to test the tentative conclusions of this study (Wunderlich 1988; Treffers 1988) and to assess likely future developments. This is essential if educational and other language-related policies are to be correctly formulated.

What seems to be happening at present is that there is a marked inter-generational decline in the use of the dialect, which bodes ill for its future:

The survival of any part of a linguistic tradition . . . depends in the first place on its continuing to be transmitted by successive generations to their offspring, and secondly on its continuing use by each generation after acquisition . . . Functional and substantial linguistic substitution within a total repertoire can (and usually does) proceed selectively, over quite a long period, involving many generations, before the stage is reached when what was once an entire linguistic tradition . . . is . . . jettisoned. (Denison 1988: 73)

At the same time there is a breakdown in the strict association beween language and domain which would have pertained ten or twenty years ago. Alsatian can be spoken with no sense of shame in many public places—though not necessarily in a school; French, conversely, is permeating the areas—male, working-class, agricultural, etc.—which were the traditional preserve of the dialect (Chapter 4). Since both languages can be used in an increasing number of contexts, the possibilities for code-switching are increasing. This situation is not unique and similar observations have been made, for example, by Mühlhäusler in Papua New Guinea:

To the extent that NGP [New Guinea Pidgin] is regarded to be on a par with English in a wide range of contexts, the choice of one or the other code is no longer strictly regulated ... Observations made by the author suggest that one is dealing with a transitional stage between a clear diglossic situation and the development of a linguistic continuum ... Such a situation appears to be characterized by the weakening of the situational and social constraints that previously determined code-choice. As a result, one encounters a degree of mixing where code-switching cannot easily be explained by either social or linguistic criteria. (1972: 169–70)

It is interesting to note the similarities, at this particular stage, between two linguistic situations whose ultimate outcomes are likely to be so different. Even in sociopolitically comparable situations in Europe the outcome of language contact is likely to be as varied as its premisses are complex (Baetens Beardsmore 1983).

In Alsace, while there is clearly some loss of distinctiveness of the two codes associated with code-switching, it is difficult to believe that a fully-fledged, pidginized third code could emerge and it appears far more likely at present that Alsatian will in due course disappear, having left its mark, no doubt, on the local form of French.

Fortunately that time is still a long way off and in the meantime European linguists can, thanks to these mixed varieties, enjoy some of the satisfactions of the early linguist-explorers and of those who work now in more exotic fields: that of discovering and describing highly sophisticated languages, hitherto unknown.

Appendix

SUPPLÉMENT

DE LA

GRAMMAIRE FRANÇAISE

POUR

L'ALSACE

OU

RECUEIL DES FAUTES QUE L'ON COMMET LE PLUS
ET DES RÈGLES QUE L'ON OBSERVE LE MOINS
DANS LE FRANÇAIS ALSACIEN.

PAR

Le Dr **J. CRON,**

PROFESSEUR AU GYMNASE ÉPISCOPAL DE STRASBOURG.

———————

STRASBOURG

AGENCE DE B. HERDER, PLACE DU DÔME, 18.
1902.

CAUSERIE ALSACIENNE.

Papa. — Allons, mes enfants, an b'r Tiſch jetz! *Ça* sonne juste midi.

Lisela. — Mais, papa, nous *n'osons* pas nous mettre à table; que *penses*-tu! Il faut attendre *sur* Tantela.

Maman. — Voilà *maintenant* encore une distraction! Tu ne *t'en* rappelles donc pas que nous avons invité tante Marie.

Papa. — Ah! oui, c'est *donc* vrai! S'iſch jo woor!

Josephela. — *Ça* pleut toujours; elle ne viendrà peut-être pas.

Lisela. — *Penses-tu! Pour sûr* qu'elle viendra! Elle aurait envoyé la bonne, si elle ne *pourrait* pas venir.

Josephela. — *Ça toque;* elle vient.

Papa. — Entrez, entrez!

Tante. — Bonjour biſamme, bonjour!

Lisela, Josephela. — Bonjour, tante!

Papa. — Comment ça va? Wie geht's?

Tante. — Merci! ça va bien chez moi.

Maman. — Et grand-papa, que *fait*-il?

Tante. — Il *fait* bien. Mais, tu sais, il n'aurait pas pu venir aujourd'hui; il est toujours *comme ça* fatigué.

Lisela. — C'est dommage; ça aurait été *maintenant* si bien, s'il *serait venu*.

Papa. — Jetz aber, Kinder, an b'r Tiſch! A table! D'abord la prière! Josephela, bet vor.

Maman. — Viens, Tante, mets-toi ici à côté de moi et de Josephela.

Tante. — So, Josephela, mets-toi bien assis; comme ça! Comment *ça va toujours*, mon enfant? Tu travailles toujours bien?

Josephela. — Oui, tante; e ſchaff.

Papa. — Jo, awer no lang nit gnüe. Pas assez, mon garçon. C'est une misère! Es isch e Elend.

Tante. — Ja, geht's denn nit?

Maman. — Non, es geht net güet; son maître m'a dit hier qu'il *restera assis*, s'il ne travaille pas plus.

Tante. — Josephela, Josephela, was müeß e here? *Pense donc*, c'est une honte, si tu *restes assis*.

Papa. — S'il ne *monte* pas, il sera cordonnier.

Maman. — Oh, oui! il vaut mieux qu'il soit petit ouvrier qu'un grand paresseux.

Tante. — Josephela, Josephela, schaff denn! Nous voulons le *laisser* maintenant; il pleure.

Papa. — Il a *déjà souvent pleuré;* mais ça ne sert à rien. S'il travaillait comme Lisela, à la bonne heure!

Tante. — Ah, oui! je sais bien que Lisela a toujours de bons bulletins. — C'est bien, chère Lisela; tu es *gentille.*

Josephela. — Oui, *aux filles on donne* toujours *rien que* sehr gut. Elles *l'ont bon, elles.*

Maman. — Tais-toi Josephela; si tu travaillais, tu aurais sehr gut aussi.

Josephela. — Notre maître ne donne jamais sehr gut. Les filles *l'ont bien plus facile.*

Papa. — Mon garçon, ne parle plus, et tâche de mieux faire!

Maman. — Lisela, va dire à Kätela qu'elle *doit venir avec le bœuf.*

Lisela. — Oui, maman!

Papa. — Des esch e güets Seppla gsin — net woor Tante?

Tante. — Oh oui, Kätela *peut* très bien cuire; n'est-ce pas Kätela?

Kätela. — D'Mamsel Marie esch halt net difficile.

Tante. — Un's Kätela esch zue modeste.

Kätela. — E bin au alt gnüa for's zu kenne. Het isch drißig Johr, daß e do bin.

Papa. — Do, bi uns?

Kätela. — Ja, Herr, brißig Johr!

Maman. — 'S' Kätela het racht; es esch het brißig Johr, daß es kuma isch.

Papa. — Des het e=n'er scho lang kenne saia. Des müeß gfirt sin, Kätela; am Dessert trinkjch mit uns G'sundheit. De holsch eina vom besta; hesch g'hert!

Kätela. — Merci, Herr! Sie sin züa güat.

Papa. — Nix do; hesch verstande!

Kätela. — Oui, Monsieur!

Maman. — Nous sommes sûrement bien tombés *avec* cette bonne Kätela. Elle *n'osera* plus jamais nous quitter.

Lisela. — Oui, papa a toujours dit que nous la *garderons*, quand même elle sera vieille. — N'est-ce pas, papa?

Papa. — Oui, fillettela, oui... Mais maintenant il faut boire! Tante Marie prendra *de nouveau* du rouge, n'est-ce pas, tante? Tu permets que je verse?

Tante. — Mais pas trop, mon cher; je veux mettre de l'eau *avec*. Merci! merci!

Papa. — Ah! mais voilà Kätela avec le Sürkrût. — Ah que ça a bonne mine!

Tante. — *Pour sûr!*

Papa. — Allons, mes enfants, nous allons voir ça!

Josephela. — *Ça j'aime.*

Maman. — Quoi? qu'est-ce que tu veux encore réclamer?

Josephela. — *Ça, la viande rouge j'aime le plus.*

Papa. — Toi tu prendras ce que *moi je te* donnerai. — Hasch des verstanden? Un jetz still!

Tante. — Oui, Josephela, tais-toi! Papa t'en donnera *déjà*.

Papa. — Ça c'est *maintenant* bon! Des Sürkrût isch herrlich güet. Elle est excellente... Il faut manger, tante; nous n'aurons *rien d'autre*.

Josephela. — Si, papa; tu sais le gros jambon?

Maman. — Tais-toi *une fois!* Tu n'es pas du tout sage aujourd'hui!

Papa. — Le voilà, le jambon!... Kätela mettez-le ici... ſo. Et maintenant cherchez cette bouteille; nous allons tout à l'heure boire à votre santé.

Kätela. — Tout de suite, Monsieur.

Maman. — Sie brengt glich au b'Gläſer, wenn Sie wel ſo güet ſin.

Kätela. — Ja, Madam!

Papa. — *Ça c'est maintenant pourtant encore une fois trop fort.*

Maman. — Quoi!

Papa. — Voilà ce sale chien qui m'a enlevé un gros morceau de jambon. 'Nüß mit'm. *Devant la porte avec lui!*

Lisela. — Geſch 'nüß, bü Böſer! *Va dehors.*

Kätela. — Was iſch?

Papa. — Rien; c'est le chien. — Viens, maintenant, Kätela, prends ce verre... Eh ben, Kätela, nous buvons à votre santé, *nous nous remercions tous pour* les bonnes choses que vous nous cuisez depuis trente ans. Un Sie ſoll noch lang, lang bi uns glückli un zufriba lewa. G'ſundheit, Kätela!

Tous. — G'ſundheit, Kätela!

Josephela. — s'Kätela ſoll lewa!

Maman. — Nous prendrons le café dehors, Kätela; il fait meilleur *que dedans.*

Lisela. — Je *veux* aider Kätela, n'est-ce pas, maman?

Maman. — Oui, mon enfant, va gentiment. Porte les tasses, le sucre et tout dehors.

Lisela. — *Je dois* faire la prière d'abord?

Maman. — Ja, Kind, nous *voulons* prier...

Papa. — Seppela, toi, tu vas maintenant me *chercher* les cigares; et ne *fais pas longtemps!*

Josephela. — Oui, papa!

Tante. — Tu *es* déjà fini, Lisela?

Lisela. — Oui, tante; tout est dehors.

Tante. — Mets ton chapeau, mon enfant, à cause du soleil.

Lisela. — Oui, tante.

Josephela. — Papa, do fin d'Cigarra !

Papa. — So, merci ; jetz 'nüß ! *maintenant dehors !*

References

AGNIHOTRI, R. M. (1987), *Crisis of Identity: The Sikhs in England* (New Delhi: Bahri).

ALBERT, M. L. and OBLER, L. K. (1978), *The Bilingual Brain* (New York: Academic Press).

AUER, J. C. P. and DI LUZIO, A. (1982), *The Development of Italian/German Alternation among Italian Migrant Children in Germany*, Projekt: 'Muttersprache italienischer Gastarbeiterkinder' (Univ. of Konstanz).

BAETENS BEARDSMORE, H. (1983). 'Substratum, Adstratum and Residual Bilingualism in Brussels', *Journal of Multilingual and Multicultural Development*, 4/1, pp. 1–14.

BAL, Willy (1981), 'Au sujet du discours mixte', in P. Wald (ed.), *Le Changement linguistique* (Univ. of Nice).

BENTAHILA, A. and DAVIES, E. E. (1983), 'The Syntax of Arabic–French Code-Switching', *Lingua*, 59, pp. 301–30.

BERK-SELIGSON, S. (1986), 'Linguistic Constraints on Intrasentential Code-Switching: A Study of Spanish/Hebrew Bilingualism', *Lang. Soc.*, 15, pp. 313–48.

BERNSTEIN, B. (1971–2), *Class, Codes and Control*, i and ii (London: Routledge & Kegan Paul).

BEYER, E. and MATZEN, R. (1969), *Atlas linguistique et ethnographique de l'Alsace*, i, *L'Homme—Der Mensch* (Paris: CNRS).

BICKEL-KAUFFMANN, M.-M. (1983), 'Les Consonnes du parler d'Andolsheim: étude expérimentale en milieu bilingue', thèse 3ème cycle, Univ. des Sciences Humaines de Strasbourg.

BLOM, J. P. and GUMPERZ, J. J. (1972), 'Social Meaning in Linguistic Structures: Code-Switching in Norway', in J. Gumperz and D. Hymes (eds.), *Directions in Sociolinguistics* (New York: Holt Rinehart & Winston), pp. 407–34.

BOULOT, S. and BOIZON-FRADET, D. (1987), 'Un siècle de réglementation à l'école', *France, pays multilingue*, i, ed. G. Vermès and J. Boutet (Paris: L'Harmattan), pp. 163–88.

BREITBORDE, L. B. (1983), 'Levels of Analysis in Sociolinguistic Explanation: Bilingual Codeswitching, Social Relations, and Domain Theory', *International Journal of the Sociology of Language*, 39, pp. 4–45.

CARAMAZZA, A., YENI-KOMSHIAN, G., and ZURIF, E. B. (1974), 'Bilingual Switching: The Phonological Level', *Canadian Journal of Psychology*, 28/3, pp. 310–18.

CARRINGTON, L. D. (1989), 'Acquiring Language in a Creole Setting: Theoretical and Methodological Issues', *Papers and Reports on Child Language Development*, 28, pp. 65–71.

CEDERGREN, H. J. (1973). 'On the Nature of Variable Constraints', in C.-J. N. Bailey and R. W. Shuy (eds.), *New Ways of Analysing Variation in English* (Washington, DC: Georgetown Univ. Press), pp. 13–22.

—— and SANKOFF, D. (1974), 'Variable Rules: Performance as a Statistical Reflection of Competence', *Language*, 40/2, pp. 333–55.

CHAMBERS, J. K. and TRUDGILL, P. (1980), *Dialectology*, Cambridge Textbooks in Linguistics (Cambridge: CUP).

CHANA, U. and ROMAINE, S. (1984), 'Evaluative Reactions to Panjabi/English Code-Switching', *Journal of Multilingual and Multicultural Development*, 6, pp. 447–73.

CHESHIRE, J. (1987), 'Syntactic Variation, the Linguistic Variable and Sociolinguistic Theory', *Linguistics*, 25, pp. 257–82.

CHOMSKY, N. (1965), *Aspects of the Theory of Syntax* (Cambridge, Mass.: MIT Press).

CLYNE, M. G. (1967), *Transference and Triggering: Observations on the Language Assimilation of Postwar German-Speaking Migrants in Australia* (The Hague: Martinus Nijhoff).

— (1969), 'Switching between Language Systems', *Proceedings of the Tenth International Congress of Linguists*, 1, pp. 343–9.

— (1981), '"Second Generation" Foreigner Talk in Australia', *International Journal of the Sociology of Language*, 28, pp. 69–80.

— (1987), 'Constraints on Code Switching: How Universal are They?', *Linguistics*, 25, pp. 739–64.

COHEN-SOLAL, A. (1985), *Sartre (1905–1980)* (Paris: Gallimard).

COLE, R. L. (1975), 'Divergent and Convergent Attitudes towards the Alsatian Dialect', *Anthropological Linguistics*, 17/6, pp. 293–304.

COSO-CALAME, F. DEL, PIETRO, F. DE, and OESCH-SERRA, C. (1983),'La Compétence de communication bilingue: étude fonctionelle des code-switchings dans le discours des migrants espagnols et italiens à Neuchâtel (Suisse)', Talk given at the Romanistentag, Berlin.

COUPLAND, N. (1984). 'Accommodation at Work: Some Phonological Data and their Applications', *International Journal of the Sociology of Language*, 46, pp. 49–70.

— (1985), 'Hark, hark the lark: Social Motivations for Phonological Style-Shifting', *Language and Communication*, 5/3, pp. 153–71.

CRON, J. (1902), *Supplément de la grammaire française pour l'Alsace ou recueil des fautes que l'on commet le plus et des règles que l'on observe le moins dans le français alsacien* (Strasbourg: B. Herder, 18 place du Dôme).

CRYSTAL, D. (1980), *A First Dictionary of Linguistics and Phonetics* (London: André Deutsch).

DABÈNE, L. and BILLIEZ, J. (1986), 'Code-Switching in the Speech of Adolescents Born of Immigrant Parents', *Studies in Second Language Acquisition*, 8, pp. 309–25.

DE FERAL, C. (1979), 'Ce que parler veut dire: essai de définition linguistique et socio-linguistique du pidgin English camerounais', in G. Manessy and P. Wald (eds.), *Plurilinguisme: normes, situations, stratégies* (Paris: L'Harmattan), pp. 103–29.

DECHERT, H. W. (1982), *First and Second Language Processing: Similarities and Differences*, First AILA Commission on Psycholinguistics International Conference: First and Second Language Learning: Similarities and Differences, Milan, 1–3 Nov. 1982.

DENISON, N. (1972), 'Some Observations on Language Variety and Plurilingualism', in J. B. Pride and J. Holmes (eds.), *Sociolinguistics* (Harmondsworth: Penguin).

— (1982), 'A Linguistic Ecology for Europe', *Folia Linguistica: Acta Societatis Linguisticae Europeae*, 16/1–4, pp. 5–16.

— (1987), 'Sauris, a Typical "Linguistic Island" in the Carnian Alps', *Isole linguistiche e culturali*, Proceedings of the Twenty-Fourth AIMAV Colloquy, Univ. of Udine, 13–16 May 1987, pp. 65–75.

DI PIETRO, R. (1978), 'Code-Switching as a Verbal Strategy among Bilinguals', in

M. Paradis (ed.), *Aspects of Bilingualism* (Columbia, SC: Hornbeam Press), pp. 275–83.

DI SCIULLO, A. M., MUYSKEN, P., and SINGH, R. (1986), 'Government and Code-Mixing', *Journal of Linguistics*, 22, pp. 1–24.

DORIAN, N. C. (1981), *Language Death: The Life Cycle of a Scottish Gaelic Dialect* (Philadelphia: Univ. of Pennsylvania Press).

—— (1984), Review of Rudolph Muhr's 'Sprachwandel als soziales Phänomen: eine empirische Studie zu soziolinguistischen und soziopsychologischen Faktoren des Sprachwandels im südlichen Burgenland', *Language in Society*, 13/2.

—— (ed.) (1988), *Investigating Obsolescence: Studies in Language Contraction and Death* (Cambridge: CUP).

EDWARDS, J. (1985), *Language, Society and Identity* (Oxford: Blackwell).

ELIASSON, S. (1989), 'English–Maori Language Contact: Code-switching and the Free Morpheme Constraint', Reports from Uppsala Univ. Department of Linguistics, 18.

Encyclopédie de L'Alsace (1985), 'Eckwersheim' (Strasbourg: Publitotal).

FANTINI, A. E. (1978), 'Bilingual Behaviour and Social Cues: Case-Studies of Two Bilingual Children' in M. Paradis (ed.), *Aspects of Bilingualism* (Columbia, SC: Hornbeam Press), pp. 283–302.

FERGUSON, C. A. (1959), 'Diglossia', *Word*, 15, pp. 325–40. (repr. in P. Giglioli (ed.) (1972), *Language and Social Context* (Harmondsworth: Penguin), pp. 232–52).

FISCHER, A. (1979), *Le Code-switching à Sarrebourg*, Mémoire de maîtrise, Univ of Strasbourg II.

—— (1982), 'De quelques aspects du code-switching à Sarrebourg (Moselle)', *Recherches Linguistiques* ('Articles for M. Philipp').

FISHMAN, J. A. (1972), 'Domains and the Relationship between Micro and Macro Sociolinguistics', in J. J. Gumperz and D. Hymes (eds.), *Directions in Sociolinguistics* (New York: Holt, Rinehart & Winston), pp. 435–53.

—— (1965), 'Who Speaks What Language to Whom and When?', *La Linguistique*, 2, pp. 67–87.

—— TABOURET-KELLER, A., CLYNE, M., KRISHNAMURTI, B., and ABDULAZIZ, M. (eds.) (1986), *The Fergusonian Impact*, 2 vols. (Berlin: Mouton de Gruyter).

GAFARANGA, J. (1987), 'Code-switching et/ou le vernaculaire bilingue au Rwanda', Paper given at the Colloquy *Contacts de Langues: quels modèles?* Univ. of Nice, 28–30 Sept. 1987.

GAL, S. (1979), *Language Shift: Social Determination of Linguistic Change in Bilingual Austria* (New York: Academic Press).

—— (1983), 'Comments on Breitborde: "Levels of Analysis in Sociolinguistic Explanation"', *International Journal of the Sociology of Language*, 39, pp. 63–72.

GARCIA, E. E. (1980), 'The Function of Language-Switching during Bilingual Mother–Child Interactions', *Journal of Multilingual and Multicultural Development*, 1/3, pp. 243–52.

GARDNER-CHLOROS, P. H. (1983), 'Code-switching: approches principales et perspectives', *La Linguistique*, 19/2, pp. 21–53.

—— (1985), 'Language Selection and Switching among Strasbourg Shoppers', *International Journal of the Sociology of Language*, 54, pp. 117–35.

—— (1987a), 'Code-Switching in Relation to Language Contact and Convergence',

Devenir bilingue—parler bilingue, actes du 2ème colloque sur le bilinguisme, Univ. of Neuchâtel, Sept. 1984, Linguistische Arbeiten, Niemeyer (Tübingen), pp. 99–115.

GARDNER-CHLOROS, P. H. (1987*b*), 'La cigogne et l'autruche, ou l'éducation linguistique dans le Cité des Chasseurs', *Enfance*, 40/1–2, pp. 27–37.

— (1988), 'How to Kill Dialects and Influence People', *Isole linguistiche e culturali*, Proceedings of the Twenty-Fourth AIMAV Colloquy, 13–16 May 1987, University of Udine, pp. 209–17.

— (1990), 'Code-Switching and Child Language: A Comparison', in R. Jacobson (ed.), *Code-Switching as a Worldwide Phenomenon* (New York: Peter Lang).

GENESEE, F. and BOURHIS, R. Y. (1982), 'The Social Psychological Significance of Code-Switching in Cross-Cultural Communication', *Journal of Language and Social Psychology*, 1/1, pp. 1–27.

GILES, H., BOURHIS, R. Y., and TAYLOR, D. M. (1977), 'Towards a Theory of Language in Ethnic Group Relations', in H. Giles (ed.), *Language Ethnicity and Intergroup Relations* (London: Academic Press).

GILES, H. and SMITH, P. (1979), 'Accommodation Theory: Optimal Levels of Convergence', in H. Giles and R. St Clair (eds.), *Language and Social Psychology* (Oxford: Blackwell), pp. 45–66.

GOFFMAN, E. (1981), *Forms of Talk* (Oxford: Blackwell).

GREEN, D. W. (1986), 'Control, Activation and Resource: A Framework and a Model for the Control of Speech in Bilinguals', *Brain and Language*, 27, pp. 210–23.

GRICE, H. (1975), 'Logic and Conversation', in P. Cole and J. L. Morgan (eds.), *Syntax and Semantics* (New York: Academic Press), iii, 41–58.

GROSJEAN, F. (1982), *Life with Two Languages* (Cambridge, Mass.: Harvard Univ. Press).

— (1985*a*), 'Polyglot Aphasics and Language Mixing: A Comment on Perecman', *Brain and Language*, 26, pp. 349–55.

— (1985*b*), 'The Bilingual as a Competent but Specific Speaker–Hearer', *Journal of Multilingual and Multicultural Development*, 6/6, pp. 467–77.

— (1988), 'Exploring the Recognition of Guest Words in Bilingual Speech', *Language and Cognitive Processes*, 3/3, pp. 233–74.

— and SOARES, C. (1986), 'Processing Mixed Language: Some Preliminary Findings', in J. Vaid (ed.), *Language Processing in Bilinguals: Psycholinguistic and Neuropsychological Perspectives* (Hillsdale, NJ: Lawrence Earlbaum Associates).

GUMPERZ, J. J. (1964), 'Hindi–Punjabi Code-Switching in Delhi', *Proceedings of the Ninth International Congress of Linguistics*, pp. 115–24.

— (1967), 'On the Linguistic Markers of Bilingual Communication', *Journal of Social Issues*, 23/2, pp. 48–57.

— (1969), 'Cognitive Aspects of Bilingual Communication', working paper no. 28, Language Behaviour Research Laboratory (Berkeley, Calif.: Univ. of California Press).

— (1970), 'Verbal Strategies in Multilingual Communication', working paper no. 36, Language Behaviour Research Laboratory (Berkeley, Calif.: Univ. of California Press).

— (1972), 'The Communicative Competence of Bilinguals: Some Hypotheses and Suggestions for Research', 1/1, pp. 143–54.

— (1982), *Discourse Strategies* (Cambridge: CUP).

HAMERS, J. F. and BLANC, M. (1989), *Bilinguality and Bilingualism* (Cambridge: CUP).

HASSELMO, N. (1972), 'Code-Switching as Ordered Selection', *Studies for Einar Haugen* (The Hague: Mouton).

HAUGEN, E. (1956), 'Bilingualism in the Americas: A Bibliography and Research Guide', *Publications of the American Dialect Society*, 26 (Alabama: Univ. of Alabama Press).

—— (1972*a*), 'The Analysis of Linguistic Borrowing', in E. Scherabon Firchow, K. Grimstad, N. Hasselmo, and W. A. O'Neil (eds.), *Studies by Einar Haugen* (The Hague: Mouton), pp. 161–86.

—— (1972*b*), *The Ecology of Language* (Stanford, Calif.: Stanford Univ. Press).

HOFFET, F. (1951), *Psychanalyse de l'Alsace* (Colmar: Alsatia).

HUG, M. (1975), 'La Situation en Alsace', *Langue Française*, 25, pp. 112–20.

JACOBSON, R. (1978), 'Anticipatory Embedding and Imaginary Content: Two Newly Identified Codeswitching Variables', in A. G. Lozano (ed.), *Swallow VII: Bilingual and Biliterate Perspectives* ed. A. G. Lozano (Boulder, Colorado: Univ. of Colorado), pp. 16–25.

JADIN, N. (1985), 'Modalisateurs dans le français contemporain en Alsace', in G. Salmon (ed.), *Le Français en Alsace*, (Paris: Slatkine).

JAKOBOVITS, L. A. (1968), 'Dimensionality of Compound-Coordinate Bilingualism', *Language Learning*, special issue no. 3, pp. 29–49.

JAKOBSON, R. (1963), *Essais de linguistique générale* (Paris: Éditions de Minuit).

JANICKI, K. (1990), *Toward Non-Essentialist Sociolinguistics*, (Berlin: Mouton de Gruyter).

KACHRU, B. B. (1978), 'Code Mixing as a Communicative Strategy', in J. Alatis (ed.), *International Dimensions of Bilingual Education* (Washington DC: Georgetown Univ. Press).

KALLEN, J. L. (1981), 'The Irish Language in the United States' (unpub. MS.).

KOLERS, P. A. (1966), 'Reading and Talking Bilingually', *American Journal of Psychology*, 79, pp. 357–76.

KUO, E. C. Y. (1974), 'Bilingual Pattern of a Chinese Immigrant Group in the United States', *Anthropological Linguistics*, 16/3, pp. 128–40.

LABOV, W. (1978*a*), 'The Social Stratification of (R) in New York City Department Stores', *Sociolinguistic Patterns*, pp. 43–70 (Oxford: Blackwell).

—— (1978*b*), *Sociolinguistic Patterns* (Oxford: Blackwell).

LABRIE, N. (1988), 'Social Networks and Code-switching: A Sociolinguistic Investigation of Italians in Montreal', in N. Dittmar and P. Schlobinski (eds.), *The Sociolinguistics of Urban Vernaculars: Case Studies and their Evaluation* (New York: Mouton de Gruyter), pp. 217–31.

LADIN, W. (1982), *Der elsässische Dialekt—Museumsreif? Analyse einer Umfrage* (Strasbourg: Salde).

LAMBERT, W. E. and RAWLINGS, C. (1969), 'Bilingual Processing of Mixed-Language Associative Networks', *Journal of Verbal Learning and Verbal Behaviour*, 8, pp. 604–9.

LAVENDERA, B. R. (1978), 'The Variable Component in Bilingual Performance', *International Dimensions of Bilingual Education* (Washington, DC: Georgetown Univ. Press), pp. 391–409.

LAWTON, D. (1979), 'Code-shifting in Puerto Rican Spanish/English', *Linguistics*, 17, pp. 257–65.

LEOPOLD, W. F. (1939–49), *Speech Development of a Bilingual Child* (Evanston, Ill.: Norwestern Univ. Press).

LE PAGE, R. B. (1978), '"Projection, Focussing, Diffusion" or Steps Towards a Sociolinguistic Theory of Language', Society for Caribbean Linguistics, occasional paper
no. 9 (reprinted in *York Papers in Linguistics*, 9 (1980)).

—— (1989), 'What is a Language?' Lecture delivered at the Univ. of York, Mar. 1988,
York Papers in Linguistics, 13, pp. 9–24.

—— and TABOURET-KELLER, A. (1985), *Acts of Identity* (Cambridge: CUP).

LÉVY, P. (1929), *Histoire linguistique d'Alsace et de Lorraine* (Paris: Les Belles Lettres).

LINDHOLM, K. J. and PADILLA, A. M. (1978), 'Language Mixing in Bilingual Children',
Journal of Child Language, 5, pp. 327–35.

LIPSKI, J. M. (1978), 'Code Switching and the Problem of Bilingual Competence', in
M. Paradis (ed.), *Aspects of Bilingualism* (Columbia, SC: Hornbeam Press).

LÜDI, G. (1984), 'Constance et variation dans le choix de langue: l'exemple de trois
groupes de migrants bilingues à Neuchâtel (Suisse)', Bulletin de la section de
Linguistique de la Faculté de Lettres de Lausanne, 6, pp. 181–203.

—— (1986),'Forms and Functions of Bilingual Speech in Pluricultural Migrant
Communities in Switzerland', in J. A. Fishman, A. Tabouret-Keller, M. Clyne,
B. Krishnamurti, and M. Abdulaziz (eds.), *The Fergusonian Impact*, 2 vols. (Berlin:
Mouton de Gruyter), ii. 217–37.

MCCORMICK, K. (1989), 'English and Afrikaans in District Six: A Sociolinguistic Study',
D.Phil. thesis, Univ. of Cape Town.

MACKEY, W. F. (1979), 'L'irrédentisme linguistique: une enquête témoin', in
G. Manessy and P. Wald (eds.), *Plurilinguisme: normes, situations, stratégies* (Paris:
L'Harmattan), pp. 257–84.

MACNAMARA, J. (1971), 'The Bilingual's Linguistic Performance: A Psychological
Overview', *Journal of Social Issues*, 23/2, pp. 67–71.

—— and KUSHNIR, S. L. (1971), 'Linguistic Independence of Bilinguals: The Input
Switch', *Journal of Verbal Learning and Verbal Behaviour*, 10, pp. 480–78.

MARCELLESI, J.-B. (1989), 'Quelques problèmes de l'hégémonie culturelle en France:
langue nationale et langues régionales', *International Journal of the Sociology of Language*,
21, pp. 63–80.

—— and LE GRECO (1975), 'L'Enseignement des "langues régionales"', *Langue Française*,
25.

MARTIN-JONES, M. (1980), 'Code-Switching as a Mode of Discourse: Some Evidence
from Bilingual Communities in Britain', Paper presented at the First International
Conference on Minority Languages, Univ. of Glasgow, 8–13 Sept. 1980.

—— and ROMAINE, S. (1985), 'Semilingualism: A Half-baked Theory of Communicative
Competence' *Applied Linguistics*, 6/2, pp. 105–17.

MARTINET, A. (1970), *Éléments de linguistique générale* (Paris: Armand Colin).

MATERS, K. (1979), 'An Evaluation of Syntactic Constraints on Code-Switching and
their Potential Application to Dutch/English', M.Phil. thesis, Cambridge.

MATZEN, R. (1973), 'Sprachliches aus dem Elsass', *Dialekt als Sprachbarriere*, pp. 77–87.

—— (1977), 'Le Français alsacien d'aujourd'hui', *Ethnologie Française*, 3, pp. 3–4.

—— (1980), *Dichte isch Bichte: Gedichte in Strassburger Mundart* (Kehl: Morstadt Verlag).

MILROY, J. and MILROY, L. (1985), *Authority in Language: Investigating Language Prescription
and Standardisation* (London: Routledge & Kegan Paul).

MILROY, L. (1980), *Language and Social Networks* (Oxford: Blackwell).

—— (1987), *Observing and Analysing Natural Language* (Oxford: Blackwell).

MÜHLHÄUSLER, P. (1982), 'Code-Switching in Papua New Guinea: Local Languages versus New Guinea Pidgin, Hiri Motu and English', in S. A. Wurm (ed.), *New Guinea and Neighbouring Areas: A Sociolinguistic Laboratory* (The Hague: Mouton).

NADKARNI, M. V. (1975), 'Bilingualism and Syntactic Change in Konkani', *Language*, 51, pp. 672–83.

NEUFELD, G. G. (1976), 'The Bilingual's Lexical Store', *IRAL*, 14/1, pp. 15–35.

PARADIS, M. (ed.) (1983), *Readings on Aphasia in Bilinguals and Polyglots* (Montreal: Didier).

—— and LEBRUN, Y. (1984) (eds.), *Early Bilingualism and Child Development* (Lisse: Swets and Zeitlinger BV).

PARKIN, D. J. (1974), 'Language Switching in Nairobi', in W. H. Whiteley (ed.), *Language in Kenya* (Oxford: OUP), pp. 189–214.

PENFIELD, W. and ROBERTS, L. (1959), *Speech and Brain Mechanisms* (Princeton NJ: Princeton Univ. Press).

PFAFF, C. W. (1979), 'Constraints on Language Mixing: Intrasentential Code-Switching and Borrowing in Spanish/English', *Language*, 55/2, pp. 291–318.

PHILIPP, M. (1965), 'Le Système phonologique du parler de Blaesheim', thèse, Univ. des Sciences Humaines de Strasbourg.

—— (1978), 'Abschliessende Bemerkungen zum Thema Dialekt', in A. Finck, R. Matzen, and M. Philipp (eds.), *Mundart und Mundartdichtung im Alemanischen Sprachraum—Situationsberichte* (Strasbourg: Institut de dialectologie alsacienne), pp. 71–81.

—— (1985), 'L'Accent alsacien', in G. L. Salmon (ed.), *Le Français en Alsace* (Paris: Slatkine), pp. 19–27.

—— and BOTHOREL-WITZ, A. (1989), 'Low Alemannic', in C. U. J. Russ (ed.), *The Dialects of Modern German: A Linguistic Survey* (London: Routledge & Kegan Paul).

—— —— and SPINDLER, S. (1984), *Atlas linguistique et ethnographique de l'Alsace*, ii. *Les Animaux, phénomènes atmosphériques* (Paris: CNRS).

PHILIPPS, E. (1975), *Les Luttes linguistiques en Alsace jusqu'en 1945* (Griesheim-sur-Souffel: Éditions Culture Alsacienne).

POPLACK, S. (1980), ' "Sometimes I'll start a sentence in English y terminó en español": Toward a Typology of Code-Switching', *Linguistics*, 18, pp. 581–618.

—— (1983), 'Intergenerational Variation in Language Use and Structure in a Bilingual Context', *Multilingual Matters*, 8, pp. 42–70.

—— (1988), 'Contrasting Patterns of Code-Switching in Two Communities', in M. Heller (ed.), *Code-Switching: Anthropological and Sociolinguistic Perspectives* (Berlin: Mouton de Gruyter), pp. 215–45.

—— and SANKOFF, D. (1984), 'Borrowing: The Synchrony of Integration', *Linguistics*, 22, pp. 99–135.

—— WHEELER, S., and WESTWOOD, A. (1987), 'Distinguishing Language Contact Phenomena: Evidence from Finnish–English Bilingualism', *The Nordic Languages and Modern Linguistics*, 6, ed. P. Lilius and M. Saari (Helsinki: Univ. of Helsinki Press).

POPPER, K. (1959). *The Logic of Scientific Discovery* (London: Hutchinson).

PRESTON, M. S. and LAMBERT, W. E. (1969), 'Interlingual Interference in a Bilingual Version of the Stroop Color-Word Task', *Journal of Verbal Learning and Verbal Behaviour*, 8, pp. 295–301.

RAMPTON, M. B. H. (1987), 'Uses of English in a Multilingual British Peergroup', Ph.D. thesis, Univ. of London.

ROMAINE, S. (1982), *Socio-Historical Linguistics: Its Status and Methodology*, Cambridge Studies in Linguistics, 34 (Cambridge: CUP).

—— (1984), *The Language of Children and Adolescents: The Acquisition of Communicative Competence* (Oxford: Blackwell).

—— (1986), 'The Syntax and Semantics of the Code-Mixed Compound Verb in Panjabi/ English Bilingual Discourse', in D. Tannen and J. Alatis (eds.), *Language and Linguistics: The Interdependence of Theory, Data and Application* (Washington, DC: Georgetown Univ. Press), pp. 35–49.

—— (1989), *Bilingualism* (Oxford: Blackwell).

RONJAT, J. (1913), *Le Développement du langage observé chez un enfant bilingue* (Paris: Champion).

RUBIN, J. (1962), 'Bilingualism in Paraguay', *Anthropological Linguistics*, 4/1, pp. 52–8.

RUSS, C. U. J. (1988), *The Dialects of Modern German: A Linguistic Survey* (London: Routledge & Kegan Paul).

SALMON, G. (ed.) (1985), *Le Français en Alsace* (Paris: Slatkine).

SANKOFF, D. and POPLACK, S. (1981), 'A Formal Grammar for Code-Switching', *Papers in Linguistics*, 14/1, pp. 3–46.

——, —— and VANNIARAJAN, S. (1986), 'The Case of the Nonce Loan in Tamil', Technical report 1348, Centre de recherches mathématiques, Univ. of Montreal.

SARG, F. (1981), *Aspects de la Robertsau* (Strasbourg: Éditions Oberlin).

SAVILLE-TROIKE, M. (1982), *The Ethnography of Communication: An Introduction* (Oxford: Blackwell).

SCHUFFENECKER, G. (1981), 'Mode de vie en Alsace', Institut National de la statistique et des études économiques, *Dernières Nouvelles d'Alsace*, 6–15 Feb. 1981.

SCOTTON, C. M. (1976), 'Strategies of Neutrality: Language Choice in Uncertain Situations', *Language*, 52/4, pp. 919–41.

—— (1982), 'The possibility of Code-Switching: Motivation for Maintaining Multi-lingualism', *Anthropological Linguistics*, 24, pp. 432–43.

—— (1983), 'The Negotiation of Identities in Conversation: A Theory of Markedness and Code Choice', *International Journal of Sociology of Language*, 44, pp. 115–36.

—— (1986a), 'Code-Switching as an Unmarked Choice and Morpheme Constraints', Paper presented at the Fifteenth Annual Conference on New Ways of Analysing Variation, 17–19 Oct. 1986, Stanford.

—— (1986b), 'Diglossia and Code Switching', in J. A. Fishman, A. Tabouret-Keller, M. Clyne, B. Krishnamurti, and M. Abdulaziz (eds.), *The Fergusonian Impact*, 2 vols. (Berlin: Mouton de Gruyter), ii. 403–17.

—— (1987a), 'Code-Switching and Types of Multilingual Communities', in P. Lowenberg (ed.), *Language Spread and Language Policy* (Washington DC: Georgetown Univ. Press), pp. 61–82.

—— (1987b), 'Differentiating Borrowing and Codeswitching', in *Linguistic Change and Contact*, Proceedings of the Sixteenth Annual Conference on New Ways of Analysing Variation, ed. K. Ferrara, B. Brown, K. Walters, and J. Baugh (Austin, Tex.: Univ. of Texas Dept. of Linguistics).

—— (1988), 'Code Switching as Indexical of Social Negotiations', in M. Heller (ed.), *Codeswitching: Anthropological and Linguistic Aspects* (Berlin: Mouton de Gruyter), pp. 151–86.

— and URY, W. (1977), 'Bilingual Strategies: The Social Functions of Code-Switching', *International Journal of the Sociology of Language*, 13, pp. 5–20.

SELIGMANN, N. (1979), 'Connaissance déclarée du dialecte et de l'allemand', Survey conducted by the Institut National de la Statistique et des Études Économiques, *Chiffres pour l'Alsace*, 4, pp. 21–30.

SHAFFER, D. (1978), 'The Place of Code-Switching in Linguistic Contacts', in M. Paradis (ed.), *Aspects of Bilingualism* (Columbia, SC: Hornbeam Press), pp. 265–75.

SINGH, R. (1983), 'We, They, and Us: A Note on Code-Switching and Stratification in North India', *Language in Society*, 12/1, pp. 71–3.

SKUTNABB-KANGAS, T. (1984), 'Bilingualism or Not: The Education of Minorities' (Clevedon: Multilingual Matters).

— and TOUKOMAA, P. (1976), 'Teaching Migrant Children their Mother Tongue and Learning the Language of the Host Country in the Context of the Sociocultural Situation of the Migrant Family' (Helsinki: Finnish National Commission for Unesco).

SOBRERO, A. (1988), 'Villages and Towns in Salento; the Way Code-Switching Switches', in N. Dittmar and P. Schlobinski (eds.), *The Sociolinguistics of Urban Vernaculars: Case Studies and their Evaluation* (New York: Mouton de Gruyter), pp. 207–15

STUBBS, M. (1983), *Discourse Analysis: The Sociolinguistic Analysis of Natural Language* (Oxford: Blackwell).

SWAIN, M. (1971), 'Bilingualism, Monolingualism and Code Acquisition', Paper presented at the Child Language Conference, Chicago.

TABOURET-KELLER, A. (1969), *Le Bilinguisme de l'enfant avant 6 ans: étude en milieu alsacien*, thèse lettres, Univ. of Strasbourg II.

— (1983), 'Switching from a Psychological Point of View', *International Journal of the Sociology of Language*, 39, pp. 139–49.

— (1985), 'Diglossie', *Encyclopédie de L'Alsace*, ix (Strasbourg: Publitotal).

— (ed.) (1985), 'Preface: Sociolinguistics in France: Current Research in Urban Settings', *International Journal of the Sociology of Language*, 54, pp. 5–15.

— (ed.) (1981), 'Regional Languages in France', *International Journal of the Sociology of Language*, 29.

— (1990), 'Emprunts et alternances lexicales en Alsace', Actes du 16ème colloque international de linguistique fonctionelle, Paris-Sorbonne 1989 (Istanbul: Istikal).

— and GARDNER-CHLOROS, P. (1987), 'Plurilinguisme', *Encyclopédie universalis*, xiii. (Paris: Éditions Universalis) pp. 852–7.

— and LUCKEL, F. (1981a), 'La Dynamique sociale du changement linguistique: quelques aspects de la situation rurale en Alsace', *International Journal of the Sociology of Language*, 29, pp. 51–66.

— and — (1981b), 'Maintien de l'alsacien et adoption du français: éléments de la situation linguistique en milieu rural en Alsace', *Langages*, 61, pp. 39–62.

TAYLOR, I. (1971), 'How are Words from Two Languages Organised in Bilinguals' Memory?' *Canadian Journal of Psychology*, 25/3, pp. 228–39.

THELANDER, M. (1976), 'Code-Switching or Code-Mixing? Sociolinguistic Research in Sweden and Finland', *International Journal of the Sociology of Language*, 10, pp. 103–23.

THOMASON, S. G. (1986), 'On Establishing External Causes of Language Change', from

Proceedings of Eastern States Conference on Linguistics, Oct. 1985, ed. S. Choi *et al.* (Columbus, Ohio: Ohio State Univ. Press).

TIMM, L. A. (1975), 'Spanish-English Code-Switching: El Porqué y How-Not-To', *Romance Philology*, 28/4, pp. 473–82.

—— (1978), 'Code-Switching in War and Peace', in M. Paradis (ed.), *Aspects of Bilingualism* (Columbia, SC: Hornbeam Press), pp. 302–15.

TITONE, R. (1987), 'The Bilingual Personality as a Metasystem: The Case of Code Switching', *Rassegna Italiana di Linguistica Applicata*, 1 (Jan.–Apr.).

TREFFERS, J. (1988), 'Code-Switching Patterns in Two Bilingual Communities: A Comparison of Brussels and Strasbourg', Proceedings of the Conference Taalcontact en Taalconflict, 2–4 June 1988, Vrije Univ., Brussels.

TRUDGILL, P. (1972), 'Sex, Covert Prestige and Linguistic Change in the Urban British English of Norwich', *Language in Society*, 1, pp. 179–95.

—— (1974), *The Social Differentiation of English in Norwich* (Cambridge: CUP).

—— (1976–7), 'Creolisation in Reverse: Reduction and Simplification in the Albanian Dialects of Greece', *Transactions of the Philological Society*, pp. 32–50.

—— (1988a), 'Norwich Revisited: Recent Linguistic Changes in an English Urban Dialect', *English World-Wide*, 9/1, pp. 33–49.

—— (1988b), 'On the Role of Dialect Contact and Interdialect in Linguistic Change', in J. Fisiak (ed.), *Historical Dialectology* (Berlin: Mouton de Gruyter), pp. 547–67.

T'SOU, B. K. (1975), 'On the Linguistic Covariants of Cultural Assimilation', *Anthropological Linguistics*, 17/9, pp. 445–65.

VAID, J. (ed.) (1986), *Language Processing in Bilinguals: Psycholinguistic and Neuropsychological Perspectives* (Hillsdale, NJ: Erlbaum).

VALDÈS-FALLIS, G. (1977), 'Code-Switching among Bilingual Mexican-American Women: Towards an Understanding of Sex-Related Language Alternation', *International Journal of the Sociology of Language*, 17, pp. 65–72.

VELTMAN, C. (1982), 'La Régression du Dialecte', *Chiffres pour l'Alsace*, 3, pp. 39–42.

—— (1983), 'La Transmission de l'alsacien dans le milieu familial', *Revue des Sciences Sociales de la France de l'Est*, 12, 12 *bis*.

—— and DENIS, M.-N. (1988), 'Usages linguistiques en Alsace: présentation d'une enquête et premiers résultats', *International Journal of the Sociology of Language*, 74, pp. 71–89.

WARDHAUGH, R. (1987), *Languages in Competition* (Oxford: Blackwell).

WEINREICH, U. (1953), 'Languages in Contact: Problems and Findings', *Publications of the Linguistic Circle of New York*, 1.

WOOLARD, K. (1988), 'Code-Switching and Comedy in Catalonia', in M. Heller (ed.), *Code-Switching: Anthropological and Sociolinguistic Perspectives* (Berlin: Mouton de Gruyter).

WOOLFORD, E. (1983), 'Bilingual Code-Switching and Syntactic Theory', *Linguistic Inquiry*, 14/3, pp. 520–36.

WUNDERLICH, D. (1988), 'Études de l'alternance en milieu de travail', Mémoire de maîtrise, Univ. of Strasbourg I.

Index